Mapping Recreational Literacies

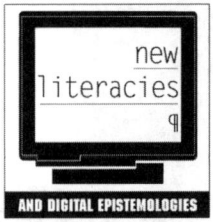

Colin Lankshear, Michele Knobel,
Chris Bigum, and Michael Peters
General Editors

Vol. 28

PETER LANG
New York • Washington, D.C./Baltimore • Bern
Frankfurt am Main • Berlin • Brussels • Vienna • Oxford

Margaret Mackey

Mapping Recreational Literacies

Contemporary Adults at Play

PETER LANG
New York • Washington, D.C./Baltimore • Bern
Frankfurt am Main • Berlin • Brussels • Vienna • Oxford

Library of Congress Cataloging-in-Publication Data

Mackey, Margaret.
Mapping recreational literacies: contemporary adults at play / Margaret Mackey.
p. cm. — (New literacies and digital epistemologies; v. 28)
Includes bibliographical references and index.
1. Literacy—Social aspects. 2. Media literacy.
3. Technological literacy. 4. Electronic industries—Technological innovations.
I. Title.
LC149.M227   302.2'244—dc22   2007015431
ISBN 978-0-8204-9706-8
ISSN 1523-9543

Bibliographic information published by **Die Deutsche Bibliothek**.
Die Deutsche Bibliothek lists this publication in the "Deutsche
Nationalbibliografie"; detailed bibliographic data is available
on the Internet at http://dnb.ddb.de/.

Cover design by Joshua Hanson

© 2007 Peter Lang Publishing, Inc., New York
29 Broadway, 18th floor, New York, NY 10006
www.peterlang.com

Printed in the United States of America

CONTENTS

SECTION II: PARTICULAR PATHWAYS

SECTION III: MEETING PLACES AND DEPARTURE POINTS
MEETING PLACES: SITES FOR RESPONSE   57

ACKNOWLEDGMENTS

Many people helped in the creation of this book, but it will be obvious to all readers that my gratitude must go primarily to the nine anonymous individuals who participated so generously in the study reported here. As usual, in a project of this nature, I start out with a generalized awareness that all readers are interested and conclude with a hugely enhanced respect for the variety and scope of different individuals' interpretive choices. In this case, I also had the pleasure of working for extended hours with nine delightful and diverse individuals.

Collecting the data was complicated by the fact that working adults are not as easily scheduled as students. In order to accommodate shifts in the pizza parlour, calls for substitute teaching, the demands of an infant, and many other contingencies, it was necessary to set up a flexible rota of graduate assistants who set up equipment, manned cameras, took notes, and made the participants feel welcome. Alphabetically listed, Sandra Anderson, Mary Braun, Kat Johnston, Mary-Lee Judah, Jyoti Mangat, Norma Anne Power, Brenda Raynard, Deborah Schamuhn Kirk, Margaret Shane, Allison Sivak, and Diana Zimmerschied worked cheerfully and cooperatively through evenings and weekends, often at quite short notice, and kept the equipment running smoothly so that I could focus on content. Sandra Anderson also contributed some of that content when she located and forwarded to me the online poem that is featured in this study. My graduate assistants over the period when the book was being written, Heather Robertson, Tanya Rogoschewsky, James MacDonald, and Dale Storie, all supplied editorial and technological help and encouragement.

Jyoti Mangat in particular went far beyond the call of duty in helping with technology that sometimes intimidated both of us. Her assistance with the Transana software used to analyze the responses to Black & White was invaluable. And I am also happy to acknowledge the Transana software itself. Freely available at http://www.transana.org/ and supported with useful helplines, it provides the opportunity to analyze video and transcript records together. Having in the past experienced the misery of annotating a print transcript with quantities of extra information from the video record, a very laborious and frustrating experience, I was well placed to appreciate the simplicity that Transana makes possible.

As usual, my audio records were riddled with the noise of digital sound effects, as well as the erratic clanking of the local heating system. As usual, Deidré Johnston did heroic work to turn out viable transcripts. Her care and dedication always improve any project of mine and I am permanently in her debt.

Eliot Khalil Wilson, the author of the online poem that is featured in Chapter 6, was very generous in his immediate consent to quote this poem and I thank him.

I am fortunately situated at the University of Alberta with a cohort of excellent colleagues. I must thank my colleagues at the School of Library and Information Studies, academic and support staff alike, who all took an intelligent interest in this project and made many useful observations. As ever, Jill McClay, Ingrid Johnston, and Anna Altmann read many drafts and offered invaluable advice; Gail de Vos was also an essential sounding board.

I am also grateful to Homerton College, Cambridge University, and particularly to Morag Styles and Eve Bearne, who took me in on a sabbatical visit and made it possible for me to do some highly focused work on the transcripts. My great friends, Jenifer and Richard Allaway, also facilitated that sabbatical trip in all kinds of ways and made it much more productive than it otherwise might have been. A special word of thanks goes to Janet Evans whose help offered new direction and new energy for this project at a time when such help was very welcome.

Like many fortunate instructors, I also owe a great debt to my students, especially those in the graduate reading and multimedia courses. They listened, questioned, challenged, and reinforced at every step of the way; the book is better because I worked with them (though, needless to say, all errors and misinterpretations are my own responsibility).

My thanks also go to Colin Lankshear and Michele Knobel for recognizing the significance and interest in contemporary adult literacy and enabling this publication to see the light of day.

I owe a different kind of obligation to the Social Sciences and Humanities Research Council of Canada who funded this project very generously and made it possible to concentrate on getting the best data possible.

Finally, and again as usual, my greatest debt is to my family: to Sarah and Beth, to Jamie and Dave, and to Terry. My thanks come with all my love.

SECTION I
INTRODUCTION

· 1 ·

INTRODUCTION

It is an irony of terminology that the phrase "adult literacy" is most often used to describe the position and needs of adults whose literacy is deficient in some way. The concept of fully literate adulthood occupies a strange default position of invisibility—the end-point and measure of literacy education but taken for granted, under-explored, and under-described.

At the beginning of the 21st century, being a fully literate adult is a condition in a complex and dramatic state of flux. Much research focuses on the changing multi-literate world of young people, but the first generation to have grown up with ubiquitous domestic computers is now well advanced into adulthood. It is time to take a look at issues of contemporary literate maturity.

The generation of 18–34-year-olds is the darling of advertisers, but they are interesting for many more reasons than their discretionary spending power. These young men and women grew up in a time of enormous and rapid change in communications media. They were the first generation to take for granted the Walkman, the video cassette recorder, the game console, and the personal computer. As they moved into their teens, they registered the birth of the cell phone and the DVD, they were among the youngest to venture onto the Internet in its early days, and they contributed to the huge success of the iPod. They were among the first to email, surf, chat, and text. As they move through the early part of their maturity, they serve as models of full, contemporary literate adulthood to the adolescents and children growing up behind them.

Yet there is relatively little research into the experiences and capabilities of this group. This book aims to begin filling a large gap in our understanding of how literacy changes and develops under the pressure of rapid technological innovation, concentrating on the importance of recreational literacies.

In this book, I present nine Western adults aged from 19 to 36 and investigate how they engage in different literate activities in their leisure time. I am interested in how literacy affects their lives for a number of reasons. Unlike their younger counterparts, they have autonomy in their tastes and choices. They may face financial constraints but they are in a position to make independent decisions about their reading, their listening, their viewing, and their digital interactions. They have grown up familiar with computers and also comfortable with the idea of domestic access to recorded moving images. The video cassette is a format that feels like old technology nowadays but actually dates back only to the 1980s, and adults in their 20s represent the first generation to take it for granted as part of their childhood experience.

At one level, the adults in this study can be described as ordinary. With varying educational backgrounds and work lives, they still have some features in common. All are capable readers, though they vary widely in their tastes, in their enthusiasm for reading, and in the time they devote to reading for pleasure. All are vastly experienced viewers of movies and television. All are competent in at least one form of digital gaming—a competency acquired in youth. All feel at home using the Internet. And all find ways to strike a balance among the many forms of literacy in their lives.

Of course, no reader is ordinary when we pay close attention. Each of these adults leads a life that is strongly and vividly enhanced and expanded by their literate choices. Exploring with them how they create a balance among all the textual options open to them will increase our understanding of the changing significance of multiple literacies in the lives of those who are at home in the digital world. And when we understand more about being a literate adult today, we will also better appreciate how adolescents are developing. Today's teenagers, after all, will grow up to resemble these new adult literates rather than reproduce the kinds of literacy I experienced a mere 30 years ago when I was in my 20s.

What is missing in these literate lives is also interesting. Although they were all relatively comfortable on the Internet, they were highly selective about how they communicated online. Rather than exploiting all the affordances of the Web, they were specific in their use of it. Only one was seriously interested in journalling and blogging. The others, for the most part, used the Web mainly as a tool to further offline interests: fantasy gaming, collecting music, preventing cruelty to animals. They were highly selective when it came to using and exploring online communications—lurkers as much as participants.

In this response, they may well represent their demographic well. Jakob Nielsen talks about an "empowerment divide" on the Internet, pointing out that "in social networks and community systems, about 90% of users don't contribute, 9% contribute sporadically, and a tiny minority of 1% accounts for most contributions" (2006, n.p.). Having only one keen Internet contributor among my little group of nine amounts to a percentage that maps well onto Nielsen's assessment of the numbers of producers versus lurkers.

The final phase of interviews in this study concluded in the spring of 2003, and there have, of course, been many technological developments since then. From these interviews I strongly suspect that these adults will continue to be very selective, choosing new options based on their priorities. They are far less likely to change their priorities to accommodate new communicative possibilities. They are, by and large, not early adopters for the sake of it, though they are cheerfully pragmatic about making use of what seems interesting to them. At a time when research, reasonably enough, often focuses on the exciting potential of the advance guard in new literacies, this little group of independent adults offers a different grounding to our developing understanding of what makes new literacies *work* for people.

Events and Practices

David Barton and Mary Hamilton offer a useful distinction between literacy events and literacy practices (1998, 7). A literacy event is singular; a literacy practice represents a cumulative pattern of responses and behaviours. In teasing out the implications of a variety of literacy *events* performed and described by the nine adults in this study, we will arrive at a better-informed understanding of contemporary literacy *practices*.

The study focuses on voluntary, self-selected events and practices rather than on the demands of the workplace or the needs of daily organization and household requirements. I am not exploring how these young adults made use of literate behaviours at their place of work. Nor am I taking any account of the literacies necessary to run their domestic lives, the kinds of behaviours and materials cited by Barton and Hamilton in a lengthy list that includes such documents as shopping lists, television schedules, junk mail, personal and official letters, bills, scrapbooks, notice-boards, recipe books, newspapers, catalogues, instructions, and many more (1998, 149). Although these obligatory forms of literacy are important and interesting, it is more often the recreational side of reading, writing, viewing, and playing that offers today's adults a ringside seat for the changes currently permeating our literate society.

"Recreational literacies," as I use the term in this book, means engagements with texts of all kinds that are undertaken entirely for their own sake, for the pleasure of the engagement and not for any utilitarian outcome. In exploring the recreational literacies of these particular adults, I am attempting to answer the call of Michele Knobel and Colin Lankshear for research into new literacies "that seeks to understand contemporary practices in their own right, on their own terms, and, so far as possible, from the perspectives of insiders to those practices" (2005, 25). Like them, I am interested to consider "[r]esearch that provides rich accounts of new social practices mediated by new technologies and multimodal texts" as a way of understanding "what the world, beyond the school gates that is mediated by these technologies and texts, *is like*" (2005, 25, emphasis in original).

The radical nature of this new world should not blind us to the fact that many old and familiar forms continue to exist alongside breaking technologies. The importance of reading is not diminished by the computer or the Internet, and in attempting to understand new literacies we may do well to draw on our understanding of the old ones. A consideration of the act of reading, for example, may help us to think about other interpretive activities as well.

Understanding Reading

The act of reading is complex, invisible, intimate, contingent, socially informed, and personally powerful. S.R. Fischer calls it "[s]omething approaching a human sense" (2003, 337). He goes on to say, "[R]eading indeed approaches thought itself. . . . [F]luent reading is 'one of the inherent powers of the mind or body' capable of things no skill could ever achieve" (2003, 338).

Such a remarkable achievement is very difficult to describe or explain, except in very vague terms or in terms so scientifically narrow that they miss the mystery of transformation altogether. We do not really understand how ink marks on paper or pixels on screen transmute in the human mind into the form of usable and evocative human images. Nor is it clear how we can observe this astonishing, yet invisible accomplishment as it occurs within the mind of any person other than our own self.

As a result, some of what we know about reading we can understand only from the inside, from our own experience of reading. Antonio Damasio draws our attention to the importance of taking regard of our own interior awareness when we discuss mental events. He describes how we must take account of ourselves under the heading of "Studying Consciousness":

> It is fine for us scientists to bemoan the fact that consciousness is an entirely personal and private affair and that it is not amenable to the third-person observations that are commonplace in physics and other branches of the life sciences. We must face the fact, however, that this is the situation and turn the hurdle into a virtue. Above all, we must not fall in the trap of attempting to study consciousness exclusively from an external vantage point based on the fear that the internal vantage point is hopelessly flawed. The study of human consciousness requires both internal and external views. (1999, 82)

The study of human reading, like the study of consciousness, requires both internal and external views. But the limitation as well as the strength of the interior perspective is that it is singular, that it is rooted in its own time and place, that it is conditioned by its own origins. One of the many paradoxes of understanding reading is that we cannot grasp how it works except from our own awareness of what we do personally—yet if we confine our understanding to that inside view, we fail to comprehend the range and variety of the multitudinous ways in which people read. Galen Strawson outlines the problem very well, talking about people who

> generalize from their own case with that special, misplaced confidence that people feel when, considering elements of their own experience that are existentially fundamental for them, they take it that they must also be fundamental for everyone else. (2004, 14)

This paradox has always caused problems for those who want to understand reading, but the ongoing media revolution compounds the complexity of that singular/plural dichotomy. What is encompassed in the term "literate" varies according to historical situations as well as according to our "existential fundamentals." In this study I worked with adults who blogged, chatted, orchestrated online fantasy games, produced Internet radio programs, developed databases to catalogue their music collections, and created websites. Yet, as a middle-aged reader, I understand the process of interpreting print from the perspective of someone who learned to read in a world without television and without computers, where books came in hard covers and were few on the ground, where a movie was an almost unheard-of treat, and where children's radio lasted for 15 minutes a day, weekdays only.

I need to acknowledge the specifics of my own history when I use (as I must) my personal, inside-out awareness of reading as a touchstone for understanding what other people tell me about their own reading experiences. Yet I must also find ways of taking account of experiences (such as learning to read in a context of computers and DVDs) that I can never know from the inside.

The gap between the kind of reader that I have turned out to be and a young, new reader is personified by an anecdote presented by Lynda Graham to a session of the 2004 conference of the United Kingdom Literacy Association. Graham was working with very young children who were writing about and illustrating topics of their own choice in a journal. One small boy drew a grid representing a bird's eye view of an urban street scene from a Spider-Man game he was creating. Graham photographed his page, which at that time was about one-quarter scribbled-out with green felt pen. When she returned to the boy a few minutes later, he had obliterated his entire drawing with the green pen. His approach did not seem to involve dissatisfaction or destruction, and Graham was at a loss to interpret his action. Her own son, himself a gamer, supplied the clue: he suggested that the child was probably using his green pen to represent the "fade-out" of the image from the screen, to be replaced by a new image (Ellis, Graham, & Merchant, 2004).

If this interpretation is correct—and it is certainly a persuasive proposition—it suggests that some new readers and writers are doing the exact opposite of what confirmed print readers like myself prefer to do. This child seems to have been using his paper to represent the transitory qualities of the screen. I am typing these words on a laptop, far removed from a printer, and the fact that I cannot create a fixed paper copy of my words is making me very uneasy. This child's attitude to the fixed image would seem to be almost the inverse of my own. Yet, given the materials with which he has learned about the making of words and images, his own adaptation of the affordances of paper to reflect the different features of the screen is testimony to his own mental suppleness and creativity as well as to the protean nature of text creation.

The gap between that child and me, between many children and many of the adults who work with them and/or live with them, is a reality of our times. Everyone comes from a particular textual and educational history, and the potential for misunderstanding is huge in a territory where one person's pathway may be very far away from another's. The gap between the conditions of my childhood and those of this little boy is very great. Add in personal predilections and divergent priorities in terms of what reading enables and accomplishes, and the potential for bewilderment is very great.

The distance between one person's experience and another's cannot always be crossed by the empathetic imagination. Greg M. Smith points out the limitations of what we can think on our own: "If investigators are limited to thought experiments about emotion, they tend to explore commonly held understandings (prototypes) of emotion rather than actual emotional data" (2003, 70). To assume that human experiences of the mediated arts and sciences have universal qualities that over-ride local differences can lead us to fall back on prototypes that no longer apply to the particular experiences of a different generation. Presuming that certain understandings are "commonly held" at all may be misleading in its own right.

Therefore, when I set out to consider questions about contemporary reading and media use more fully, I turned to other readers as well as to my own current experience. To explore the potential for a generational shift, I asked today's newest adults to help me understand what part print and other media play in their lives.

Exploring a New Landscape

Literacy is a complex and multi-stranded phenomenon. The best answer to the challenge of creating a better understanding of such a complex capacity lies in a multiple approach, described helpfully by Jacobson and Spiro in terms of geography:

> Just as a full appreciation of the nuances of a landscape emerges after "criss-crossing" the terrain from different geographical perspectives, so . . . a rich and flexible understanding of a complex conceptual landscape will emerge only after the learner has made numerous traversals of the domain from different intellectual perspectives. (1995, 303)

In this project, I have criss-crossed the complex landscape of contemporary literacies by as many routes as possible, and have also engaged other readers to help with the mapping. To stretch the landscape metaphor, perhaps to breaking point, the nine participants in this study have acted as guides to an area where I am lost if I explore by myself. They have been able to point out new perspectives on the complex scenery.

Newman (2004, 114) has pointed out the difference between a map and a tour. A map offers a bird's-eye view but abstracts the qualities and features of the territory, eliminating local detail. A tour is a much more partial perspective, but it moves *through* the landscape at ground level, offering a felt experience of the paths. In this study, I make use of both tours and maps.

When I speak about this work to audiences of teachers, librarians, and parents, I invariably find that many of them feel lost in the world of fast-changing textuality. Their mental and emotional maps of this strange new life are not unlike the early charts of the old explorers, with vast zones of terra incognita, and warning signs that say, "Here be dragons." The "dragons" of what they do not understand, as they look at the behaviours of the young people they live with and work with, are all too easily called up: video game violence and misogyny, mindless and isolating computer sociopathy, Internet predators, constant pointless Instant Messaging, endless and frivolous time-wasting and brain-numbing. The older adults I speak to are often baffled by the idea that their children, who are so bright and intelligent and lovable, are plunged into this world of dragons in incomprehensible ways.

Yet there are delights as well as dragons in the new literacy world. With nine young women and men acting as tour-guides, I explored much further into this new territory than I could have managed on my own.

Criss-crossing a New World

My routes across this complex conceptual landscape include the following trails of data, all developed from the research project:

- detailed exploration of video and transcript evidence of nine adult readers' behaviours in relation to particular texts in a range of media formats;
- a broader investigation of general themes and individual details that arise from these participants' focused conversation about their literate lives, exploring common patterns and personal idiosyncrasies;
- some limited contextual exploration of the cultural and commercial frameworks within which particular texts are located and understood by participants.

In addition, three sets of "maps" from already established sources inform my criss-crossings and in turn are sometimes challenged by the data from the readers in this project:

- a variety of theoretical and descriptive discussions of different contingencies that affect how and why we read the printed word;
- new theoretical discussions of media other than print that help us investigate how our understanding of interpretive processes in a contemporary context may be illuminated by a wider scholarship;
- my interior understanding of my own personal interpretive processes, which inevitably colours my capacity to understand how other people engage with different media.

This book takes account of the nature of the gap between my own personal understandings and the new maps that are being developed. Awareness of the gap between readers with different experiences is a very important feature of the contemporary literacy landscape. Neither those who rely largely on print nor those whose experience has always been more multimodal exactly understand what it is they do not know about the other group, but the feeling of incomprehension and the lack of vocabulary with which to attempt a closing of the gap are important aspects of the current scene. Adults are baffled by the young people in their care; kids are frustrated by the lack of comprehension they perceive.

No single path across this complex conceptual territory can capture all the paradoxes of how we make sense of texts. I hope my criss-crossing will help to illuminate corners of this landscape-in-transition that might otherwise escape attention.

There is much important conceptual work on the subjects of space and landscape, but this book is not about theories of space and place. Nor did I explore the settings where literacy events took place in the lives of the participants in this study; all our meetings took place in the building where I work. Instead, I have taken Jacobson and Spiro's landscape metaphor as an organizer and used it to help marshal a large data set.

The opening section, "Particular Pathways," introduces the nine adult participants in this project and explores the marked distinctiveness with which each makes selections among the huge range of textual worlds on offer. In the second section, "Meeting Places and Departure Points," I explore the participants' responses to selected examples of *particular* texts (a computer game, an online poem, a picture book, a graphic novel) and investigate the commonalities and the differences in how they react. I also look briefly at participants' priorities in making choices about which texts to enjoy. In the third section, labelled "Contour Lines," I turn from *events* to *practices* and develop some significant themes that mark the developing territory of contemporary literacies. Finally I look at the map as a whole, exploring new perspectives that have arisen from this project.

The Project

Between late 2001 and the spring of 2003, nine women and men worked with me, allowing me to record them as they responded to texts in a variety of media, including print. I met with each of them separately for a total of ten hours apiece, giving me 90 hours of videotaped and transcribed sessions of varied textual encounters. This data set lies at the heart of this project, and in this section I outline the details of how it was acquired.

One aim of this study was to explore as precisely as possible the interpretive behaviours of individual young women and men engaging with particular texts in a broad range of media. Another intention was to use these media encounters as a springboard for participants to discuss their own personal habits, tastes, and behaviours with regard to different recreational media. Thus, in these sessions I both offered specific common texts to participants for immediate response and talked with them about their own cultural choices and tastes, particularly in relation to their recreational decisions.

The Sessions

Nine men and women, aged 19 to 36, took part in this study. Each of them attended five 2-hour sessions in which they engaged with sample texts in the following media and formats:

- Print on paper;
  - the first page of each of seven novels, followed in each case by a browse of the novel itself;
  - a complete short story, chosen by the participant from a set of three alternatives;

- a print book organized along hypertext lines, *The Interactive Book*;
- a sampling of *253*, the paper version of an online hypertext novel;
- Print and image on paper;
  - a complete picture book, *The Three Pigs* by David Wiesner;
  - a sampling of 11 graphic novels, all browsed and one read further;
- Print on paper with sound;
  - a sample reading from an issue of *McSweeney's* literary magazine (actually a hardback) with a CD of associated music that was fastened into the cover;
- Moving image;
  - the opening scenes of six movies;
  - a sample scene from the television series *The Sopranos*;
  - a selection from *The Geek Album*, a CD-ROM of performances by Three Dead Trolls in a Baggie, a satirical group that has often performed live at the local Fringe Theatre Festival in Edmonton;
- Digital game;
  - opening scenes of five computer games;
  - more extended play of one computer game, *Black & White*;
  - sample play of one PlayStation 2 game, chosen by the participant from a small selection;
  - sample play of one GameBoy game, chosen by the participant from a small selection;
- Onscreen print, with or without images/sound;
  - a sampling of *Victory Garden*, a literary hypertext;
  - a sampling of *253*, an online hypertext novel;
  - two complete readings of "Designing a Bird from Memory in Jack's Skin Kitchen," an online poem with background images, music, and sound effects;
  - an exploration of websites related to *The Sopranos*;
  - a range of websites regularly or occasionally visited by the participant, located and displayed by the participant;

A complete list of all the titles used appears in the appendix.

In addition, the participants filled out two brief questionnaires, responded in detail to general questions about their recreational use of texts in a variety of media, and supplied examples of favourite titles.

The Participants

Of the nine participants in this project, six were men and three were women. Their occupations were diverse at the time of the interviews. This list presents them in ascending order of age.

Jeremy, 19, had taken a year to work in a computer store while completing the single course he needed for his high school diploma. At the time we met, in the early fall of 2002, he had just begun his first year at university. He was contemplating a major in history but was not yet committed to that idea.

Ben, 21, had also recently obtained his high school diploma. In the fall of 2002, he was taking a one-year course in computer networking skills, while simultaneously working part time in a pizza restaurant.

Denise, 23 in late 2001–early 2002 when we met, had completed a bachelor's degree in microbiology and had also qualified as a certified massage therapist, with a view to finding employment.

Damian, 24 in the winter of 2002, was a Reservist in the Canadian Armed Forces and was taking some academic courses in a local college. He was unclear about his future career and was mulling over the possibility of becoming a firefighter.

Courtney, 26, had a bachelor's degree in education and was qualified to teach secondary English language arts, though she had done very little actual teaching by the time in late 2002 when she came to the sessions. She had a new baby, born in June 2002, and was also newly married. At the time of our sessions, she was mostly at home with the baby.

Drew, 27, had a certificate in the management of computer networks but was finding it extremely difficult to get work locally. Newly married to Courtney and a new father, he was aware that moving to find work would be more complicated now than in the past. During the course of the sessions, in early winter 2003, he began employment on a computer helpline, but he did not like the job and considered it a stopgap.

Seth, 28, had steady employment as a nurse in late winter 2003. His job involved many night shifts, a fact that had definite consequences for his reading habits in particular.

Jocelyn, 31, was Seth's partner at the time of the sessions in late winter 2003. She also had a steady job, as a middle manager in a local shopping mall.

Isaac, 36, was looking for work as a substitute teacher. During the time of our sessions in August and September 2002, he was hopeful about one or two long-term contract possibilities, but by the time the sessions finished he had found only day jobs and was becoming discouraged.

The Recruitment Procedures

The nine women and men were recruited in a variety of ways. Denise was recruited through a personal contact for a pilot exercise, and she recommended her friend Damian as a text user very different from herself. (These two participants, as pilots, sampled a smaller and slightly different set of texts from all the others.) The contact with Courtney was also made through a personal connection, and she similarly recommended that her partner, Drew, would provide an interesting contrast, with a very different set of interests from her own. Isaac, Jeremy, and Ben all responded to a sign-up table located outside a "second-chance" high school designed for students who did not matriculate in the regulation three years. Isaac was teaching there, and Jeremy and Ben were taking courses to complete their high school diplomas. One of the research assistants on the project recommended Jocelyn and Seth, whom she knew through an outside work connection. In both cases where couples were involved (Drew and Courtney, Seth and Jocelyn), the partners agreed not to talk with each other about the project until it was completed. I have no way of verifying that they actually kept this commitment, but they did all talk about how difficult it was to keep quiet, so I am confident that they at least tried. Drew's sessions were all held after Courtney's were finished, but Jocelyn and Seth's sessions overlapped.

The case of Courtney is a little different from all the others. I had interviewed five participants at the time she was recruited, and none of them showed any particular interest in writing on the computer or joining chat groups, although it was manifested by this stage that the participants were all very different from each other. The idea of a literacy that was productive as well as receptive was of interest to me, so in the cause of augmenting the set of volunteers, I asked people I knew whether they could suggest any likely person who would particularly use the computer as a communication tool in this way, and Courtney's name came up. In no other case did I attempt to recruit a participant with a particular set of interests. It is noticeable that none of the more randomly recruited participants demonstrated any current interest in writing for the Internet or any other kind of public forum, though one or two of them had done some private writing in the past. Thus, Courtney brought a distinctive set of interests to the table, and I was happy to have recruited her. Her introduction of Drew, whose fantasy game-playing experience was unique within this little group, also widened the cultural range of the study.

Because of the personal contact, I was very slightly acquainted with Denise and Courtney before the work began. In all other cases, I did not meet the participants until they came to the project.

Because of the small size of my set of participants, I made no attempt to accomplish any kind of random sample, nor did I worry unduly about my slight personal connection with Denise and Courtney. This is not the kind of scientific study where such factors are particularly significant. My aim was to hold focused conversations with readers other than myself who could tell me about diverse interpretive processes that might otherwise remain closed to me. The variety of textual tastes and habits manifested even in such a small group meant that my aim of plural perspectives was successfully accomplished.

The Records

All sessions were audiotaped and transcribed. All sessions were also video recorded by two cameras: one trained on the participant and one on the text under consideration (page or screen). In particular cases, transcripts and video records have been loaded onto the coding software Transana for detailed analysis. This software allows the video image and the transcript to appear side by side on the screen, and facilitates the addition and coordination of coding tags.

This method of recording and mounting onscreen allows for fine-grained analysis of participants' interpretive procedures in their encounters with particular texts in specific media. The fact that they frequently engaged in more general conversation about their own recreational tastes and behaviours also makes room for a coarser-grained reporting of how they described their personal tastes and habits.

Commonalities and Differences

This is a small set of individuals, recruited through diverse channels. It is very difficult to speak of them as a group in any way, yet some descriptors apply to all or most of them.

Awareness of Western Popular Culture

Not all the participants were white, not all were born in Canada, and not all of them spoke English as their first language. Nevertheless, they all demonstrated easy familiarity with North American popular culture, and there was no sense of any language barrier with anybody. I recruited these people to explore texts and did not ask many personal questions. Only one participant volunteered much information about family background, describing, in very relaxed and comfortable terms, an immigrant childhood and the experience of learning English at the age of about 5. The remaining eight participants mentioned their childhoods only in relation to particular media experiences (most often gaming).

Computer Skills and Tastes

All nine participants were confident and relaxed with many aspects of computer use. All of them were adept with at least some kinds of digital games, though Denise and Isaac both initially described themselves as non-gamers. Denise, however, was skilled with the GameBoy, a fact she attributed to long car journeys. Isaac, who said he never played computer games, seized the mouse with considerable aplomb and skill, and then described his high school years as largely spent at video arcades. All the other participants played some recreational digital games on a regular basis. All nine described themselves as very comfortable with using the Internet.

Reading Skills and Tastes

Similarly, all of them read for pleasure, though not necessarily all the time. Jeremy seemed the most desultory reader of the group, but he liked Terry Brooks and would read a whole series of books if one caught his attention. Isaac read only Piers Anthony; Ben read nearly as narrowly, favouring Terry Goodkind. On the other hand, Courtney, Seth, and Jocelyn were regular and avid readers. Drew and Damian were intermittent readers, and Denise read selectively. In general, all the participants spoke of reading as one viable choice among many recreational options, and all of them spoke of the pleasure associated with reading.

Economic Limitations and Uncertainties

Another common ingredient, and one that I had not anticipated, was that with the partial exception of Jocelyn and Seth, both in regular employment, all the other participants described a certain degree of economic insecurity. Seth and Jocelyn did not express any major economic concerns, but did, from time to time, talk about the price of different forms of entertainment and how some options were simply not affordable.

Of the others, Jeremy, perhaps because he was the youngest and the most firmly locked into student mode, manifested uneasiness about his economic future rather less strongly, but for Ben, Isaac, Courtney, Drew, Denise, and Damian, concern about long-term employment was a substantial theme. It was also a problem with differential impact on their media-related behaviours. Participants spoke of the expense of going to see a movie in the cinema, of being able to afford only the most basic package of television channels, of not subscribing to a daily newspaper but looking at news online to save money. On the other hand, most owned some form of sophisticated media technology (gifts in some cases); some participants could best be described as hardware-rich but software-poor. Jeremy, Ben, and Denise still lived with their parents, which enhanced the availability of certain media but also meant they sometimes had to share access. Jeremy and Ben spoke of the virtues of having equipment in their own bedrooms that was easier to control; Courtney and Drew both mentioned the pressures of having to share one computer.

That these Canadian participants, all young, healthy, in possession or pursuit of useful educational and vocational qualifications, and living in a prosperous Western economy, should be so concerned about uncertain economic futures at first seemed startling . However, they are not alone (one of my graduate students, hearing this account, said, "That describes everybody under 30 that I know"). A large-scale study of Canadian college and university students, released just after the sessions concluded, shows that many Canadian young people are uneasy about their employment potential. "Half of the university students polled and four in 10 college students say they anticipate having trouble finding a job" (Alphonso, 2003, A8). Taking a longer-term perspective, Robert Wright confirms that young people are right to be pessimistic:

> Taken as a whole . . . Canadians born in the wake of the baby boom are far less affluent, which has meant increased poverty for working class youth and increased economic dependency for the children of the middle class. Young people's real wages have been declining more or less continuously since the 1970s, while the costs of higher education have soared by over 100 percent in the 1990s alone. Canadians who came of age in the late 1980s and the 1990s have inherited a world in which very little is possible—a world of low wages, high unemployment, and downward mobility. . . . In short, youth *are* alienated—not from books, but from a culture of

extraordinary opulence in which they have been largely marginalized, stigmatized and silenced. (2001, 215)

So the economic uncertainty expressed by the participants was by no means unique. Its impact on various aspects of their media behaviour was significant, however. One reason I initially chose to work with this age group was that I thought it would be interesting to see the cultural habits of a population with greater control over their own discretionary spending than the adolescents and children I had met in previous projects. My little set of participants demonstrated that my expectation was simplistic and that economic factors perceived as outside their control actually constituted an important element in their relationship to the culture at large.

The fact that many of their media tastes were expensive—even if they already owned the requisite equipment and hardware—also affected behaviours. Library access to different media formats is variable, and any mention of library use was confined to borrowing books. Whatever the economic status of these participants, it was clear that they perceived it necessary to acquire some particular texts, so their budgets would be shaped accordingly.

Cultural Agency

Despite the financial misgivings of many of the participants, the other common element that manifested itself very strongly was that all nine people were comfortable in their cultural skins. I expected that the first session would naturally involve a certain amount of "guess what teacher wants," a checking out of what might impress the university researcher. A bit of such inevitable jockeying occurred, but less than I had anticipated, and by the second session all nine gave every appearance of being happy to talk reasonably freely about their tastes and habits. I have no doubt that some tastes and habits were suppressed—though Isaac did speak of lurking on online dating sites and Seth mentioned "dabbling in pornography," so not everyone was entirely governed by the most obvious forms of circumspection.

By the second session, all the participants were aware that they were infinitely more competent in dealing with computer games than I was, which I believe helped to diffuse the mystique of the university researcher and aided in the development of more open and reciprocal relationships than might otherwise have been created (though it would be naive to think that issues of power imbalance ever evaporated completely).

In general, people seemed pleased to articulate their tastes, and confident in describing those materials that interested them most intently. They were active participants in the culture that surrounds them. Their sense of cultural agency seemed to be secure, using Brenda Laurel's Aristotelian definition of agent as "one who initiates action" (1993/1991, 4) and Janet Murray's definition of agency as "the satisfying power to take meaningful action and see the results of our decisions and choices" (1997, 126). Making selections among the wide range of available texts and media, deciding on the level of commitment to a particular narrative or format, making personally and socially organized connections to a story world—all these activities added up to meaningful action for these literate adults.

I do not intend to sit in judgment on these nine people's cultural participation in any way, nor am I qualified to probe their decisions for implications concerning issues of personal or political identity. I would have to know these people much better—and also to operate under quite a different ethical license and relationship and a different set of personal and professional competencies— to feel comfortable about making any kind of psychological or political assessment of their tastes and choices. Instead I will deal with what has been called a "presentation of self" (DiPardo & Schnack, 2004, 21; Newkirk 1997; Goffman, 1959). The participants manifested and described behaviours in connection with texts; the specifics of these behaviours and texts and the implications for how we understand processes of interpretation are the subject of this study. I will leave other kinds of interpretation to different projects.

My analysis of my own interpretive behaviours undoubtedly also involves a measure of self-presentation. I attempt to be candid, but I am sure there are many murky internal corners where my introspective light never shines. To achieve anything else would be to write a very different book. In this discussion, I occasionally refer to my own text-related behaviours simply as a different kind of route through a complex landscape.

SECTION II
PARTICULAR PATHWAYS

· 2 ·

PARTICULAR PATHWAYS

This book describes and alludes to a vast, varied, and complex cultural land-scape. In working with the nine participants, I tried to find ways that would enable them to show me parts of their cultural worlds, as well as inviting them to join me in exploring areas already familiar to them and new zones of cultural expression they had not encountered before.

As the project progressed, the element that was most startling to me, and that was a major topic of discussion with the research assistants at the end of almost every session, was the distinctive individuality of each participant and of his or her approach to the cultural universe. I kept expecting that sooner or later I would encounter some repetition, some major overlap between par-ticipants and their stances towards texts, but such duplication simply did not occur. Perhaps if I had been able to collect all the participants together in a group, some commonalities would have emerged from the discussion—but in four of the nine cases, I was dealing with partners who presumably talked to each other all the time, and Jocelyn and Seth, Courtney and Drew were as utterly divergent as any of the single participants.

What kinds of engines fuel this individuality? What are the implications of such potential for particularity in contemporary Western culture? These men and women function in a "mass" market culture, and many of their tastes draw from that popular culture—but the outcome is anything but "mass."

In terms of the controlling metaphor of this study, I focus in this section on the individual and particular spaces and paths these participants have traced for themselves through the crowded landscape of contemporary culture. What follows is a brief, thumbnail outline of some cultural tastes and predilections of these nine individuals. Space constraints make it impossible to do real justice to their distinctiveness, but I hope to convey some measure of that individuality.

How We Met: Research Situations and Relationships

The connections I made with the nine participants in this project were unlike any other social relationships in my life. In each case, we talked for five two-hour sessions. In ordinary daily social life, it would take a long time to build up the intensity of ten hours' more or less uninterrupted conversation. And yet, it was a relationship in a kind of bubble. I knew nothing of these people except what they chose to tell me, and our connection ended at the close of the fifth session (with the partial exception of Denise and Courtney, and by extension, Drew, whom I recruited through personal links and about whom I still hear occasional news). In addition to this formal limitation on our connection, all our conversation was conducted in public and recorded on two audio tape recorders, filmed by two video cameras, and summed up in the notes of the two research assistants who were present at each session (not the same two each time, either; the vagaries of scheduling meant that there was a rota of helpers and a participant might expect to meet a number of different assistants over the term of the project).

The exchanges between participants and research assistants before and after each session were not recorded. Yet the easy-going banter that often occurred at these times created a kind of interview "paratext" that was often helpful in establishing a more relaxed mood.

Undoubtedly the public and recorded nature of the sessions affected what was said. All the participants were very accommodating, indeed often non-chalant, about the paraphernalia of the video-recording in particular. But they could never forget that the setting of our conversation was artificial; I am very grateful to them for their willingness to talk at length in such circumstances.

Pilot work with Denise and Damian took place in my office and was recorded using only one camera. After that, the second camera was acquired and all subsequent sessions took place in a small meeting room in my university department. Participants arrived to find the cameras and tape recorders in place, and a box of sample texts waiting to be explored during that session.

The outside world intruded in only minor ways: Ben was first apprehensive and subsequently exhausted when the pizza parlour where he worked part time took on an enormous order for a school pizza lunch. Isaac had to postpone a session when a day's contract teaching materialized at short notice. Seth's interview schedule had to be slotted around his night shifts. Babysitting arrangements had to be made for the infant Joanna, who often accompanied one or both of her parents (Courtney and Drew) to the campus. The equipment acted up from time to time, and more than once it was a participant who helped to get it working again.

For the most part, however, once we shut the door to the interview room, the focus was intensively on that day's texts and the conversations that arose from them. The conversations were both intimate and artificial, and involved performances both by the participant and by me. Although I relied heavily on my assistants to keep things moving, I found part of my mind was very often distracted by the potential for something to go wrong. The computer games and the PDA were especially likely to cause trouble (more than once, the PDA lost its full-text reader), and I was never completely convinced that the PlayStation would connect smoothly with my department's old television set. Another part of my mind was occupied with a kind of "host" attitude. I not only hoped that each participant would like the texts on offer and would have plenty to say about them; I also worried a little bit that nobody would be embarrassed by any kind of breakdown in comprehension, either mechanical or skill-based. Paradoxically, the first session (involving books and movies only, so with minimal potential for mechanical problems) was the most taxing. I was meeting participants for the first time, hopeful that they would find the project interesting enough to continue, unsure how they would react to the kinds of novel I had on offer, and intent on persuading them that there could be no such thing as a wrong answer. Simultaneously, I was presenting myself to them, setting up conditions for our encounter, anxious not to be rejected (for both intellectual and personal reasons).

At the end of the fifth session, there was a moment for detachment, and in each case this farewell was difficult. I liked each of the participants, I was genuinely grateful to each, and I was inevitably very sorry to see our fascinating meetings come to an end.

After the end of each session ensued a lengthy interval while the transcriber wrestled with the audio and videotapes, battling with the interference caused by so many of these texts: the game sound effects, the movie soundtracks, the occasional gales of laughter from everyone in the room. During this time, I mulled over the larger picture but naturally forgot many of the details; as I read the transcripts for the first time, these details leapt to life once more.

Meeting to transcript, participant to data: the transformation is significant. And at this point, my job is to recreate something of the vividness of the original sessions, to draw threads together and report on these different people without simply turning them into avatars of my own thinking about multi-literacies. The most difficult part of this book to write was the section that follows, the nine thumbnail sketches of the very different human beings, presented here in alphabetical order, who guided me across their own corner of the landscape of contemporary literacies. Space considerations squeeze my accounts of these fascinating and complex people, and I know I have not done them justice, but I hope some of their lively and varied personalities, and their very different ways of responding to texts, can be conveyed.

Ben (Age 21)

Ben was a student on a year-long computer course, working part time in a pizza parlour. He was a person who made deep commitments to particular stories. The two fictions that dominated his conversations through all our sessions in the fall of 2002 were Terry Goodkind's print fantasy series *The Sword of Truth* and the movie *Spider-Man*, which was released on DVD during the time we were meeting. Earlier he had watched *Batman Forever* "every day for about two months," and he anticipated equally intensive viewing of *Spider-Man* once he got his hands on it. Waiting for the movie to appear on DVD, he located a pirate copy on the Internet and watched that, rather than spending $15 at the theatre every time he wanted to look at it. With the Goodkind books, he bought the new hardback of each title in the series on the day it appeared, and if he had a new Goodkind novel in hand, all other media took second place.

The appeal of *Spider-Man* was quite clear to Ben: "He started off as a normal guy so it makes the character a bit more dreamable for people." But Ben's way of dreaming this story involved immersion in a singular telling to the point where he expected to be able to recite long stretches of dialogue.

In addition to the Goodkind books, Ben attempted to read *The Hobbit* and enjoyed the *Harry Potter* books. Although he made intense connections with particular movies, he actually watched a much wider variety. He estimated that he watched two dozen different movies on average in a month, and said, "I can watch almost anything, I just don't always enjoy it."

Ben owned seven different game consoles (four Nintendo variations, PlayStations One and Two, and a Sega Genesis), as well as three versions of GameBoy, plus his computer—11 game platforms in total. However, he said, "The games are more important than the system is." To Ben, the storyline was generally the most important element of a game, followed by the game play. He estimated that he owned between 55 and 60 different games for these platforms and had played most of them right through to the end. He saw advantages to both console play and computer play: "The PlayStation would give you more limited controls but slightly easier, where a computer would give you more complex controls but it would raise the difficulty, so it's debatable."

Not surprisingly, given his predilection for deep connections with fictions, Ben would play digital games "for hours at a time till my body is exhausted." He played one game of *Final Fantasy* X for a total of 101 hours (he estimated his average game play at about a dozen hours a week). He was eloquent on the virtues of playing for extended sessions:

> If you play it on a long term you're going to have your mind still working on it and anything that you notice or you're paying attention to and the storyline is going to go and become a little bit more understandable to you and you'll like, be able to work on it perhaps easier if you're playing it for a long stretch. But if you're going and you're doing breaks in between, then you've had a chance to go and get away from it and you're not getting frustrated with perhaps a problem, and you may easily have found a solution by just stepping away from it for a while.

Yet Ben resisted the lure of the largest online games, "because they require that you have to have no life whatsoever and simply be attached to your computer."

At home with time to kill, Ben would often flick onto Yahoo Pool and play with an online partner, but given a choice between real and virtual, he would choose to play real pool.

Ben liked both the ebook and the PDA reading experience but would prefer something between the two—lighter to carry than the ebook but not so small as the PDA, which he thought would be too easy to lose.

He enjoyed live entertainment such as festivals, but found live concerts often so loud they hurt him physically, and he would prefer to play sports than go to watch them.

Courtney (Age 26)

Courtney was recently married and a new mother; the baby Joanna was five months old at the time of the first session in late 2002. Courtney, who was qualified as an English teacher but had very little actual teaching experience, was at home with the baby at this time, and references to Joanna larded her conversation. She was a committed reader, estimating that she spent as much as 60 hours a week reading before the baby's birth, and even now averaging about 10 hours a week. Compared with other participants, she was also a very literary reader, and made references to the appeal of being "well read." Her experience showed in remarks such as her first response to page one of *Middlemarch*: "Umh, interesting, it's got, it's got an underlying sense of humour that you really have to read between the lines to get." She had already read two of the titles on offer (*Sophie's World* and *Cat's Eye*) before the sessions began, and she said she would read a Margaret Atwood book "because of her acclaim." She described her reading tastes as bifurcated: "Things that make you think, I guess, more intellectual and then again I like my fluff [*laughs*], you know." Her favourite books were Philip Pullman's trilogy *His Dark Materials*.

Courtney's book reading was personal and intense; her accounts of movies indicated a much more social framework. Her husband (Drew) had encouraged her to watch background information on DVDs; she was not a big fan of parody but talked about enjoying *Galaxy Quest* with the right group of friends, or picking a "fluffy" movie for a night out with the girls.

Courtney reckoned that her current computer time, now that she was home with the baby, ran from six to eight hours a day (it is tempting to assume that as the baby grew older, this number would diminish). She could get lost in *The Sims*, but she described it as a different kind of engrossment from reading: "When I play the Sims, it's something that I can pay attention to while paying attention to other things." Much of her time on the computer, however, was spent in communication with others or in writing her online diary and lurking on message boards (some involving parenting issues) or in working on writing sites that offer editing advice.

> When Joanna was very small and she used to stay up very late at night then it became quite a habit. She was very comfortable with me sitting in front of the computer and she would fall asleep there and so we would—that became our nightly routine was, I would go online and I would lurk while she lulled herself to sleep.

Courtney and Drew watched little television at home, and received only the basic channels. She acquired her main news information online. If she got involved in a complex television series, her preference was to watch it on DVD, rather than being at the mercy of TV schedules.

Courtney mentioned her poor hand-eye coordination every time a digital game was on offer, and she used keyboard controls for preference. She was not enthusiastic about most of the games, even though she played *The Sims* a lot at home.

She was the only participant who had a single positive thing to say about *Victory Garden*, the hypertext novel.

> I would probably keep going for a while. Umh, as you click and you get, you know, little gamuts of the story here and there, those parts are interesting enough that you want to keep going from screen to screen, but not—not interesting enough that I'd want to spend, you know, ten hours trying to figure out what they're actually trying to say.

She was lukewarm about her connection with the characters in this hypertext novel, but she did say, "It would be great to write this kind of text." She preferred the paper format of *253* to the online version, however, and said that generally paper is her first choice. She was comfortable with different options, however, and said, "I think that reading materials just evolve with the people that read it."

Courtney liked the ebook and said, "It does give you a book feeling." The PDA was less appealing: "It's not terrible you know, [but] it doesn't have the same illustrations and it's not as aesthetically like a book. I mean, it feels very computerish."

Courtney was a big fan of live entertainment and hoped to be able to keep going to festivals even with the baby. "Being in an audience is always different than being just, you know, in your home."

The web was, in some ways, like a second home for Courtney, a place where private family life could be recorded. She mounted baby pictures, dealt with parenting queries, reflected on her book reading, and kept in touch with her friends online. Little Joanna had a web presence from the very beginning of her life.

Damian (Age 24)

Damian was a Reservist in the Canadian Armed Forces and working towards a BSc. He was not entirely clear about his future, but wanted a job that involved action (firefighting was one promising option). He was fond of sports and would happily go to games if he could afford it; failing the price of a ticket he would rather watch with company in a sports bar than home alone. He also liked to take in a broad range of live concerts and theatre when he had the money—even including some opera.

Damian was a reader (favouring best-sellers for the most part), but to enjoy a book he had to see his way clear to finish it in a reasonable span of time. He drew a comparison with digital games; in both cases, he preferred a good run at a story rather than a series of short fragments, such as a couple of pages at bedtime. Flow was very important to him in both instances. He would play a game for hours (but would not turn down a social outing in order to keep playing). Similarly, he was not a fan of chatting; he would rather talk to his friends in person. He made a number of references to the appeal of blood and gore, and liked the twisted aspects of *American McGee's Alice*, a computer game parody of *Alice's Adventures in Wonderland*. But gore was not the only factor that appealed to him. For example, looking at the graphic novels, he said, "The big thing with graphic novels and whatnot is if there's an intelligence behind it or not. It could make it or break it." Even with *American McGee's Alice* he commented on the importance of a compelling character for his enjoyment of the game. And in some ways his favourite movie was still *The Princess Bride*, in part because he saw it when young.

Given the electronic book, he said he *could* read it quite successfully but he would hate to think of the classic books he owned being read this way. "They have a mystique, they have the smell of the book. They have just the—act of reading, but certainly I could read a book with this [ebook]." He would use one for locating information, he said, but his final judgement was, "It's part of the whole—it's not a book!" Nevertheless, he anticipated that some electronic version of extended reading will eventually take over.

Damian played games for many hours of the week ("I think I have spent far too much of my life playing video games"). He described himself as an "embarrassingly literate" game player. "I don't know, there's not very many games out there that I can't figure out quickly." He rejected the idea that it might be an improvement to find short games that he could play for half an hour a night and let it go at that: "You don't quite get the whole mental engrossment."

Damian spoke at some length about the priority of connecting with related texts in the right order:

> If you watch a movie first, it'll ruin the book and if you watch well, say, I don't know of any movie that's lived up to a book. Uh, but yeah, generally it's much better reading the book because at least for me I get more out of the book, and then you can see the movie and someone's interpretation of it, you can go, oh, that's neat.

Playing two versions of *Harry Potter*, on the GameBoy and the computer, Damian commented that knowing the book was helpful. ("This would be hard to follow if you hadn't read the book.") He did not simply draw on content knowledge of *Harry Potter*, however; he commented that it is even more important to recognize standard platform moves and conventions since the game of *Harry Potter* is run on a recognizable engine that is used for a number of games.

Denise (Age 23)

Denise was the first pilot study participant, and consequently looked at fewer texts than anyone else, since I added items to flesh out alternatives as a result of her sessions. At the time of our meetings in late 2001/early 2002, she had completed an undergraduate degree in microbiology but was also training as a certified massage therapist in the belief that this qualification was more likely to lead to employment.

Denise liked to read and was slogging her way through *The Fellowship of the Ring* when we first met, saying she would wait to see the movie until she had finished the book and complaining that trailers for this first movie in *The Lord of the Rings* trilogy kept spoiling the story for her. Of the books I showed her, she was most interested in *Monster*, but she was moderately positive about all of them. In speaking of books she enjoyed re-reading, she was the only participant to single out a book read in school for particular praise; her selection was *Things Fall Apart* by Chinua Achebe. Her general preference was for books over movies:

> Just because I do get my own image and I get fairly locked into them so that this is what I saw happening, this is where I saw it going, this is the image of this that I got and if my image and director's image are too far apart, then it's really hard to let go what I saw of it. I prefer to read the book than see the movie in general.

She said she has more staying power with a book.

I'm way more likely to get part way into a movie and say, "forget this" than to—with a book I'll persevere, I'll keep going because it's bound to get better as opposed to a movie. If it hadn't got me by half an hour in then, then it's not going to happen.

Denise was a very visual reader indeed, and said that, on re-reading a book, she was capable of adding details to a previously visualized scene as she came across them. Her mental incarnation of the story was visually robust and she would expect to create the same images on subsequent readings. Her virtual relationship to the story as a spectator depended partly on how the story was written but possibly even more intensely on how well she recognized the story as similar to something in her own life.

Denise liked her movies to have some substance.

There are movies that have too much point and there are movies that have too little. I like my movies to have something to say whether it's something to say about the world or something about a specific issue or problem. It depends on like, the mood I'm in and there are days when I'm perfectly happy going and watching some fluff movie, but those don't tend to be the ones that I watch over and over again or they're not the ones that I'm willing to invest money on. The ones I prefer to invest money on are the ones that are a little bit more thinking and I can watch them again and say, "okay I see something a little different this time."

Denise was not much of a computer user. She rarely chatted, and she used email only to keep up with half a dozen out-of-town friends; she resorted to the Internet for study purposes only when hard copy material in the library failed to produce what she needed. If she felt like wasting a little time on the Internet, she would check out the Martha Stewart website, but this activity did not propel her to watch Martha Stewart on television or to buy any books or magazines. She rated her comfort level with the computer at about medium (partly because she was prepared to experiment in confidence that her younger brother would come to her rescue if she got in real trouble), but said she was close to the minimum in terms of actual use.

Watching a clip of *The Sopranos*, and looking at related Internet sites, Denise was scornful about people who create *Soprano*-like recipes and eat them as they watch the television program. That is getting too involved, she said. What is the difference between that and an 8-year-old playing at being Bart Simpson, I asked, but Denise was adamant that there was a big difference:

Because that's what kids are supposed to do!!! [laughter] Kids are supposed to explore their world in that way by becoming part of it, as opposed to if you know, you're grown up . . . you don't necessarily need to experience your TV show that you're watching.

She was mildly intrigued by the hypertext *Victory Garden*, a little more so by *253*, but not enough to want to pursue them extensively. A big hockey fan, she chose the *NHL* game for the PlayStation and took a lively interest in the onscreen proceedings, even though she claimed to be awkward in using her hands. As with many games, she said, she was happy just to bang along and see what happened; control and competitiveness did not seem to be major components of her gaming.

Denise was not especially skilful with any of the computer games until we gave her a GameBoy handheld console. Suddenly she was able to handle the buttons very adeptly, a skill she attributed to long car journeys in childhood. The contrast with her diffidence in using many other kinds of computer control was very marked.

Drew (Age 27)

Drew was newly married and a new father when we met (the baby Joanna was between 6 and 7 months old at our first meeting in early 2003). Certified to work with computer networks, he was struggling to find satisfying full-time work. During the time of our sessions, he started with a computer helpline, but he disliked this work (at least in part because he was not allowed to use his initiative but was ordered to follow the script) and was still looking for something better.

Drew's relationship to the many texts in his life might fairly be described as intense. He liked big, sprawling, multi-text worlds, revelled in detail, and diagnosed himself as a perfectionist. His Monday night fantasy gaming group frustrated him sometimes because his partners did not take the stories as seriously as he did; when he was game-master he put much planning and preparation into his presentation of the story.

Drew said he would look at websites downloaded onto the ebook or the PDA, but he would be much less interested in reading fiction through these vehicles because the technology would interfere with his craving for complete immersion.

The fantasy gaming group appeared to be his main creative outlet at the time that we met, but he had written stories in the past, and he reacted positively to *The Light Fantastic* on the basis of a comparison to his own work, explaining his enthusiasm for the first page in the following terms:

> Well, one is the writing style; it's a lot similar to my own. Ah, I like the use of imagery and just because it's very fantastical, it's very, very different and so I guess that grabs me more so I just try to understand it.

He described himself as drawn to 19th-century material as well as fantasy, but said he was less interested in obviously 20th-century worlds. Nevertheless, he was positive about *Atonement*, saying it appeared to be "sort of ah—a thesis on morality which draws me," and liked the look of *Sophie's World* because of his interest in philosophy.

Drew's devotion to reading was intermittent, wavering according to other circumstances in his life. A friend got him hooked on reading fantasy at the age of 14 and he read voraciously, but a few years later, at 16 or 17, he decided that 90% of what he was reading was trash and cut back radically: "I didn't want to read anything if I—if there was a chance that it would be bad, so I basically just stopped reading." Computers were becoming more significant in his life at this point, putting pressure on his time.

At the time of our meetings, however, Drew's computer time was reduced as a consequence of having to share a single computer with a wife who wanted to use it as much as he did. Courtney was a heavy reader, which had also influenced Drew and given him a pool of books to make use of. He also read magazines when he could, mentioning a diverse list that included *Discovery*, *Scientific American*, *Military Quarterly Journal*, *Realms of Fantasy*, and *National* and/or *Canadian Geographic*, and said he would like to be able to afford subscriptions. Online reading on these journal sites was better than nothing, he said.

Drew often needed some warming up to movies, liking them better on a reviewing than on the first encounter. Once he took to a film, he was interested in background books, magazines, and DVD extras. He watched little television at the time of our sessions; he had been a big viewer in the past but quit more or less cold turkey when he moved to his sister's acreage, where reception was limited. He tended to watch selected movies on DVD rather than viewing whatever happened to be on television, and he binged on a film when he first acquired it. The soundtrack was very important to him, and he made many knowledgeable comments on film music, particularly on its emotional values and resonances.

Drew liked big computer games such as *Civilization*. He was not a fan of console games: "Yeah, I don't like the input device, the controller—it's too limited. I need a mouse and keyboard for a lot of them . . . . [A] console is just controls; it's more action oriented." It was interesting to watch him tackle games new to him; more than once he said he would keep going simply to learn how to master a set of unfamiliar controls. But his approach to gaming was subtler than just developing mastery. He liked *Alice* for a number of reasons:

I'm finding it enjoyable, it's really cute, I especially enjoy the cat, but he's always been one of my favourite characters, but the big appeal for me is that it is atmospheric. It's got a certain ambience to it. A lot of games nowadays don't seem to have that really.

Perhaps predictably, Drew liked the fact that *The Sopranos* was not based on the unit of the single episode, and said that for preference he would watch it on DVD so that he could control the experience (not be interrupted by the telephone, for example). He liked the background materials too, especially the big book that emphasized the fictional back story: it would "give you more of an in-depth history and environment to really aid when you watch it, to believe in the show."

The eclecticism of Drew's interests is reflected in his account of websites he has bookmarked on his own computer: he mentioned art and photography, his job search, some *Dungeons & Dragons*-related sites ("wizards.com, which is the publisher, and some cute fan sites that have interesting adventures or interesting characters or good artwork"), military history ("especially the War of 1812"), and medieval history ("some of it's revisionist and some of it is not really what you would consider history in the timeline of events, but rather umh, it's more study of the culture and you know, the dress and the music, so it's more about the people").

Drew's reading of the short story was among the most sympathetic of all the readings in this project, and he was interesting in his observation of how he marked up the story when something caught his attention:

You're—becoming immersed in the story at the beginning, so you are marking it more because you are taking yourself away from yourself, and you know, by the time you get to the mid-point, or the later parts of the story, you are already drawn into the story, so there is less—variation of emotion. You're kind of locked into the story.

But Drew was also good at *locking himself out*. Of all the participants, he was the one with the largest set of ideological barriers. More than once, he rejected materials if he did not like, or thought he would not like, the politics of the text.

Isaac (Age 36)

Isaac was working as a substitute teacher when we met, with intermittent work assignments. His print reading was largely confined to Piers Anthony's *Xanth* novels, which he normally read in one two- or three-hour stint a week. He did not read newspapers or magazines. He had definite ideas about what made a book appealing, rejecting several for being "too wordy." Isaac liked books that explore "the inner workings of the mind." And, despite his distaste for wordiness, he did not appear to be too keen on something completely straightforward; he disliked his short story, "The Red Queen," because it was

> too straightforward. Yes, it kept me detached . . . . So there was no reason for me to invest myself emotionally in the story and it was, it was laid up very factual . . . . It was just the facts. It didn't really have [sighs] a point—an outcome—a goal for either of them. It was just a scenario that happened and concluded.

Asked about his favourite movie, he mentioned *Powder*, for reasons that also stress an emotional link:

> Human connection. Underdog—compassion by certain people . . . ah, I can't think of the right words—miraculous isn't the right word, but in the ending something happened that was amazing, special ah, a little bit fantastical, umh, but touched everybody in the movie and outside the movie.

Isaac did not watch a lot of television series, but his description of *Scrubs*, his favourite, sounded similar:

> Comedy, drama, umh, ah—narrative dialogue, umh, heart—heartstrings being tugged on. So like, when you've got twenty eight minutes of comedy and then all of a sudden the last minute and a half it's just all of a sudden this thing that makes your eyes well up with tears and it's like, "holy cow."

What he did watch on television was movies: at least one a day, more or less, throughout the summer months (we first met in late summer, 2002). There is such a thing as too much watching, he said, "but I try not to let that stop me!" He rarely visited a movie theatre, partly because of the expense, but when he did go he chose the big action films:

> Yeah, you have to be able to be enveloped by it. You can't really do that at home. Umh, whereas at home, yeah I mean, last night I watched this sappy almost Harlequin romance type of a thing which is cool, umh, but I'm never going to pay to see that in the theatre.

Isaac referred to his book life as "fairly narrow"; his film life, in contrast, was very broad and he resorted to outside information to help him decide what he was going to watch: "The advertising and previews, or if I rent it or watch it on TV, what's on the back of the box or in the TV guide." Yet he claimed that books actually meant more to him. "I don't know, I think I value a book and what's in it and probably who wrote it more than a movie and what it's about. [Movies are] more recreational. Whereas a book, it's making more sense to it."

Talking about the importance of music to a film, Isaac shifted to discussion of his enormous collection of CDs (he owned 2,200, all carefully catalogued, mostly 80s and Christian contemporary music) and of his intensive music research processes, mostly online. He had strict criteria for what made a website useful as an aid for his collecting: it should have a complete discography, preferably with a visual of each recording and the opportunity to listen to some sample music. It should also offer links to other sites, and provide sources for acquiring CDs.

Isaac also occasionally visited the Internet to lurk on online dating sites. He said he did not play many computer or console games, though he did spend his high school years in arcades, so he was comfortable with many game controls. He also expressed interest in a different kind of comfort, with recognizable elements in *American McGee's Alice*:

> Comfort zones appeal to me . . . . If it's got familiar portions to it, then it's easier to learn and adapt because I know that I liked the other so therefore if it's got part of it you know, then I'd probably like this one too.

I asked him about the computer game's potential for telling stories.

> It can. *Alice* does, *Oni* could if I got that far . . . Kids like the new, everybody likes the new computer animations. It's more realistic and probably therefore it can flow better. Umh, and because you can do so much more with it, it's different than just sitting and watching a movie about the exact same thing. Umh, so for storytelling because you're actually—mmm—helping write the story—so yeah.

Isaac's passion for completeness dominated many of our discussions. He wanted to read all of Piers Anthony, but was not really interested in taking the short cut of a graphic novel version of an Anthony book. Nor would he prefer the graphic novel *Mort* (though he liked it a lot) to the prose versions of Pratchett's Discworld series:

> If it's something that interests me, I want to read it because I want all the detail in a way that, music wise, if I really like an artist, I will want to try and get all their

previous stuff, even if it was reviewed as crappy . . . . So I like the detail, the depth and the whole growth process. So that, you don't get everything with a graphic novel. A graphic novel is good to grab attention and to spark interest.

Isaac was unusual among the participants in expressing even a fleeting enthusiasm for *Victory Garden*, the hypertext novel. He started off thinking it was "cool," but too many opening sub-plots soon dampened his enthusiasm. He was also interesting about the practicalities of reading it: "But that's too little [i.e., too few words on the screen] so that when I click ahead, there's so little there that I kinda still need some of the old, probably, to help it." Looking at the story map discouraged him because it made the story seem so enormous that he thought he would never have any chance of working through it and understanding the whole thing. "If I don't know the story is ever going to end, everything for sure is going to tie together and make sense, I've got no incentive to read it." He preferred *253* in its hypertextual form because he had a greater sense of the structure and the workings of the links. Having read about one passenger, he could click onto another.

I go back, I pick up where I left off, but with added knowledge. Umh, which to *me* is how a story really should be written. As the story goes along, isn't that what a story is? You keep building on it and building on it.

Jeremy (Age 19)

In the fall of 2002, Jeremy had just completed a year of working in a computer store while he finished the one course he needed for his high school diploma. When we met, he was just starting his first year at university, considering a history major but not completely decided.

Jeremy's highly social approach to all kinds of text manifested itself from the outset. His main criterion for relating to any kind of text included the intervention of other people in one way or another. When, in the first session, I asked him whether it would make a difference to know that Terry Pratchett is famous as the most shoplifted author in Britain, he said yes (uniquely in this group—nobody else cared). Knowing that even shoplifters choose Pratchett would affect his reaction to the story. He rejected *Middlemarch*, but social input in the form of a friend's approval of the book would change his mind, he said. A personal recommendation would cause him to take any book more seriously, though he would always consider the source: "If it was from my sister then

I probably wouldn't read it [*laughter*]. If it was from one of my male friends I would probably at least give it a go. Even if I didn't like the first part of it."

In addition to including social points of reference, Jeremy also used genre as a filter, preferring science fiction and fantasy, some history, and the occasional mystery. His description of his own reading habits was telling: "Usually I have a novel going. Sometimes I won't, but ah—I'm not a huge reader, but I do read casually, a couple of books a year. A couple of novels a year."

Jeremy was a moderate movie viewer, and watched maybe an hour of television a day. He had a few favoured programs such as *Buffy the Vampire Slayer* and *Star Trek Enterprise*, and would watch and re-watch episodes of *The Simpsons*, but often he simply watched whatever was on. He had "never bothered to look at the extras on a DVD," and was indifferent to directors and producers.

Jeremy described his involvement with the computer game *Half-Life* in social terms:

Jeremy: Well there's a number of different cases to it. There's the single player which is quite good, it's got a real storyline. It's the typical sort of game where you go around and shoot things, but with *Half-Life*'s case it has a good storyline. It has a lot of interesting sub-sections to it, but the real thing that got me interested was the online play. There were some modifications to it that were just regular people who build around the game and it didn't have anything to do with the company and I've played through a lot of those and I ended up meeting a lot of people over the Internet playing these games.

Margaret: Right. So there's a whole Internet community happening?

Jeremy: Yes, it's massive.

Margaret: Do you have any association with any of these people outside the *Half-Life* game or are they just your *Half-Life* buddies?

Jeremy: I have actually had associations. I met a bunch of guys around my age that were in Edmonton, through the game and it actually turns out they're going to the U of A now as well, so I hang out with some of these guys. As well as I've met other people now in a barbeque that they've had in Calgary and another one in Edmonton.

I asked Jeremy about these Internet friends and he replied, "I don't just think of them as another part of the game. I think of them as real people even if I haven't met them." He described his online life as a mix of chatting and gaming.

Like, I could just be sitting on my computer chatting with people, and then we'll decide to go off and play a game together and in half an hour we'll come back, spend another talking to each other and surfing the Web and what not.

If he were to sit down to browse the Internet to pass time, Jeremy would be most likely to explore sites discussing various forms of computer equipment. He had been interested in computers since the age of about 10. I asked him what drew him to computers at that age.

> I had some friends that were into it. That was probably really it. Just that they were doing the same sort of things like playing games and looking at BBS's and stuff and chatting with people. Pre-Internet obviously. So I wanted to be doing the same things as them.

Jeremy's fascination with computers had lasted, with one or two short interruptions, ever since. But devotion to computers and gaming could occasionally cause problems:

> Umh, I think in the past it has been a problem. Umh, neglecting going out. To a certain extent, neglecting to eat, not seriously a problem, but just that I would rather continue sitting there playing the game instead of getting up and making something to eat.

At the time we met, Jeremy was thinking about computers in fairly negative terms.

> For a little while, getting involved with computers was a positive force and I think if I had kept it at a reasonable level it would have been a positive force as well, but I, for a while at least, during high school I spent too much time playing and I think that's where it started to negatively impact me.

He had resolved to stop playing games. I asked him whether he thought he would go back to gaming in the holidays.

> I'm hoping that I won't, and I tend to feel, actually, a little bit angry at times that these games have taken a lot away from me. But, there's also the other side in that I have met other people that aren't just online. I know a bunch of people at the U of A here now, which I don't really even play with them anymore; I just talk to them around campus and such. But, I don't think I'm going to get back heavily into the games.

Although he spoke so positively of the social aspect of games, Jeremy also mentioned the downside of playing socially: if you are committed to play online for an evening, you must show up, or "these are real people that are going to be angry at me."

There were physical aspects of the computer that Jeremy was lukewarm about also. Offered a choice between 253 on paper and online, he opted for paper. "Less straining on my neck for one. The flicker of the screen which I don't really like either. I spend a lot of time on the computer. And I've come to find that it can be pretty annoying."

In general, Jeremy seemed less positive about computers than he had been in the past. In part, this decline in interest relates to the reduction in challenge of being competent. "Oh, maybe one of the reasons is because they're becoming a lot more common today that there's a lot more people that are able to produce things like quality web pages without much thought. It's also that I found I was spending a lot of time on computer."

When Jeremy was most heavily involved with computers, it was the social networking that seemed to appeal to him most strongly. In all his references to different media, his default position was to revert to conversation about the social aspects of text use. He was completely consistent in this bias over the full 10 hours of our interviews, and the varieties of social contact enabled by different forms of text clearly provided him with much pleasure.

Jocelyn (Age 31)

Jocelyn worked in middle management in a shopping mall. She was very quick at deciding for or against anything we presented. "Unless I like something in the first paragraph, I usually won't read the book," she said, and in some cases the cover alone decided her. She liked horror and true crime, but most of all she liked to be hooked before the end of page one. "I love buying twenty-five cent books and reading ten books at a time if they're all real good." Yet, offered hardcover and softcover editions of a *Sopranos* book, she preferred the hardcover even though the paperback was newer: "Because I love books and I've always wanted to have a library so I like hardcovers better." Her favourite author was Dean Koontz, and he was one of a very small number of writers whose work she might consider re-reading.

Similarly, if Jocelyn saw a movie on television, she had to be grabbed early or she would abandon it for housework. Again, she preferred horror and suspense. The movie that appealed to her most strongly of all she had seen recently was *The Ring*. "It freaked me out and movies don't usually freak me out and ah—I like the ending. You think it's over, and then at the very end it's not and I was like, 'Ah, that's what made it for me!'"

Jocelyn preferred realistic material to fantasy, but when I suggested that horror represented a kind of fantasy, she answered thoughtfully. "I see it as—kind of the unknown, so I guess in a way it is fantasy, but . . . I see it like, something that will really grab me and it's not like everyday and you know, it's just kind of—I don't know—I just like that fear."

She was equally swift to make up her mind about the computer games, rejecting all of the alternatives I offered her except for *American McGee's Alice*. "I liked the kind of horror sort of aspect of it, but I also—it wasn't as complicated, like, you could just start playing it, you don't have to read instructions and they guide you along and easy. I liked it. It was fun." The cover told her instantly that she would like it, she said. The novelty of *Sophie's World* caught her briefly but she was not very patient with it.

She used her computer for messaging to both local and Internet friends, and for email, and for occasional research, where the virtue of the Internet was that it is quick. "I like quick." She had produced two websites about animal welfare, one for a friend, but she found it frustrating and did not enjoy the process.

Jocelyn was not interested in the graphic novels, and was lukewarm about the PlayStation games, though she did get some pleasure out of playing *Men in Black*. I asked her how she would design a PlayStation game that would really appeal to her and she said it had to have lots of action and use straightforward controls. She added, "It would always have to catch me, it would have to have interesting characters. Like, really, characters."

Although she said she had never played one before, she immediately liked the GameBoy, and warmed to her game of *Mario*, which she remembered from playing Nintendo. She disliked the hypertext *Victory Garden* and was only slightly less hostile to *253*, a more controlled hypertext. The online poem "Designing a Bird from Memory" caught her interest to a much greater extent, surprising even her; it was as if she decided she liked it before she had time to reject it. She found the ebook "cool." She liked it better than the PDA, which was too small. When I told her I knew of someone who was reading *The Lord of the Rings* on PDA, she reacted with some horror:

> Wow! That's bizarre! I don't think I can do that. Like, to me the whole thing too about books is it's like, the smell of books and the feel and the look and, like, this [the PDA] isn't a book. I mean I might use that one [the ebook] once in a while, but still—I would still have a library.

In general, Jocelyn preferred recorded entertainment to attendance at live events of any kind.

> I think if you're live there's more distractions and I'd probably—I'm the type that I
> probably wouldn't pay attention, like if I hear somebody saying something, I'd be like
> looking and I'd be like checking people out. I like to see what people are wearing,
> you know.

Yet if the show was a musical, she would much rather see it live, and she does
like to go out dancing. Paradoxically, she spoke more enthusiastically about
live music than most of the other participants.

Jocelyn's capacity to accept or reject a title in any medium on an instantaneous, hair-trigger basis was quite remarkable. In some cases she rejected a
book before it could even be handed to her. She appeared to rely very heavily
on a kind of informed instinct about cover design, and any feeling of doubt
whatsoever led to instant rejection. The idea of being hooked—and then
preferably surprised—by a story was very powerful to her, and she expressed
little interest in the kind of background information that appears on DVDs.
Her responses were consistent across all the options shown to her.

Jocelyn also testified across media to the importance of an emotional connection with a text. Her responses could often be best described as visceral,
and it did not matter which medium she was addressing.

Seth (Age 28)

Seth was a nurse who worked shifts. He was a big reader, with very wide-
ranging tastes.

> I try to read at least one or two books a week depending on the size of them. It helps
> my night shifts go faster. But I go from books like novels ah, like screenplays, maga-
> zines, like not tabloids or trash or anything like that, to anything—comics. I guess
> I'm just a big kid.

Seth said he would read all the books I showed him, with a slight caveat
concerning *Sophie's World*. *Middlemarch* made him think of *Little Women*. He
said he would read it: "I mean, I read *Bridges of Madison County* so I guess I'm
open to anything . . . . I might have a tough time staying consistent with it,
but, umh, I would go back to it over time." He tried never to leave a book or a
movie unfinished. "I guess it's just a way to escape reality whether I get thirty
minutes or two hours to read it."

Seth found it difficult to remember authors' names, and said, "It's sad
because they're the people that put those feelings and memories into you, so

they're not getting the true credit that they deserve, I guess." He was uninterested in prizes: "No. I don't tend to follow everybody's public opinion. Like, if somebody raves and raves about something, I'll go out of my way to avoid it just because everybody else loved it and I mean, that's just how I am. I don't want to fit the norm."

Seth was equally interested in seeing all of the movies I showed him; some, he had seen already. Generally he preferred to watch movies at home, though for the big-effect films or ones he wanted to see straight away, he might go to the theatre. He generally found the theatre spoiled by people's cell phones and other forms of inconsiderate behaviour.

Seth had varying standards for digital games:

> It depends on what type of game it is. Like, if it's a sports game umh, I want it to be as real as possible. Simulated action. Like fantasy games and stuff I mean, they're fantasy, so it doesn't have to be to . . . just anything with good graphics really. Umh, you know, something you enjoy watching as well as playing.

He liked *Oni*: "It was like watching a cartoon that you're in control of, so—it's pretty cool."

The reduced consequences of digital games appealed to Seth, something he mentioned several times. Talking about *The Sims*, he said,

> And there's no consequence, so it's probably just ah—like something similar to ah— one of the games I was playing, Grand Theft Auto on PlayStation. You know, you're a thug basically, so you get to do a lot of, you know, hit a guy with a bat and there's no consequences. It's just an outlet I guess. Ah, I think sometimes people get a little, you know, carried away and ah, they don't know when to draw that distinction between reality and a video game and that's ah—you know, that's too bad because these are just meant to, you know, played in fun.

He found it hard to get worked up about winning and losing. "Like movies too, I just take games for what they are. Face value. So if I don't finish level one or something, I'm not going to lose sleep over it."

As with the books, Seth balked at the digital game of *Sophie's World*, one of the few titles in the whole project that gave him pause.

> I'm not so philosophical. So, I don't see this as really a game as much as it is umh, I don't know what to call it to be honest. A realization! You know, it's kind of neat, but I don't think I'd have the same fun with it that I would with some of the other games. I think honestly, I just don't understand it. That, or I don't care [laughs], one or the other.

Unlike most of the participants in the project, who generally could not afford an extensive (and expensive) cable package and therefore had never connected with *The Sopranos*, Seth was a huge fan of this series. He owned the DVD sets, and, during our session, looked at the background books with great interest. He was also happy to look at the HBO website but said he would not be interested in chatting online about the show.

> No. No I mean, it doesn't matter what chat site or chat route you go to, it always ah—like, sometimes I'm looking at—I enjoy car audio, okay. You know, and installing and everything, [but] you go to a car audio [chat site] and somebody is always trying to get laid in there, you know what I mean, and so I don't waste my time. There's too many real people I can talk to here than spend my time doing that.

Seth used the Internet for information about car audio, and also talked about recreational online use, playing online pool, for example, after a hard day's shift. "Okay, I've dabbled in porn too," he said.

Seth played the NHL hockey PlayStation game with great gusto, talking about the investment of time to make your skills automatic, and comparing it to the real-life thrills of playing. He was a poor skater so played only street hockey in real life, but he found the PlayStation games very compelling. He spoke eloquently about sport, extolling the virtues of seeing a game live, of following it on the radio (sometimes even while in attendance at a live game), of following the team. I asked him which was more inviting, attending a game or playing the PlayStation version:

> Umh, I don't know, it's pretty close. You know, I like the atmosphere at the game, the environment, it's fun. You have more control here of making the [Edmonton] Oilers win than you can do in real life—but not right now [his virtual Oilers were being outshot 14–4 as he spoke] . . . . I'd probably just go to the game because this will always be waiting for me at home.

But the single most striking quality of Seth's approach to all texts was his reluctance to say no to any of them. Of the graphic novels, he said,

> Umh, like I said before, I'm very easy going. I'm—I believe you have to have an open mind, otherwise there's no like, point to coming here if I was just to go through the motions. You can't base any judgments or decisions on anything if you're like, you know, narrow-minded because then you're not really being true to yourself that way and you won't know what's, what you enjoyed, what's not something—.

Seth's other strong characteristic was his propensity for making intertextual connections. Over and over, he compared one text to another. His links were sometimes idiosyncratic on the face of it (*The Three Pigs* and *The X-Files*, *Middlemarch* and *Little Women*) but invariably contributed helpfully to his ongoing interpretation of the text in hand. On separate occasions he drew links between *Time Code*, the film with the four-way split screen, and *The Sopranos*, with its intricate interlinking of different stories; and between *Time Code* and *253*, the hypertext novel with its enormous cast of characters.

Seth not only enthused about nearly every title we showed him; he also hated to sample, preferring to commit his attention to whatever materials he happened to have in his hand at any given time. It was easy to get him to start looking at any text, much harder to get him to stop.

Coda: Theme and Variations

In many parts of this project, I set up frameworks to capture individual responses, but in at least one area, the participants framed their own cultural lives in vigorous terms. Although I had paid only perfunctory attention to music when I began to shape the project, every participant introduced personal perspectives on music into the discussion. The topic of music offers the potential for a kind of core sampling of a particular aspect of many distinctive cultural lives.

The project as I set it up included music only in secondary ways: on soundtracks, as part of the online poem, in the magazine/CD package of *McSweeney's*. Nearly every participant chose to discuss the role of music in their lives at some length, however, and the topic provided an interesting sampler of some significant issues. The range and variety of musical tastes was extensive, with very little duplication among the participants. Many of them linked music with other media in various ways. Although it was not officially on the agenda as a separate topic, the discussions about music turned out to present one microcosm of the vast range of options and possibilities that are on offer in contemporary Western culture, and to offer some insight into the great potential for individual variation in how people choose to participate in this cultural world.

Music was ubiquitous and important in the lives of these participants, associated with numerous other activities. That sentence, however, is just about the end point of statements that can be made in common for this group of people. How, when, and what they chose to listen to was widely divergent. In this short section, I will present a few of the activities that were important to different participants in this study.

Music as Background

Ben listened largely to modern and classic rock; he did not really like pop music. He listened "a fair amount," either to the radio or to his own CDs.

> When I'm at work usually I just listen to the radio. Other than that, when I'm at school I bring CDs with me and I can listen to CDs while I'm working on whichever project or whatever I'm doing. At home I occasionally listen to CDs—not really that often.

Denise listened constantly to music, suiting her choice to her activity. She was able to be very precise in her descriptions:

> I have music going in the background while I'm doing pretty much *everything*. Umh, if I'm cooking it's usually just the radio or something random in the background. If I'm studying, it tends to be more classical music on CD because it's something like, it's in an environment I like to control a lot more. So if I put in a CD I know exactly what's coming and whatever. If I'm driving, I always have the radio on.

Jocelyn was also a constant listener. "If I'm cleaning—music! If I'm getting ready to go out—music! Always! I always have to have it and then, if not, I'm watching on TV on *Much Music*." But she pointed out a potential problem. Asked whether music on the computer would help her to work, she said,

> Yeah, if it's low enough, but sometimes I can get distracted. Like, if a really good song comes on I'll just start singing away. . . . When I was going to school at nights, sometimes I'd listen to the radio and then I'd find myself reading, but listening to the song, you know, so I was like "whoa," so I just turned it off.

Courtney was clear that she was not a multi-tasker when it comes to music, although she liked to sing.

> I'm not the kind of person that can listen to music and read at the same time. I find it very distracting. I can either read or I can listen to music, unless it's wordless, kind of like study music, you know, that I can just have in the background. But I wouldn't actually be listening to it.

Music to Own

Jocelyn was a big downloader: "I love getting it free, so I download tons from the Internet." Seth also downloaded, and would burn CDs if he owned a CD burner.

Denise had not yet figured out how to download music, so when she really wanted something she asked her brother to find it, download it, and burn her a CD. She felt a bit lost in the world of online music:

> I still have noooo idea. I end up with a whole bunch of stuff that I don't want and it's just—I haven't been able to find out how to either filter it properly so I'm getting exactly what I want or I just don't have the patience to look through it all and listen to a whole bunch of stuff that I'm not looking for.

Damian's problem was inadequate equipment. He said that all that prevented him from downloading music was the absence of software and anywhere to do it, "but given the chance I probably would be [a big downloader]."

Ben downloaded some music but not a lot. He had rules for buying a CD. "For me to buy any CD I have to want more than two songs on it, and I've only broken that rule twice. I don't like buying a CD for just one song or two." He played a new CD "quite frequently and stuff, and it'll go to, like, really frequently, to in rotation, to kind of sit there for a while, and then just occasionally." The words are generally more important to him than the music, "but even if it's a good song and there's really crappy background music, it's really hard to listen to. But the words are quite a bit more important to me."

Music as Memory

Denise was very keen on musicals, a specific taste tied into a specific memory with strong emotional overtones.

> I love old musicals. Most of my personal video collection in the house are old musicals. I have the whole Rogers and Hammerstein set. I have a bunch of other, Bing Crosby movies and stuff of Nat King Cole and all that kind of stuff. . . . My dad's parents are huge musical fans and so, like, one of the first movies I remember seeing was *Brigadoon* and I loved that movie.

Seth, on the other hand, expressed a more general link between music and personal memories.

> I find a lot of music that—music I listen to has a significant, umh, time period in my life where it brings back, you know something good or bad. And you know what, it was a learning experience that goes back, and I enjoy it for the music, whereas before when I was younger, I was, like, "I'm never going to listen to this again, it sucks."

Books [won't] necessarily [do the same thing]. I don't share books with people on intimate levels as with music.

Music as Dramatic and Emotional Emphasis

Drew liked movie music but in completely different ways from Denise. He preferred to listen to soundtracks of movies he had already seen.

> Generally I like the music because it is good music but I wouldn't, in the most part, I wouldn't listen to it on its own, without that emotional thrust of having seen it. For instance, all of my scores that I own, they are all to movies that I have actually seen, so I can tie in the music with specific events in a movie which can relate to specific emotions.

He owned the soundtracks to *The Fellowship of the Ring* and *The Two Towers*, but at the time of our conversation had seen *The Two Towers* only once in the movie theatre, as opposed to having watched the special edition DVD of *The Fellowship of the Ring* "say seven or eight times." He had much to say about the contrasting listening experiences:

> So you have certain musical foundations or themes that you know, the really high pitch whiny strings that start off is sort of the [*takes a deep breath*], it's almost like a narration theme. It's sort of a set-up theme. Then you have something more of the Shire theme, and then you have you know, the big horns, the industrial might of Saruman and—so with the *Two Towers* CD you can pick up the themes and they give you, not even an emotion, but like a base feeling—a base idea, a base foundation, emotional foundation to build on, but because I have only seen *The Two Towers* umh, once I cannot really place pictures to it. There is a lot of—I'm not sure where the music actually ties in. So in that case, I appreciate it more for its actual music value. For instance, the Rohan theme in *Two Towers*, and I read this in the sleeve notes, is actually—it's actually driven by Norwegian strings and I never noticed it in the music, or in the movie. It was just sort of strings, but when you listen to it, it is really powerful, so I guess I appreciate that song more now, for its musical value. Then when I actually have *The Two Towers* on DVD it will shift more of a, sort of a—an emotional tie into the movie at certain points.

Drew made a point of reading the sleeve notes carefully, as well as exploring background information on the DVDs, saying, "I think that it enhances—I think it brings—it makes it more of a complete picture when I see a movie."

Like Drew, Isaac paid careful attention to movie music, but, for him, more of the emotional impact was tied up with the words.

Most movies sound, the songs on the soundtrack—oftentimes they will leave out the lyrics, but then when they play it during the credits at the end, or you buy the soundtrack, the CD, it's got the lyrics, and then those lyrics are meaningful in relation to the story and you do want to listen to it.

Music as Collectible

Isaac described himself as a musical person and listened to "pretty much anything except ah, umh, real heavy metal. Not the Balance and rap and most jazz and blues, but otherwise I've got a huge CD collection and I've always got a radio on or CD on or something." His preferences were for 80s music and Christian contemporary. He bought CDs rather than downloading music, but he used the Internet extensively to research his bands, judging websites by the quality of their discographies. Looking for a sample website to show me, he typed Kylie Minogue's name into google.ca because he had found a good website that provided a list, a visual of the CD covers, and the chance to hear sample music—all good elements but without a discography "so it's not a good complete website."

Isaac had an extensive list of specifications that make a website useful to him, but he said there was no systematic way to trawl the Internet for information.

> There's never a set way. Umh, websites can be gone. I mean, I don't necessarily want to go with UK websites because I can't really import stuff from the UK. I'd rather it be an American based website. I'd rather it be an official website rather than a fan created website. Umh, and the big companies are my last resort because they don't usually deal with all the small details.

Isaac kept a running list of what he wants—"a constant mental list." Once he acquired a new CD, he played it to saturation point and then put it on the shelf. "But I won't part with any of them. . . . I'm a person who, when the mood hits me, if that song pops to mind, I want to walk over and be able to play it."

Isaac struggled to explain his attraction to Christian music. He did not say whether he is Christian himself, and I did not ask, though I gave him many opportunities to tell me (I considered that if Isaac did not want to volunteer such personal information in a semi-public context, I was not really entitled to ask for it within the terms of our ethical agreement). The main appeal that he could describe was that he was much more likely to enjoy the whole CD.

> [Silence] You know, it's odd that—most Christian CDs are, like, the whole CD. Umh, and usually umh, more musically. Umh, [pause] I think lyrics are often a background

thing for me that umh, that I could like. I mean, Ozzy Osborne, I love his tunes, his lyrics I couldn't care less about, but certain tunes he does, musically, are just very appealing to me. Umh, lyrically if I were to evaluate Ozzy Osborne overall I would probably not want to listen to his stuff. Umh, now Christian artists yeah, I like the lyrics if I sit down specifically, intent—ah—in-tent-ly analyse lyrics, but most Christian CDs that I have, I like the whole CD, it—ah, every song musically is appealing to me. Many secular artists, you get like a couple really musically appealing songs on a CD and the rest are all just something else that they threw on the CD kind of thing it seems.

He added, "I don't know. I've thought about that many times, umh, why I find Christian CDs musically, the whole CD generally to be good."

Music as Communication

It was Jeremy, not surprisingly, who found a sociable way to enjoy his music. He downloaded material and used it with his friends to produce a little online radio station, a precursor to podcasting:

Every once in a while, pop it up on weekends for a couple of hours and some friends will jump on and listen. . . . It's pretty private. I have to send invitations. I don't want everybody to know, it's not advertised.

He enjoyed the challenge of programming:

It's fun, you know, just because it's mostly between friends, and I don't think I would ever do anything professional with it, but it takes a fair amount of preparation to get everything going in it, so to organize how long each person is going to play a set for, and just keep it going, and all that sort of stuff.

The station ran for as much as three hours at a time, with participants each taking half an hour to an hour, "depending on how ambitious we are feeling," introducing and playing their songs.

Music as Live Entertainment

Of all the participants, Jocelyn expressed the strongest enthusiasm for live music (though, paradoxically, she also presented a strong preference for most of her musical experience to come in recorded form). "I like concerts. Like, if I really like a group. Because, you know, I'm totally, totally into music and I'm totally into dancing and that kind of stuff, so if I'm—usually it will capture me totally." She liked concerts that not only offered the opportunity for dancing, but that also offered "lots of things for me to watch and put on a good show." She also sang along. She had gone to the ballet "and stuff like that," but was not a big theatre-goer. If she did go to the theatre, her first choice would be a musical, preferably "the big and famous ones because I know the songs and I know I'll love it." These big and famous musicals did not appeal to her as movies. With a live performance, "you just get so into it, and then you get to see their faces, you know, if you're sitting close up, and then, I don't know—I got *so* into it. I would never watch it on a movie, ever. I tried once watching *Les Mis* a bit and I turned it off. It wasn't the same."

On the other hand, she enjoyed watching music videos, at least for one single viewing. "I love watching videos once and then I'm good. I just like to know what the artist is doing." I asked why she would go to the trouble of locating the video to a song she likes in audio form and she said,

> Because I might interpret the song different than the singer. Maybe I don't know the words and then sometimes I'll see the video and I'll be, like, "Oh!" You know, or maybe I'm just listening to the song and not even thinking about what it's about, I'm just singing along without even realizing what the words mean, and sometimes I watch the video and I'm like, "Okay, that's what they meant," so I kind of like to see their point of view sometimes.

Music as Engineering

Seth was an aficionado of car audio systems. Asked to display some Internet sites he might normally look at, he clicked straight through to car audio sites. His explanation of the appeal of what might seem a fairly arcane interest combined interest in music with interest in engineering systems:

> I don't know, it's just something that I enjoy doing. Putting in, you know, whether it's just a CD player or a tape deck, and you know, the sound, all the different music you can listen to. Like . . . I'm always looking for a cheap car to buy that you know, "Oh it's going to have the factory deck and in the glove box is the real deck and over here the CD changer and secret compartment," and I don't know, I just want a good clean, like a good level of sound quality for all the music I listen to. I'm not one of the like, the little punks with the big subs and I mean, I like bass, but they all sound the same.

Seth would like equally splendid home audio equipment but found the costs of systems made for cars to be closer to his own limit.

Discussion

We are so used to thinking of computers as a factor in visual literacy that we often forget their major role as audio machines. There was some mention of radio in these transcripts, and Denise mentioned video, but for the most part the participants' musical references were digital, from CDs and DVDs, to aspects of downloading and caching and reproducing, to the niceties of digital audio systems.

None of these participants expressed any enthusiasm for spoken word audio; their interest in audio forms was entirely musical. Only Jocelyn talked about singing or dancing herself, and no one mentioned playing an instrument, yet listening is clearly important to just about everybody (and Jeremy turned listening into a kind of production with his Internet radio station). In varying ways, some of them also tied listening in with experiences of viewing. Some used music as background to other media encounters; others were not able to merge two different semiotic channels in this way.

From the descriptions, it was clear that music seeped into their daily lives and was intimately entangled with their most personal memories. Yet there was wide variation in their approaches to acquiring access to music and their attitudes towards what kinds of music they actually liked, and why.

The individuality of the different participants and the broad range of possibilities in forms of media use were highlighted in their discussions of music, but such distinctiveness was present in almost every discussion we had. It was not even so much that their tastes in texts were necessarily different, though there was certainly some of that. What was particularly striking was the varied *use* they made of musical and other culture.

SECTION III
MEETING PLACES
AND DEPARTURE POINTS

MEETING PLACES: SITES FOR RESPONSE

In this section of the book, I will investigate particular texts and the reactions they garnered. The emphasis will be much more strongly on the interaction between one text and a number of interpreters.

In pursuit of the landscape metaphor, I have referred to these texts as meeting places, but it is important to remember that these "meetings" are virtual, in that every participant met the same text in each case, but never at the same time. I exploit this metaphor in my headings. Two sets of theoretical exploration are presented in short chapters entitled "What the Maps Say"; readers anxious to pursue the responses of individual participants may choose to skip these chapters and move straight to the rather longer chapters entitled "What the Travellers Say."

For reasons of space, I have been highly selective in the texts I investigate, attempting to choose options that were productive of a broader understanding of new forms of literacy. This section presents reactions to and reflections on a digital game and a variety of polysemic texts that involve words plus other elements: an online poem, a picture book, a set of graphic novels.

·3·

PLAYING THE GAME:
WHAT THE MAPS SAY

Introduction

The participants in this study sampled a relatively large variety of digital games. They played the opening moves of five different computer games; they looked through a stack of games for PlayStation 2 and selected one for a modest amount of play time; they did the same with a set of games for the GameBoy Advance. The most extended time they spent with a game (indeed with any text in this project) was a session of about an hour and a half playing *Black & White*, and it is on this relatively extended play that I will report in this section.

Of course, 90 minutes for a computer game is a drop in the bucket, and I do not hope to provide a substantial account of their game-playing proclivities with this small snapshot. However, the combination of their play and their commentary on that play proved to be quite informative about how individual players can vary in their approaches and satisfactions.

Before I investigate that play by the nine participants, however, I will take an extensive look at some of the theoretical observations about the cultural life of game playing. Every year sees an exponential increase in the quantity of such observations, and I am well aware that I am not doing justice to a complex and expanding field. My own playing capacities are extremely limited and I also take the opportunity to reflect on the pros and cons of a researcher investigating a relatively unfamiliar territory.

In short, any section marked "limitations of this study" would be extensive. The gamers played for a very short period of time, the investigator possesses almost none of the skills she is exploring, nobody in the room had a real chance to open up the world of *Black & White* to its full potential, and any description of this game will be inadequate by definition. Nevertheless, and in full cognizance of all these limitations, I think this part of the project opened the door to a number of interesting and potentially useful insights into interpretive behaviours.

Theoretical Approaches to Understanding Gaming

The digital game calls for a new set of literate strategies and skills, as well as a new way of thinking about story-making. *Black & White* is a computer game with a substantial narrative component and potential for significant narrative variation. Here, I will explore a sample of the commentary on digital games in particular and interactive texts more generally.

When I began to look at theoretical approaches to gaming, I started from a position that many non-gamers will probably recognize: perplexed, intimidated, eager to find some familiar links that would reduce the strangeness of this format. No doubt I began my study with a bias in favour of viewing games as a new form of narrative production. But as I explored the available literature about gaming, it became clear that making a story is only one element of the gaming experience. Setting oneself in relation to a fictional world is a multi-dimensional exercise; there are many angles of approach to this form of literate experience.

The Game as Fiction

The world of the digital imaginary is a complex, hybrid form. It certainly involves stepping into the fictional world of *as-if* (Bruner, 1986; Pavel, 1986; Ronen, 1994; Walton, 1990). But this world unfolds in different ways in a game than in a story.

One way of exploring some of these differences involves the tense of the verb implied in the exploration. Gonzalo Frasca talks about the distinction between narrative and drama in terms of tense; a told or written story is located in the past, while a game is oriented towards the future because all the parts of the story have yet to be assembled at the moment of play:

> It is common to contrast narrative and drama because the former is the form of the past, of what cannot be changed, while the latter unfolds in present time. To take the analogy further, simulation is the form of the future. It does not deal with what happened or is happening, but with what may happen. Unlike narrative and drama, its essence lays [*sic*] on a basic assumption: change is possible. (2003, 233)

Frasca would seem to be distinguishing between drama and simulation on the basis of the open-ended nature of simulation versus the always-already-known ending of the drama. But Thomas Elsaesser throws a different light on that open-endedness with a shrewd observation that this future is in significant ways still virtual:

> While the ideology of a self-selected narrative and open-ended storyline suggests freedom and choice . . . [t]he user colludes with being a "player," whose freedom can be summed up as: "you can go wherever you like, so long as I was there before you"—which is of course precisely the strategy of the "conventional" story-teller (or narrational agency) whose skill lies in the ability to suggest an open future at every point of the narrative, while having, of course, planned or "programmed" the progress and the resolution in advance. (1998, 217)

In other words, the digital text is not completely open-ended; there is a component of pre-craftedness about it that life simply does not offer. It is arguable that the massively multi-player online role-playing games, which are assembled by players through time with only the framework pre-planned, do actually offer something different, a genuinely open-ended story whose conclusion is not yet determined. But *Black & White*, the game we explore in greater detail in this section, is published on a CD-ROM, where the future laid before the players in this study, who did not experiment at all with any online version, is indeed virtual in this sense of having limitations pre-set upon it.

Barry Atkins offers yet another perspective on the question of tense, and interestingly ties it to issues of the player's gaze:

> The screen does not represent the present, let alone the future, on which the player is focused. Rather the screen represents the past of play. It presents us with a report that conveys information about the game state that is essential to successful play, but the player's gaze actually lingers elsewhere. The player is not fixed on the image that has been revealed as anything more than a confirmation of the success or failure of

past action, or as an indicator of possible futures that may yet be revealed. . . . To the player [the screen] is full of rich possibilities of future action, pointing always off to the moment at which it will be replaced by another image and then another. Its purpose, if it fulfills its function, is to insist on its own erasure as it prompts the player to move on and look elsewhere. (2006, 135)

The Game as Procedure

The player intervenes in the game to build up the elements that create the plot, and the repertoire of conventions, strategies, and skills that is required to play a game successfully contains considerable procedural understanding. A number of writers have considered the implications of this procedural level of game playing.

For example, Torben Grodal, who has written in very interesting ways about narrative processing in other media such as film, makes the case for considering games as different rather than inferior forms of stories, looking at the procedural component as an essential part of his argument:

> Playing video games demands a detailed richness and specificity in cognitive maps of spaces and opposing agents, of causal inferences that do not only have to be vague premonitions as in films or novels in which the author/director is in control, but precise ideas in order to work. The perceptions have to be fast and precise, the motor control coordinated with the perceptions, and thus the computer story demands the acquisition of a series of procedural schemas. From another point of view, therefore, video games are not imploded stories, but on the contrary the full, basic story that the retelling has to omit, including its perceptual and muscular realization. Video games are based on learning processes and rehearsals and are therefore stories *in the making*, sketches of different stories, different coping strategies. (2003, 147–148, emphasis in original)

Jesper Juul addresses the idea of a game as a form of "imploded" story from a different perspective, looking at the time of the story events, the time of the telling, and the time of the reading, which are separated in print reading but much more closely aligned in game playing. Interestingly, he tweaks the idea of tense in slightly different directions again:

> If we then play an action-based computer game . . . it is hard to find a distance between story time, narrative time, and reading/viewing time . . . .
>
> It is clear that the events represented cannot be *past* or *prior*, since we as players can influence them. By pressing the CTRL key, we fire the current weapon, which influences the game world. In this way, the game constructs the story time as

synchronous with narrative time and reading/viewing time: the story time is *now*. Now, not just in the sense that the viewer witnesses events now, but in the sense that the events are *happening* now, and that what comes next is not yet determined. (2001, n.p, emphasis in original.)

It is clear from these assorted thinkers that the issue of tense and the question of distinction between the events of the story, the telling of the story, and the reception of the story are significant in describing different forms of literature. The idea of a narrative game as a story need not disappear in this distinction; it may be more useful to think of it as a story that is communicated under different conditions—or a set of conditions that make the story possible though not inevitable. And of course not all games are narrative in nature.

The Game as Performance

Ideas about performance can also contribute to our thinking about digital games. Every encounter with an aesthetic object involves some kind of performance, but often these performances are largely internal and invisible, as with reading or looking at a painting. As with the performance of drama and music, digital game playing offers a kind of presentation that provides some external indicators. As with the performance of drama and music, it begins with a script and develops a public instantiation of the notation, and also opens the door to an exploration of issues of practice and improvisation, both of which are important in the development of game playing.

The idea of performance leads us to the question of the performer, who always inhabits a body. Jenny Sundén, writing about an online community she names WaterMOO, draws our attention to the importance of not forgetting the typist: "[T]he physical body of the typist is seen as an intrinsic part of the making of these online texts. Physical bodies not only exist as textual figurations continuously brought to life in online narratives, but 'the body typing' is itself indispensable to their production" (2003, 49). Many observations are lost if the physical specificity of the performer is overlooked. Charles Rosen, talking about playing the piano and improvising, also emphasizes the significance of the body, though with a different emphasis:

It may not be completely true to say that the fingers of the pianist have a reason of their own that reason knows not of, because improvisation is not exactly unconscious, but it is clear that the fingers develop a partially independent logic which is only afterward ratified by the mind. Perhaps one should add that interpretation, too, works very much like improvisation. In playing a Chopin ballade, an interpretation can be as much an instinctive muscular reaction of the body as a reasoned approach. (2001, 31)

Such physical reactions are surely part of game playing as well, both for experienced and skilful players and for beginners (certainly my own muscular ineptitude is very much part of my gaming experience, whatever my reason wants me to do). Bodily intelligence is a factor in smooth playing, and the absence of swift physical responses is as much a reason why inexperienced players struggle with games as lack of familiarity with conventions. It is more than a question of fluency of access to the story world, however; James Newman rightly reminds us of "the significance of the 'feel' of the game and the kinaesthetic pleasures and challenges of spatial navigation" (2004, 110).

Specific performances also run into other complications, such as interruption. Kristin Thompson rightly points out that "psychologists have devoted little or no research to the effects of interruptions on the comprehension of narratives" (2003, 17). She is talking about television, and it may be that television viewing actually trains us to deal with breaks in storytelling, since its essential format is the serially told story, which is often further subdivided by advertising breaks. Newman (2004) pursues this question of interruption in the playing of digital games, discussing the importance of breaks between levels of play and cut-scenes (inserted video segments where no interaction is possible) to the overall structure and management of the played game (2004, 71–90).

Clearly specificity and physicality deserve an important role in any account of game playing; understanding how to approach the information on the screen is also highly significant.

Mastering the Conventions

Conventions are useful only when they are recognizable mutually to the producer and the receiver of a conventional text. How do game players go about establishing what conventions are going to work in a particular game? Trial and error is an obvious possibility, but more sophisticated actions are also possible.

The work of Peter Rabinowitz (1987) on what he calls "rules of reading" illuminates some interesting crossover points between the interpretation of print fiction and the interpretation of digital games. I have previously made use of this connection (Mackey, 2002), but would like to make brief reference to his rubric once more—and then to explore some observations by game theorists that raise telling questions about the potential for overlap between print and game.

Drawing on print texts of the 19th and 20th centuries, Rabinowitz (1987) talks about four categories of "rules"—really conventional understandings—of reading: rules of notice, configuration, signification, and coherence. In a nutshell, rules of notice help us to decide what is worth attending to in a book, since every detail cannot be of equal significance (titles, opening and closing sentences, single-sentence paragraphs, and so forth feature under this heading as helping us to decide priorities of attention). Rules of configuration apply to how we assemble the parts we have decided to notice to make plausible patterns. Rules of signification involve deciding how to attach importance to patterns and their detailed workings. Rules of coherence (very often acting retrospectively after the reading is over) are applied with a view to assembling a maximally satisfying overall sense of the story.

Working with pairs of young people playing *Starship Titanic* (Adams, 1998), I found that Rabinowitz's rules (with the addition of a fifth category for strategic considerations) provided a comfortable and useful fit for describing much of their activity. *Starship Titanic*, however, is a game with a very strong narrative set-up at the outset of the game, and not all digital games work on the basis of such an opening premise. Indeed, Markku Eskelinen and Ragnhild Tronstad suggest that at least some games may actually work on an inversion of the understandings described by Rabinowitz:

> [I]n art we may have to configure in order to be able to interpret, whereas in games we have to interpret in order to be able to configure, and proceed from the beginning to the winning or some other situation. (2003, 197)

Thomas Elsaesser makes a comparable point, using different language:

> No longer would a story be the exploration of a world thanks to narrative. The CD-ROM or interactive video game is more like the exploration of a narrative thanks to a "world." The setting or set, the fiction, the collection of information functions then as background to a new kind of (serial) activity: a sampling or sorting information [sic], making connections in the form of montage, or more likely, following the connexions laid by others. . . . We enter a territory in order to explore its map, rather than use a map to explore a territory. (1998, 217)

Trying to understand the logic that organizes a "map" of procedures in some forms of digital game can be a substantial challenge. When a different group of children played *Myst* with me (also reported in Mackey, 2002), they started with almost no narrative information at all (the game begins very enigmatically), and had to come to at least some initial form of interpretation before they could begin to assemble information in any useful way. Holland, Jenkins, and Squire supply the productive phrase "performance of understanding" (2003, 32). Tom, aged 11, provided a telling example of misinterpretation, leading to a lapse of configuration, in what could be called a performance of misunderstanding. He expected the game to involve the accumulation of tools and weapons. As a consequence, he spent some considerable time not noticing a letter lying conspicuously on the grass; it was not germane to his initial interpretation and was thus invisible to him.

Readers of print fiction, of course, are equally capable of missing salient details because they are operating on an overall misapprehension of authorial intent. Nevertheless, the configuration of a story is more substantially already laid out *for* readers than for gamers, and the print story flows forward regardless of how the reader reacts. Tom, on the other hand, spent a great deal of time going round and round the same little area of the *Myst* island, unable to make progress because he could not establish how to bestow and *perform* his attention.

The predilections and preferences of players offer a different way of looking at game playing, and it is to this aspect of the theoretical "map" that we turn next.

What Players Contribute

In 1990 and then again in 1996, Richard Bartle undertook a classification of ways in which different players approach MUDs (multi-user dungeons, which involve purely verbal fictional worlds created collaboratively by their players). MUDs are progenitors of the open-ended worlds now mostly displayed in massively multi-player online role-playing games, which include visuals normally provided by a game company. Bartle therefore is discussing an "unclosed" form of computer game, and to that extent his categories may not map completely with the activities of the participants in this project, all of whose encounters with computer games involved finite texts. But the overlap is suggestive and worth exploring further.

Bartle asks a significant question:

Are MUDs

- games? Like chess, tennis, AD&D (*Advanced Dungeons & Dragons*)
- pastimes? Like reading, gardening, cooking?
- sports? Like huntin', shootin', fishin'?
- entertainments? Like nightclubs, TV, concerts?

Or are they a combination of all four? Perhaps individual players even see the *same* MUD differently from each other? (1996, n.p.)

Bartle returns to these questions at the end of his analysis, which he developed as a response to six months of online discussion among highly experienced MUD players during 1989 and 1990 around the question of what people want from a MUD. He concludes,

> Abstracting the various points that had been raised, a pattern emerged: people habitu-ally found the same kinds of things about the game "fun," but there were several (four, in fact) sub-groupings into which opinion divided. Most players leaned at least a little to all four, but each tended to have some particular overall preference. (1996, n.p.)

Bartle says his categories were "generally well received by those who had par-ticipated in the debate." (1996, n.p.)

Bartle's four categories are as follows:

- Some players are achievers. They "give themselves game-related goals and vigorously set out to achieve them."
- Some players are explorers, who "try to find out as much as they can about the virtual world."
- Some players are socializers, who "use the game's communicative facilities, and apply the role-playing that these engender, as a con-text in which to converse (and otherwise interact) with their fellow players."
- Some players are what Bartle labels killers, who like to impose on oth-ers; they "use the tools provided by the game to cause distress to (or, in rare circumstances, to help) other players." (1996, n.p.)

Bartle elaborates on these categories quite extensively, but I will simply leap to the concluding summary, where he returns to his opening questions:

To answer the questions posed in the preface:

Are MUDs

- games? Like chess, tennis, D&D?
  Yes—to achievers.
- pastimes? Like reading, gardening, cooking?
  Yes—to explorers.
- sports? Like huntin', shooting' [*sic*], fishin'?

Yes, to killers.
- entertainments? Like nightclubs, TV, concerts?
  Yes, to socialisers. (1996, n.p.)

I discuss the participants' approaches to the game in a later section, but here I want to remark briefly that this taxonomy corresponded rather more closely to the data from my study than I first suspected when I read these categories. When I thought carefully about the participants' game-playing styles, it turned out to be not only easy but also productive of useful further thinking to assign participants to each heading. Jocelyn, Ben, Isaac, and Drew are achievers. Seth and Courtney are explorers. Damian is a killer. Jeremy is a socializer. None of them fits perfectly into a category, but I found that the predilections of these players do validate these rough groupings at least to a degree and with a certain amount of overlap.

So, establishing that my own data do ground these headings as potentially helpful, I turn to the theoretical consequences of Bartle's taxonomy. There are two particular points of interest. One is that none of these categories involves the idea of a story. It may be that the open-ended nature of the MUD is simply antithetical to being compared to something as pre-shaped as a story. It may simply be that Bartle and his online colleagues overlooked this aspect of the creation. In any case, I think there is potential for exploring whether any of the players of *Black & White* showed signs of validating its story components above other elements, whether the label "story-maker" should be added to the existing list.

The second point that I find interesting in Bartle's list involves the plasticity of the form he is describing. The MUD is a creature of *potential*. And here I think it is useful to return to the issue of tense: as we have established, the computer game is staged somewhere between the present and the future (though in the case of a finite game, there is, theoretically at least, no possible future where the creators have not always already been, although creative sabotage cannot be eliminated in practice). Obviously there is room for interpretation in any kind of story, but the qualities of protean openness to being played that manifest themselves in Bartle's list are a little more unusual, and may represent one aspect of digital gaming that offers something new to our arsenal of story composition.

Players and Challenges

Several researchers report that game players value the challenge of the game. In his overview of our current understanding of videogames, James Newman emphasizes this point:

> All of these [research reports on game players] point to the importance of player activity. A videogame must provide novel or exciting situations to experience, stimulating puzzles to engage with, and interesting environments to explore. Moreover, it must offer the player not merely suitable or appropriate capabilities, but capabilities that can be earned, honed and perfected. Sherry *et al.* (2001) note also the importance of challenge in their study of videogame uses and gratifications. It is essential to note that players want to work for their rewards. Gratification is not simply or effortlessly meted out. . . . [P]layers expect to fail. . . . [A]t least part of the pleasure of videogame play is derived from the refinement of performance through replay and practice. (2004, 16–17)

Players make other decisions about how they will conduct their game. Frasca, drawing on various game theorists, draws a distinction between the outcomes of different kinds of game playing, specifically whether there is a winner or loser. It is possible to use the noun "play" to describe an activity without winners or losers and the noun "game" to describe an activity that includes the possibility of victory. Frasca suggests a distinction between "paidea" and "ludus," where paidea exists for the pleasure of the activity and ludus is an activity aimed at the outcome of victory or loss.

Importantly, however, Frasca insists that the final decision lies in the hands of the player. "It is the player and not the designer who decides how to use a toy, a game, or a videogame. The designer might suggest a set of rules, but the player always has the final decision" (2001, 14).

Such a distinction needs some modification to apply to an interactive narrative, but it is not too hard to envisage the successful achievement of the story's end as being a form of winning. Certainly it was possible to observe participants in this study switch between goal-directed and aimless behaviour. Seth, in particular, stopped hunting for objects to further the story and engaged instead in a kind of manic slaughter of peasants just for the fun of it—and because, as he explicitly observed, it was "not consequential."

The distinction between ludus and paidea, or game and play, might also need to be filtered through Bartle's categories. A killer or achiever might well engage in undiluted ludus, but it seems likely that explorers and possibly some socializers would veer towards forms of paidea. The distinction provides another useful descriptive tool for exploring the behaviours of different players.

The Discourse of the Game Itself

What do the official texts of Black & White have to offer to this discussion? The *Official Strategy Guide* begins rather bizarrely by quoting two verses of William Cowper's 1774 hymn "God moves in a mysterious way." However, it moves on straight away to say, "There's no right way to play *Black & White*" (Evans, 2001, 5). On the next two pages it outlines four modes of play:

1. story mode, "an evolving narrative which spans five different landscapes" (Evans, 2001, 6);
2. the gods' playground, a practice zone;
3. skirmish mode, "all the fun of Black & White's expansionist gameplay, but without the evolving storyline" (Evans, 2001, 7);
4. multi-player, the online version.

Already we see the plural nature of the game. There is a story, one which "evolves," but skirmish lets you have the competition without the story, and the gods' playground not only lets you learn to master the controls but "also gives you the chance to play around with a village without being threatened by an enemy or bogged down by part of a storyline" (Evans, 2001, 11). If we match these schemas to Bartle's (1996) player categories, we may find that the explorer chooses the gods' playground, the killer goes for skirmish, and the socializer takes the online route. By subtraction, that would leave the achiever in the story zone, an intriguing and suggestive outcome. The achiever may value the accumulation of points rather more than the completion of the story, but it is certainly possible to contemplate reaching the end of the story as an achievement in its own right. The issue of what constitutes achievement in this context is one to which we shall return.

Discussion

The overall consensus among these many commentators is that games offer a particularly plural and plastic form of fictional engagement. On the other hand, Peter Rabinowitz's rule of thumb for configuration (the relation of events to each other and to the overall shape of the story), though it derives from conventional print fiction, still applies. He says, "First, it is appropriate to expect that *something* will happen. Second, it is appropriate to expect that not *anything* can happen" (1987, 117, emphasis in original). This generic limitation also applies with equal significance to game fiction.

The collapse of tense, so that the story event, the moment of telling, and the moment of reading or performing all meet, means that player stance is a powerful agent in the creation of the final plot. The challenge of understanding may be performed differentially, with many different—but related—outcomes in different played versions of the game.

The rhetorical structure of the game organizes attention, and we will return to this topic later. First, it is time to look at some of the specific qualities of *Black & White*, and at the different ways in which it was played in this project.

· 4 ·

PLAYING THE GAME:
WHAT THE TRAVELLERS SAY

Black & White: Inside The Game

I spent some time attempting to play *Black & White*, but my own clumsy movements shed rather less light on the more experienced play of the project participants than I would have hoped. To me, the surface of the game was indeed opaque, but not in any playful or constructive sense. I spent so much time looking from what my hand was doing with the mouse to what was being accomplished on the screen (mostly some rather wayward forward motion) that it was impossible for me to move more transparently into the world of the game. I was the exact equivalent of the child "barking at print" who is too busy decoding to be able to interpret.

Nevertheless, I made the effort and will describe the early scenes. No player managed more than a sample slice of the game and I will not attempt to recount the whole story.

As the game is loaded, day breaks on a landscape that features a rugged, rocky seashore and includes several places where a light beams straight up into the sky. The game itself begins with a video cut-scene: a child wanders into the sea and "you" are invited to rescue him. "You," in the form of a giant hand, do just that; there is no interactivity at this point and "you" are not given the option of refusing. The parents of the boy greet you as a god, and invite you to the village so you can be worshipped properly. You meet the two voices of your conscience, cast as a white god (complete with beard) and a black devil (this game is not ideologically subtle). They serve as information sources (telling you how to make particular moves) and as prompts to good or evil action, flying into a scene without warning to coach and tempt you.

In the village you are invited to help the villagers complete the building of their temple by assisting with the movement of materials and provisions. At this point, you gain some control over your actions on the screen. The conscience figures show you how to move wood and grain to the temple, and soon, if you accept this request, your giant hand is flying across the landscape.

All the words spoken in the game are repeated in a script line at the bottom of the screen. Each line shrinks in size and scrolls down the screen after you read it, so the reading order is inverted from normal page arrangement in that the unread line lies on top of the previously read material rather than below it. Movement is achieved by using the mouse or the keyboard or a combination of the two, and your two consciences spell out procedures for you. My own game did not develop far beyond a primitive grasp of the essential mouse actions, which were intuitive to a point. You move the cursor forward into the landscape, then click the mouse and drag it so that the cursor moves towards that point. Unlike some game movements, it actually feels physically analogous to an actual action: like grabbing a handhold and pulling yourself towards it. Not all the players liked this form of movement control, as some were much more at home with other methods of propulsion. Having few prior preferences, I found I could at least "feel" my way forward with this arrangement.

A further design feature of the game reinforces your analogue relationship with the screen: throughout the game, the cursor is represented on the screen as a large right hand. Metaphorically, it could be said to stand for the "hand of God" and Ben was interested to observe that it actually casts a shadow on the landscape. In terms of haptic play, it is a surprisingly literal reinforcement of what your own hand is doing with the mouse.

Once the temple is completed, you are invited to meet a challenge. Sable, the gatekeeper, suggests that you might like to collect three gatestones, which will enable you to move beyond the great gates. The first one you have apparently already passed on your way from the seashore, where you rescued the boy, to the temple. The second one is retrieved as a reward after you rescue a sick man from the woods, and the third must be carved by a local sculptor after you have located an appropriate stone for him. All of these ventures involve exploring the surroundings of the village and making yourself familiar with the possibilities of this location. You use your "hand" to pick up the stones, though there is little simulation of grasp and the giant hand most often resembles the shape of a hand holding a mouse.

Along the way, you may find the opportunity to practise particular skills such as throwing rocks at a target. You may also start to learn a few tricks of the trade of being a god: how to help your villagers with supplies or food or by reshaping the landscape by transplanting trees, for example. You may discover the gods' playground, which is essentially an arena both for practice and for just playing around, removed from the forward movement of the story.

Newman, in his survey of game theories, draws on a number of predecessors in his distinction between the "map" and the "tour" (2004, 114). In a nutshell, the map provides a bird's-eye view of the game; the tour takes place at ground level. The zoom control in *Black & White* actually allows players to alternate freely between these two approaches, though, possibly in response to the scale of territory to be covered, most of the players in this study elevated themselves above the ground-level view most of the time. But even the possibility of moving through rather than above the terrain alters the dynamics of player relationship to the territory.

As I experimented with finding the gatestones, I discovered that it was not only my literal grasp of the manual controls that was inadequate. My capacity to differentiate specific parts of the landscape and then remember them in relation to each other was very faulty. I am poor at this kind of noticing and relating in real life, so perhaps it was not entirely surprising, but it was clear to me that I also lacked experience—both in spotting significance in the pixellated landscape and then in assembling an overall mental picture of the territory. I persevered, but with very little finesse.

When you finally accumulate all the gatestones the big gate creaks open and you move through to meet the Creatures. You are invited to choose one to work with you: either a cow or an ape or a tiger. You are able to train your selected Creature by showing both approval and disapproval—you may stroke or slap him. You are given a few tools of the trade, such as a leash, and invited to turn your Creature into a force for good or for evil, as you wish. I chose the cow, though with little conviction or investment in its welfare, and mostly because I found it somewhat less annoying than the other two.

Again, the stroke and the slap are rendered in ways that relate convincingly to the actions of the player's own hand. Rubbing the mouse over the mouse pad directs the cursor hand to rub over the body of the Creature. The slap is administered by a sharp back-and-forth movement of the hand on the mouse. The sound effects of the slap and the reaction of the Creature inflate the power and cruelty of this motion. As Newman says, "Videogame spaces are experienced viscerally with the whole body. The exploration of video game space is a kinaesthetic pleasure. It is important, therefore, to consider the ways in which players virtually exist within these spaces" (2004, 125). The sound of the slap and the cringe of the Creature certainly had a visceral impact on me, even though I would not have described myself as fully involved in the game at this point.

In reaching this stage of the game, I found myself truly daunted at the prospect of abusing even a cartoon Creature, yet bored with the notion of simply being a good god, and anxious that my own pitiful scruples would get in the way of my understanding the appeal of the game. Unlike several of the participants who were actively pleased to be set up as a god, I felt diffident and actually rather excluded. My own preference would be simply to explore this very attractive world—and that is certainly one possibility within the parameters of the CD-ROM—but I felt some professional obligation to experience the story potential instead.

Overall, my experience was not particularly positive, nor, even now after watching so many variations of the game, do I feel any strong urge to play it further. I found access to the story difficult because of my limited skills, and I was not particularly gripped by the prospect of behaving like a god. At this stage of my life, I have neither the time to invest in the quantity of practice it would take to turn me into a good gamer nor the patience to put up with performing badly for hours.

If, by some alchemy of skill acquisition, I could effortlessly improve my gaming capacities, I have little doubt that I would become an explorer. My personal bias is always towards paidea; I have never been interested in winning or losing in my own playtime, and I avoid card and board games for this reason. I cannot see how or why I might suddenly convert into a point-accumulating competitor simply because the format is different.

The Role of Researcher Ineptitude

I present the questions that arise out of this obvious gulf between my own capabilities and interests and those of the participants as frankly as I can because this sort of barrier is all too substantial and all too common.

For many adults, the notion that "I'm no good at this game" translates all too readily into "therefore this game is no good." I offer the evidence of my own lack of competence partly to show that this bridge is faulty. It is not the first time I have watched other people play games that substantially defeat me as a hands-on player; this time, as before, I found watching and analysing a variety of game play to be a very worthwhile exercise and one that taught me much about interpretive processes, conventions, and skills. As in my previous encounters, I also ended up with considerable respect for the game's makers as well as for the players who worked with me.

Am I arrogant to feel I can comment on something I am manifestly unable to perform myself? I lay out my limitations because they are bound to affect what I notice and value—but I do not feel that I have nothing to offer. My interests lie in exploring the ways in which experiences in different media feed and cross-fertilize each other, and such a quest certainly involves the inclusion of digital games. My own experience is a factor in how I assemble my powers of observation to explore the games of other players, but operating from a position of personal expertise is not the only possible or valuable stance.

In contrast, being a vastly more experienced reader of print fiction than some of the participants probably disqualifies me in different ways from analysing their actions sympathetically (though this kind of disjuncture of skill level is less often perceived as problematic). I want to be honest about my limitations but I do not want to retreat behind a wall of false modesty. In some ways my ineptitude was actually very helpful in creating an atmosphere of reciprocity in the project; in some sessions, there were times when I clearly knew more about the course of the proceedings than any participant, but with the computer and console games it was manifest to every participant that I obviously knew very little indeed.

I think there are at least two ways of looking at the role of my own incompetence in this study. Jenny Sundén quotes Donna Haraway on the importance of risk in ethnographic work, something she claims is important for online ethnography as well (2003, 18). I would not call this project ethnographic, but I think the idea of researcher at risk is a productive one. There were many risks in this project; if the game went wrong and I could not figure out how to fix it, the project itself might collapse. (In fact, the game often did go wrong, particularly at the loading stage, but the participants came to my rescue time after time, finding a way to get the game going.) If the participants were so scornful of my incompetence that they lost confidence in the overall project, then there would be a different kind of breakdown.

A second way of looking at this issue involves the related question of expertise. Evelyn Arizpe and Morag Styles have spoken about the nature of the zone of proximal development in this kind of project. (Vygotsky defines the zone of proximal development as "the distance between the actual developmental level as determined by independent problem solving and the level of potential development as determined through problem solving under adult guidance or in collaboration with more capable peers" [1978, 86].) Working with young children and picture books, Arizpe and Styles discovered that the research process itself had affected the outcomes of the children's engagement with the books. They speak of "the unintentional pedagogical interventions" that they made in talking with the children.

> Our interactions with children may have shaped their responses in ways which were not planned and which are now, after the event, impossible to identify with precision . . . our research procedures themselves became inseparable from a complex teaching/learning process through which the pupils became more accomplished at looking, talking and thinking about pictures. (2003, 243)

In my study there was generally a zone of proximal development surrounding each conversation as the discussion itself stretched participants, but the question of who was the more competent interpreter genuinely changed throughout the course of the different activities. Although I hope I always made it clear that I greatly valued the responses of the participants, there were clearly some sessions where I was more knowledgeable than they. But of the five two-hour sessions, three contained some work with digital games and there could have been no question in these sessions that every participant was showing me things I genuinely did not know.

I began this project feeling apologetic about my dire want of gaming skill, but in retrospect I think it was useful. I could not have successfully pretended to be as inept as I truly am, but I think all the participants recognized my genuine incompetence and in some cases it made them relax about their own misplays. I do not want to be sentimental about the power relationships in this or any other research project—clearly it was my project and the aura of many different forms of authority rested on me. Nevertheless, I believe that this want of expertise in particular areas was not neutral and probably had a positive impact overall.

Other researchers have taken different approaches. James Paul Gee (2003), for example, has offered an exploration of many different games from the perspective of a middle-aged newbie. Some of his observations relate to my own experience with games, and some reflect his own apparent ability to play these games more wholeheartedly than I found myself able to manage. For example, he observes,

These are limitations in the real-world me as a game player (an identity intersected by a good many other identities), limitations I have to live with if I want to play and eventually get better at games. One sort of limitation video games certainly bring up to real-world baby boomers like me is that they do not reward—in fact, they punish—some of my most cherished ways of learning and thinking (e.g., being too quick to want to get to a goal without engaging in sufficient prior nonlinear exploration). (2003, 57)

Even bearing in mind my own taste for exploring rather than achieving, I can certainly sympathize with Gee's lament on the strength of my experience with *Black & White*. He, however, has persevered with games much more intensively than I have done or am likely to do in the future.

This project is focused not simply on digital games, but, more broadly, on the ways in which different literacies cross over and fertilize each other. The general span of new hybrid literacies is my main focus, and game playing is just one part of that picture. My limitations as a player are part of the lens through which I view this picture.

Black & White: What the Travellers Say

Black & White offered the same set of potentialities to all participants, but their play provided a vivid reminder of how broadly this story could vary within the constraints of the introductory framework. A glimpse of the highlights of different games played will provide some sense of this variety.

Ben

Ben was not familiar with the game but he immediately liked the idea of being a god. "I think I'm going to like that part. . . . I used to joke a while ago around that I was going to create a religion and, like, screw with everybody's head."

He was good-tempered about being trained by the game. I asked him how he managed to remember what he was being told. He said, "Well, a large portion of it is pretty similar to other things so you can just remember that it's like similar to this—."

He was doing more than remembering what he recognized; he was also paying attention to the structure of the game.

One thing I noticed is that it's the—the nice conscience guy that's actually teaching you how to do things. The only thing your bad side of the conscience has gone and said, "Yeah this will be the focus point of your power!"

Later he returned to the structural importance of details, observing, "They've actually depicted a god as simply a hand out of the sky though and it's not just a thing because they've actually gone and put the effort into making it have a shadow. So it is actually a physical hand that is—drifting in the sky." But a real god, he continued, wouldn't have to put so much effort into fulfilling the requirements of the game. (Variations of this particular observation were made by many players.)

If there was a waiting point in the game (such as when the sculptor is creating the third gatestone), Ben took the opportunity to practice a new skill. "A lot of games," he said, "come with, like, tutorials in the very beginning. They go and step you through it and it's at least my opinion to go and try and do them because you at least need to know what you're doing in the rest of the game." Later he commented, "It's always better to be really patient at the beginning of any game so that you can at least try it out before you go and you say you don't like it or something."

Ben chose the ape to be his Creature ("Just because he looks the most goofy") and postponed exploring aspects of his relationship with the villagers in order to find food for his new friend. But he gave his Creature very mixed signals, stroking it and slapping it in response to the same activity. As his play drew to a close, he said he would probably keep on playing given the chance, and described how he thought his game would change.

Margaret: What would you expect to happen if you did keep playing it?
Ben: Umh—I'd probably go and—be a lot less nice.
Margaret: Why is that?
Ben: Just because it would be more funny for me, to go and get people or drop them and throw them across the world.
Margaret: Would you train your creature to be evil or would you continue to mess it up with mixed signals?
Ben: Oh, I'd mess it up. Scratch its butty, scratch its belly, and then smack it across the face.

He rated the game at about 7/10, but anticipated it would improve:

Ben: Yeah. Well, when you get into like, more advanced features; it would go and become a lot more interesting.
Margaret: Right. How long would you expect to have to play before you got to the point where it kind of took off on its own?
Ben: Mm—well, it already started taking off when you go and have a pet too—so it's already started, so you know when, the next time would be.

Ben's connection with his Creature was drawing him into a more transparent relationship with the game, at the same time as his power over the controls became more automatic.

Drew

Drew had played the game for a couple of hours once before, some time ago, and he was apparently a bit surprised at what he remembered when he put his mind to it:

> Well, shockingly I remember the maps. For some reason my strong mnemonic is position. So I can remember the map very clearly. I can remember, actually quite a lot. . . . Unlike most other people I had seen something similar to it before so I was not quite so taken aback. Although I mean the game concepts, the way they took it was unique about god.

Like Ben, Drew was happy to perform as a god, and actually signed himself into the game as "God," choosing a thunderbolt as his icon. He disliked the game controls almost from the very beginning, and experimented with using the keyboard to see whether that suited him better. He muttered remarks to the screen and commented more than once on his frustration.

Drew was extremely systematic and thorough in his exploration of the temple and the countryside. He clicked on anything that looked as if it would offer further information, and diligently read the information scrolls that dot the landscape.

Relatively early in the game, he said that if he were playing by himself he would restart at this stage because his current game had too many errors: "At this point generally I would—I would have ah, restarted the game because it is not perfect at this particular session of the game. Or I might continue on with the purpose of doing that later, but just screwing up now."

He said more than once how much he disliked being "led by the nose" through the training exercises; he wanted his training to be discretely organized and labelled, so he could get through with it and then move through the countryside with more "free will." He said, early on, "It likes to kind of go over the training, so that's kind of a detraction."

Drew often short-circuited the words on the soundtrack, clicking ahead before the speaker had finished, so I asked him whether he was simply reading the titles on the screen. His answer was a bit more complex than my question: "I read I guess, the easiest way is that I read it for the content, but I listen to it for the emphasis, so that is generally how I do it." He also enlivened his game by talking to the screen: "I would talk to the screen. I have—a bunch of snide comments for them, especially when they walk you through by the nose like that."

Drew wound up with the tiger as his Creature, but said he had not selected it; "I just clicked on him once to see what it would say." His commitment to the tiger may have been a bit half-hearted, but he stroked him kindly and I asked another question.

Margaret:	This is a bit of a silly question. When you do that do you feel as though you are patting him or are still just playing the game? Do you have any sense of contact with him imaginatively?
Drew:	Mm—my—my first thought was that he reacted well. Not necessary good or badly, but the way he *did* react was programmed well, so I guess it's more of a sense of playing the game.
Margaret:	Right. So you do not feel any strong connections to your tiger?
Drew:	Not really because he is really ugly.
Margaret:	Yes, he is. [*Laughter*]

Drew continued the game politely, but it made him cross. In the following extract it is possible to perceive him talking alternately to the screen and to me. He was diligently practising throwing his rocks but did not seem to be enjoying himself, and I asked him whether he was finding it annoying. He replied:

Very, because it is hard to judge the depth using this, so it is always behind, but you can't tell. Ugh—see that is what I am trying to do. It is also strange because I'm used to having to hold down and then release the throw, so I'm screwing that up quite a bit—no that's too far. *Yeah—grab-the-stone—grab it—that's*—see, as long as it is below the green here, it wants to be along the earth so I can't lob it. *Ugh—get big stone—grab it, grab it, oh heck—ha, ha, ha*—this isn't bowling! Whoops! Yeah, it doesn't like that one. See now this is deliberate. Ugh—good enough. Let's do something else.

Despite his complaints, Drew entered into his kingdom with some panache. I asked him what he was doing.

Well, I am giving people something to do—all this chilling out is just not cool. Production, production, production! No I wouldn't—not that I really need the resources I don't think—hey, fishing! [*inaudible*]—how do you fish?

Drew's game play was aimed at finding control. He did not at all care for the feeling that the game was making decisions for him. He wanted the training sessions to be clearly delineated so that he would know when he was on his own. And he wanted to play a clean game with few errors.

Jocelyn

Jocelyn was the quickest of all the participants to make a decision about whether she was likely to enjoy a text, and by far the most dismissive and fretful when asked to persevere with something she did not like. She was manifestly interested in the overall project and eager to be helpful, so her negative responses did not arise from an unwillingness to cooperate. It was very clear that whether the texts are books, movies, or games, her approach is equally binary, very much yes or no with no grey area in between.

True to form, Jocelyn was suspicious about committing time to an unknown game. "Am I going to want to throw the computer out the window?" she asked at once. "Tell me if you do, and we'll figure out something," I replied, and the game began. Almost from her first glance at the box, Jocelyn was intrigued, though she instantly instituted a gender change.

Jocelyn:	[*looking at the white side of the box*] Ooh Supreme God of the Land—Goddess!
Margaret:	Yeah, you can fix that.
Jocelyn:	I like that.
Margaret:	Yeah, I wondered if you would.
Jocelyn:	[*giggles*] That looks cute.
Margaret:	Turn it over [*to the black side of the box, which also opens revealing an alternate universe*].
Jocelyn:	Mm—even. Oh, and this one too. Oh—[*inaudible*] [*silence*] Okay.

Having concluded that she was indeed interested, Jocelyn launched herself into *Black & White* in very systematic and careful ways. Almost at once, she took up the option of moving into the gods' playground in order to practise rotating, a move she found difficult. She continued to struggle and the conscience/coach continued to prod her:

Jocelyn:	This is really annoying.
Margaret:	Do you want to leave the god's playground and go back to the—
Jocelyn:	No because I kind of want to do it.
Margaret:	Okay. [*Laughter*]

And, as she continued with her rotation practice, she pointed to the "good" conscience, and said, "I like that little dude!"

When she finally left the gods' playground and returned to the island of the main story, Jocelyn was equally systematic in clicking on the signposts bearing question marks that dot the landscape. Each, when clicked, reveals a hint on playing the game.

Margaret:	Now if you were playing this at home, would you go at it until you checked all those questions marks? Would you be that systematic?
Jocelyn:	Yeah.
Margaret:	And you'd do that before you did anything else?
Jocelyn:	Yeah.

Because of time constraints I asked her to leave this operation and actually activate the quest for the gatestones. Jocelyn soon got lost on the island, and unlike many players, turned very readily to the instruction book for help. It did not help her, and she said that, at this point, if she were playing at home she would quit. By quit she meant save and return on another occasion, not abandon the game entirely. Since this possibility was not an option in our artificial framework, she obligingly played on.

It took her a long time to find the first gatestone and her response on being asked to find a second was, "Oh heck!" But the second task was easier and was leavened by irresistible hilarity when she dropped the second stone on one of the houses and damaged the roof. Much of the subsequent dialogue on the tape is inaudible because everyone was laughing, but as Jocelyn continued to struggle with keeping a firm grasp on her gatestone, she said, "All right—I guess I'm the evil goddess! Oh crap—where did it go now? Where did that guy go—I hear people scream!"

Escaping from the havoc she had created by finally getting the gates to open, Jocelyn chose the cow to be her Creature and set about finding food for it. When on her travels, she was met by a group of boat builders asking for help in finding more wood, she obliged by fetching them some wood (they instantly started asking for grain—"Oh man!" said Jocelyn).

Margaret:	So far you've taken every opportunity to be kind, you haven't taken one chance to be evil.
Jocelyn:	Yeah.
Margaret:	Is that because you're just a nice person?
Jocelyn:	Well I don't know—it's—yeah I guess it's just nice.
Margaret:	Would you play it through again taking all the evil choices or would you find that upsetting?
Jocelyn:	Mm—yeah probably not. I don't think I'd like it.

Jocelyn was very positive about the game, talking about a kind of emotional investment, particularly with her cow and the white "good" conscience.

Margaret:	So what do you make of it?
Jocelyn:	I like it, it's fun!
Margaret:	What do you like about it?
Jocelyn:	Mm—I *really* like the cow. [*Laughter*]
Margaret:	Yes.
Jocelyn:	And umh, I like that ah—well it is cool that you can be nice to people and it's kind of cool you get to pick which you want to do.
Margaret:	Yes.
Jocelyn:	And it's just funny little things like, when you can make that this type of [*inaudible*] and they go "wahoo!" Like, it kept me interested I think with that stuff.
Margaret:	Right. So it's the detail as much as the giant scheme of things?
Jocelyn:	Yeah. I like just little things like that [*inaudible*] guy that you have to find the stones for and that little white—whoever he is.
Margaret:	Yes. And do you like this kind of miniature world effect?
Jocelyn:	I've never played it, but I do like it yeah. I didn't think I would, like I probably wouldn't have given this a chance really. I didn't think I'd like it, but I do.

And later she reinforced this positive judgement.

Margaret:	So assuming you stayed this interested and you kept finding new things to fool around with, how long do you think you would play this before you gave up on it?
Jocelyn:	Oh I think I'd play this a lot. I can see myself becoming obsessed with this one.
Margaret:	What does obsessed mean? Would you come home from work every night and [*inaudible*] do it?
Jocelyn:	Yeah probably.
Margaret:	Uhuh. For the whole evening or just a couple of hours at a time or—?
Jocelyn:	I'd probably do a couple of hours at a time because then I feel guilty and I'll do stuff around the house too, but I can see like a weekend playing this for a few hours a day or something.
Margaret:	Right. Would you play right to the end?
Jocelyn:	Yeah probably. Like it depends because I really do like this, but a lot of times with games, I never finish them.
Margaret:	Right. You have to keep on liking it?
Jocelyn:	Yeah.

Jocelyn clearly values some kind of emotional connection with the story. Both her enthusiasm for particular characters (the cow and the white god, for example) and her reluctance to hurt her people suggest that there is some feeling in her relationship with this story.

Isaac

With Isaac's game, we ran into the kind of problem that drives non-technical people wild. For no reason that I could ever establish, we found it impossible to enter the game at the beginning, and we wasted a great deal of time uninstalling and reinstalling the game. Isaac was amazingly patient and admirably good-tempered throughout this frustrating procedure. As we waited for the game to load, he consulted the instruction book. When we got the game finally started, however, after wasting some 20 minutes, he was eager to get going and found the introduction unnecessarily lengthy. He also disliked the keyboard controls and rejected that option right from the beginning.

Isaac grasped the concept of the game even as he was still being trained in forms of movement, during the building of the temple: "Okay, well considering I had a good and evil conscience, I was ex-, expecting that I was going to have the choice so that I could help them build it or that I could, like, flog them and make them build it in a hurry." He tried clicking F2 for entry to the gods' playground for some practice, but that did not work for him, possibly because he was still in the training loop of the game.

Isaac would have explored the temple very thoroughly and took some interest in the information scrolls but, because we had lost so much time, I encouraged him to move on with the game. He moved around the island very surely, though he was often unhappy with his point of view; he found himself too high above the island more than once but could not succeed in lowering his perspective enough to suit him.

As he moved gatestones around the island, he paid attention to the little people scurrying along the ground, and noticed that some were called "Disciple Breeders." He was not impressed at the game pushing him forward to find his Creature before he could sort out the mystery of these people, and resorted to the instruction book to see whether he could find further information.

Isaac chose the ape and spoke kindly to it as he found food for it (though he was a bit surprised when the ape ate a peasant he had accidentally picked up along with the grain). Despite this benevolent beginning, however, when instructed how to slap his Creature, he gave it a vigorous thrashing.

As we moved through the game, Isaac described himself as somewhat interested and somewhat frustrated. He said if he owned the game he would work away at it, but not as a priority. "It would be, like, I would run over and do a little bit during a commercial or something."

Isaac made an interesting point about the increased story value of the evil choices.

Isaac: [The story] doesn't seem to be going anywhere; it's just an existing storyline. So, I was just supposed to hang out in this village that, that and fiddle around and figure out what's going on and what everybody is. Um, [laughing] and it's actually more fun to uh, do the, the evil stuff like trying to set down that stone for the sculptor and it knocked him over. Um, picking her up and uh dropping her and she squealed and tumbled over . . . . What I wanted to do was to see what the uh, because, you know basically what is going to happen if you feed him good food and that, that's it. Or if you pet him. Well, no, I wanted to see what happened when I slapped him around a bunch. Because the other's predictable. I want to find out the things that are going to be different and amusing.

Margaret: Uh huh, and do you think evil's more likely to be amusing to you?

Isaac: Well, the good things are going to be what I would expect to happen which is like everyday life. So, why would I want to live my every day life on a computer screen? That's why *The Sims* doesn't really interest me. Now, doing, the, the, the evil stuff, evil influenced stuff is kind of like, lets say more [*inaudible*], it's not what you're expecting, it's not the norm, it's not complacent. I don't want, I don't want to play a game that's just all complacent. It's kind of— boring, so. Um, boredom level and frustrated, combined with frustration level.

For Isaac, it seems that at least one part of appeal is the development of story events, something he thinks more likely to arise out of evil choices.

Margaret: Do you think if you brought your Creature up to be evil, if somebody was to cause mayhem, it would get more interesting?

Isaac: Ooooh—yes, because there's nothing, there would be something that's obviously running around on it, so creating havoc—there is nothing to create havoc right now. Or challenges, I guess if I got to the point where I could create challenges and know that these people have to do them or I could assign them to go out and do it and then just, they're going to go off and try and attempt it, and then I could check in and see if they completed it or how they screwed it up or um—yeah, so okay, maybe it's still too early, I'll—[looking at the screen] what the heck is this thing that keeps moving around all over the place? That must be that chick. [Silence] Oh, I betcha that's probably the Breeder running around for whatever purpose. Okay. Oh, so, to find out what each of the people does, like if she's running around breeding, like if I leave this for x amount of time, while all of a sudden the village would be like overfull. . . . Can the people starve, if I, if I ignore them long enough will my village hit a point of—of a—fear of disintegration or—or—yeah.

From this level of story development talk, Isaac went back to discussing his problems with managing the zoom control, moving from a question of story to one of access. Overall, however, it was the shaping of the story that caught his attention. He was not interested in emotional connections, as Jocelyn described; he was more interested in making his story intriguing.

Earlier I raised the question of whether there could be a player with a pre-dilection for story-making as a significant stance in relation to a game. I would argue that Isaac's interest in mayhem involves just such an approach. It is clear that he wants something to *shape* the nature of the challenge being offered to him by the game. He refers briefly to the possibility of entropy as one form of challenge, and speaks more than once about the potential of evil to create some interest in the story. At the same time, he wants to be able to move more fluidly about his domain, to explore and understand more freely.

Jeremy

Unlike the other players, Jeremy was familiar with *Black & White*; a year before we met, he had spent a week with it, playing about three hours a day. After that time, he started to find it repetitive and therefore boring, and gave up.

In order both to give him a new impetus with the game and to take advantage of his experience and expertise, I asked him to give me a play-by-play account as he moved through the game. As a consequence, his game was both informative and somewhat more artificial than the other games played in this project.

Jeremy had spent the year before we met working in a computer shop, and was familiar with very many games as a consequence of his need to act in an advisory capacity to customers. He is also a very sociable player, talking to his friends about games and checking online sites for extra information. Routinely, when he gets a new game he checks the web for any relevant patches to upgrade his game before he even starts playing. His explanation for preferring mouse controls to keyboard controls indicates his level of comfort with game playing: "The reason that I say that I would prefer to use the mouse for movement because often times in games there's a lot of other shortcuts on the keyboard that you can use that for and I don't like having to switch back and forth."

Jeremy fed his villagers early on, and I asked him about his relationship to the little figures that scurry around the landscape.

Margaret: Do you build up any kind of emotional attachment to these little characters?

Jeremy: Ah—not really to the characters, but I did to my Creature. Just because you
             spend so much time with it, I think, training it and such.
Margaret: Right. Did he have a name, your Creature in play?
Jeremy: I can't remember. I think maybe it was something like "Cow" or "Tiger" or
             something.
Margaret: So it wasn't a name full of emotional resonance?
Jeremy: No. I don't think so anyways. I can't remember. So, the game is building up
             in complexity as he's teaching me what to do.

Jeremy's quick switch back to the challenge of the game both reflected his
aim of explaining the game to me and also his relative lack of interest in the
emotional implications of his relationship to his Creature. What really appeals
to him about a game, he made it very clear, is an intelligent storyline. "This
has a storyline to it. Quite a good—actually—oh it has a storyline to it and
sometimes it's like a book where you just can't put it down."

The best game he ever played, said Jeremy, was *Baldur's Gate*. I quote an
extensive part of our conversation here because Jeremy was so interesting on
the subject of games and stories.

Jeremy: It's the same thing; if it's not intelligent it can get quite boring with the same
             thing over and over again. What I liked about *Baldur's Gate* is that it was more
             based around the story rather than a story lightly based around the action, which
             is what it is in a lot of games. They think of making the game first and just throw-
             ing in the story so that you have somewhere to go and kill guys.

I suggested a distinction between a story that operates as a path and a game that
behaves like a maze, with dead ends and doublings back and asked, "Which is
more satisfying of the two, a maze or path or does it depend on the medium?"

Jeremy: It depends on the medium. If I'm playing it on the computer or a gaming console
             I don't want it to be linear step after step. I want the possibility of being differ-
             ent every time I go through it. Which is good in something like this, as well as
             in *Baldur's Gate*, because you have the option of being good or evil. Parts of the
             story are affected by your reactions so every time you go through and play, it's
             not going to be the same thing every time.

I asked Jeremy how difficult it was to remember the moves in such a way that
they were second nature. He said most of them were coming back to him but
certain "tid-bits" were missing and he would have to re-learn them. This game
included more unique moves than many, he said; many first-person shooters
are generically similar.

Jeremy:	Yeah, it would be like learning to ride a bike, you'll be really used to riding your own bike, but you'll also ride another one.
Margaret:	Right, that's a very good analogy. And how do people get to that stage where it feels intuitive?
Jeremy:	Oh umh, it gets to the point where it depends how good you want to be especially if it's online. There's always someone that is better than you so you can just keep getting better and better and better.
Margaret:	Right. And how much of it is explicit instruction from the better players? Not necessarily formally, it can be very informal. How much is tips from other players that goes into making it [*inaudible*]?
Jeremy:	Quite a lot of it.
Margaret:	Uhuh, so it's quite a social arrangement learning to be a good game player?
Jeremy:	Yes.
Margaret:	And how does that social arrangement get started?
Jeremy:	There are a number of different ways. If you are just on the public server with other people you can just type in "generally chat" mode and if there happens to be a couple of nice people playing they might tell you. A lot of time they won't because they couldn't be bothered to tell someone that they don't know what to do. There are other things, gaming groups and such that play with each other and you get to know these people quite well and they will readily tell you and help you out a lot more. . . . With more advanced techniques and shorts, strategies you learn from other people, it's a lot easier to learn from other people rather than figure it out on your own.

It was striking to what extent Jeremy's game comments kept returning to relationships with other players, even as he spoke of the single-player game *Black & White*. If a game got boring, he ceased playing without compunction, but the network of friends and allies seemed to be an ongoing priority to him.

Seth

Seth took a quick look at the instruction book, but then said, "I have a general idea. I'm too excited to read, I want to play. Typical kid!" We had problems loading the game, but he quickly grasped the gist of the "god" plot, bringing wood to the temple for the "little wieners" running around on the ground, and saying grandly, "Use it well, my wieners!"

Unfortunately for the progress of his game, Seth made an early error, dropping the first gatestone into the sea. Although the conscience figure prodded him to go find it again (suggesting that this error was silently erased by the game program), he chose instead to mess around in the landscape. Finding the silver scroll that prompts a player to throw rocks at a big stone, he practised for a long time and finally threw a sheep at the stone. Although he was frustrated at not being sure whether he could proceed with the game properly in the absence of the first gatestone, he said he was enjoying the game.

Eventually he relocated the gatestone but still had trouble finding the gate. "I just want to wreck things now," he said, laughing. Back in the gods' playground, he continued to struggle with purposeful movement across the landscape. When he finally improved and the voice of the conscience congratulated him, he said, "Yeah, it took you two hours—the god is angry. He wants to play—hurry up."

Seth continued his play as a vengeful god, snatching people from the ground and hurling them into the air. He talked to himself and/or the screen as he played, but (possibly because the audiotape had to be changed, which reminded him he was playing in public, in a manner of speaking, but possibly just because he began to feel uneasy about his own imaginary cruelty) he suddenly stopped talking to himself and spoke to me.

Seth:	*Come on pick it up.* I'm going to plant it on somebody's head—in the house—*there you go.* Let's see—ah—so he thinks the—by doing that it was for a good reason. [*Laughs*] I'm so immature—it's great! Okay let's throw her against the wall—okay I'll pass. You know if I had powers in real life, I guess I shouldn't talk [*referring to the tape change*]—
Margaret:	The tape recorder's running.
Seth:	Oh okay, if I had powers in real life, I'd use it for good. This is only 'cause it's non-consequential. *Get up—what are you doing—what does that mean? I need some rocks—need some rocks. What's happening?* Okay, that's the wood.

I asked him if he would keep on playing in the face of such frustration if he were at home.

At home I'd probably have one game where I'm doing all the good things and everything, then one game of just fun. I know I'm never going to get to play this again, so I just want to have some fun with it and just, like, wreck things, just because I get to be god for a day, for an hour.

Finally, Seth got the first gatestone in place and was sent to find the second one. At this point in the game, the bad conscience suggests that rather than searching for the sick brother, the god could simply smash the house where the gatestone is kept.

Seth:	Why don't I wreck the house?
Margaret:	Go for it.
Seth:	How do I do it—I can't, the nurse in me says to go look for this guy.

But nurse or not, Seth kept experimenting with pestering his subjects. When he found the third stone for the sculptor to carve, he dropped it on top of the man instead of beside him. He was delighted to see that his "belief" score increased with his violent deeds.

| Seth: | *It's going to take you a while, man—holy!—here, you little pecker!* [*Laughs*] It's like they're being sacrificed—I've got seven belief [points]. That's awesome! *Oh you're lucky. Are you still alive? Yes, two men!* They all listen to the rock. They're tough people. |
| Margaret: | They would have to be with the likes of you around! |

Seth picked the ape as his Creature. "Ah—you're pretty homely. I will take you." When the ape hurt Sable, the trainer, and she instructed Seth to slap his Creature, he refused. "Screw that man, I like him like that. [*laughs*] That's what I want him to do." When he learned how to lead his Creature around with the Leash of Learning, he marched him into the sea, saying, "All right, Stinky, time for a bath." His main complaint was that he would have preferred to play with a joystick, but he played with the limits of the game, and was very reluctant to stop. He said he would play extensively if he had this game at home.

Seth:	You know—I don't know—sometimes if I get into something [*laughs lightly*] I don't know, five, six hours. I mean, I could go if it's got my attention. I can always stop, go to the fridge, do whatever, go to the bathroom, I'll keep playing yeah.
Margaret:	And you would with this?
Seth:	Yeah, I'd see what—what else I could do.

I asked him what would frustrate him to the point of stopping playing but he did not seem to think in such terms.

| Margaret: | What about when you were trapped looking for that stone round and round, would that stop you under normal circumstances? |
| Seth: | Well—not necessarily. Like I said, I guess it would depend on what setting. Like, you know how I said I would have one game when I'm trying and one just for craft and stuff. Like, if I was playing for real and stuff, I'd go onto the Internet and look for game plays or something like that. |

He would, he explained, read just enough to go back to playing, a common example of reading acting as a kind of pointer to other forms of interpretation. It is interesting to note that he also makes explicit reference to the issue of interruption, saying that if his interest is sufficiently aroused, it will override any problem with a temporary cessation of play. He distinguishes between messing around and playing seriously, but seems to enjoy both.

Courtney

Courtney responded almost at once to the images on the screen: "Goodness—is it an old game?" When I told her it was from 2001 (this session was held in mid-December 2002), she replied, "The graphics are very blocky. You know, it's like *older* computer animation."

More than any other player, Courtney played in long and intensive periods of silence. This observation does not necessarily reflect a totally different stance towards the game; we had unusual problems with the video recording of this particular session, and an alternative or additional explanation may be that I was simply too distracted and fatigued by this technical hitch to prompt her as regularly as I did with other players. The reality of the data-gathering exercise can never be completely extracted from the findings.

At any rate, Courtney moved through the introduction and the temple-building exercise without comment. After a bit of searching, she located the first gatestone, and it was while she was conveying the sick brother to the sister with possession of the second gatestone that she made almost her first observation. As the hand carrying the brother swerved against the swirling background of the island's forests, she said, "Poor guy, if he wasn't sick before—! [*laughter*]"

But the third gatestone eluded her for a very long time. She searched very patiently, shifting between the mouse and the keyboard in what appeared to be systematic fashion—using one control for certain actions and the other one for the remainder. She went round the island many times. After a while, I wondered whether she was simply searching out of politeness, but she indicated that this was not the case:

Margaret: What's your sense about the frustrations—the couple of times you had the second gatestone lined up, but you didn't have it quite spot-on, so you have to go back and retrieve it. And then you've been hunting and hunting for the stone, for the third one. Umh, is that just part of the deal with these games? Do you get fretful about them?

Courtney: No, I just think that's just the way it is.

I tried again to explore this question as she came to the end of her time with the game.

Margaret:	Okay, let's just talk about this for a little while. How patient would you be if you were doing this at home? Would you still be playing?
Courtney:	Possibly. Umh, if it were my first time?
Margaret:	Yeah.
Courtney:	Umh, I would probably look at it a little bit longer. Probably enlist some help. I would go back and I would watch it, and I would watch it much more carefully so that I could see, you know, maybe what the—you know, if there was a certain inlet or if it was by a certain—you could see anything else, you're not—it's like a five-second clip [when you are first shown the location of the stone as the voice speaks of it].
Margaret:	How good is your sense of spatial relationships?
Courtney:	It gets easier. Umh, it's very difficult just to do it with just the mouse, I find.
Margaret:	Yeah. Yeah, I notice you were switching back and forth quite a bit.
Courtney:	Yeah, but the keyboard—when it said that it gave you a keyboard option that was a really good for me because, umh, like with other games that we've played, you know, I just had to rely on the mouse, then it became difficult for me you know, to try and manoeuvre, but because you had the keyboard option making it a little bit easier certainly.
Margaret:	But you don't use the keyboard the whole time?
Courtney:	No, umh, personally because I couldn't really figure out how all of the keyboard—I think if I knew just all the keyboard commands, then I would probably just use the keyboard. Umh, the mouse I don't find is that handy. I think it would be different if it was a trackball. Like if when we have the stationary mouse, with just a trackball. And I think that would be a little bit simpler because then you wouldn't have to shuffle the whole mouse around to do what you want it to do. Umh, you know, with the pushing and pulling and running off of the mouse pad, it's really difficult. If you had a trackball and it was just, you know, a matter of moving your fingers where you wanted the ball to be, then it's different.
Margaret:	You'd have more finesse, more control.
Courtney:	That's right, that's right, I think that you would.

Courtney yearned for a trackball; Seth would have preferred a joystick. They were the only two who mentioned a different control mechanism, and maybe they each would have been less lost on the island with a manual control they were happy to use. The capacity to reach conclusions both about what is plausible in the story and also about what is reasonable for you to do next, and to implement these conclusions with swift and organized action is an integral part of playing a digital game, and players do get used to particular manual responses. Drew used the mouse but disliked the actual movements needed to move through this game. Jeremy stuck to the mouse so he could keep his keyboard reactions for shortcuts; it is easy to see long-term patterning in these responses.

Courtney was very clear that a gamer's job is to notice details and assemble them into a useful mental map.

Margaret [after much fruitless searching]	Do you know what you're looking for?
Courtney:	I'm looking for a rock with sparklies on top of it.
Margaret:	Okay.
Courtney:	I know that they had shown me a picture of where it was and if you pay close enough attention then you'll be able to figure out where on the island it is.

And again, later, she referred to one of the difficulties of game play, the absence of a rewind button or the ability to look back through earlier pages: "But where? Over here at this [*inaudible*]? You see, it was helpful when they first gave you a picture of where it was. And if you go back to that picture, it would be helpful."

Summing up her response to the game overall, she spoke again of this mapping facility.

Courtney:	It would be nice if they gave you a map to refer back to.
Margaret:	Right. How important is it that you develop a map of your own in your own head?
Courtney:	Yeah, I think that's part of it that you know, exploring the island a number of times so that you know when they say, "it was by the ravine" that you can know, "yeah, the ravine—of course", you know. Whereas in the beginning, like the ravine— wherever that hell that is, you know. If I knew where that was, then I guess I could find the rock, but yes, it's quite difficult. I think even if they gave you a map that said, "Quarry is here" you would still have to look around the island to find where on that map is, you know, this quarry.

Courtney considers most of these challenges simply to be part of how the game is made. She never did find the third gatestone and we talked about the development of the Creature's personality and the potential for choosing good or evil, in purely hypothetical terms. However, her patience for the game was considerable and she did not seem to be frustrated by her long hunt. It appeared that her pleasure in exploring and her appreciation of scenic details comprise one major component of that patience.

> Courtney: In the temple—it was beautiful in the temple and you could see all the different things and play with the different buttons and go through doors and all that. The ambience of it is very much a part of it.
>
> Margaret: Right. Now you explored the temple fairly methodically; you explored the island fairly methodically. How important is that when you're playing these kinds of games?
>
> Courtney: I think pretty important. On the one hand, it's nice just to appreciate all the work that went into it, even seeing all the little birds flying around—you know, the waves that lap on the shore—and you can hear it and you can see it and it's really interesting. Umh—I think that it gives you a better appreciation for the game itself.

Experience with other games and a strategic awareness of the importance of a slow but thorough start are obviously also factors in her approach.

Damian

Damian was a pilot participant and his sessions did not proceed in the same order as those of the final seven participants. He did play *Black & White*, but for considerably less time than the later players. Nevertheless, as a very experienced player, he made good headway in a short time and chose the cow to be his Creature.

Damian's predilection for violent talk, which I observed on every occasion that he encountered any kind of digital game, soon manifested itself in the play of *Black & White*. Even during the introduction, as the voice addresses him as a god for saving the boy, he says, "Squish him, squish him!" and a cull of his remarks to himself over a very short span of time includes the following lines:

> Now let's fight somebody.
> Let's get to this fighting.
> Better start smiting soon!
> Let's kill him.
> Tap . . . smite!

Damian's response to the overall game, however, was more complex than this list of quotes would indicate.

> Margaret: If you carried on playing this for longer, would you be choosing good or evil?

Damian: I don't know. It would depend on, I don't know, it would depend on a lot.
            Many different paths to go on.
Margaret: Would you try to balance them out?
Damian: I doubt I—
Margaret: You'd take one or the other?
Damian: I'd take one extreme completely.
Margaret: And then would you go back and play it again to see the other extreme
            or would one do you?
Damian: I might, yeah I'd probably try and go through as evil as I could and as good
            as I could.

Asked which he would choose if I offered him only one choice between
Black & White and the PlayStation game *Ever Grace*, which he also played
for an extended period in this session, Damian plumped for *Black & White*
"because I get to smite people."

Although his interest in "smiting" never waned, Damian's responses to
all the different computer games involved other elements as well. He spoke
eloquently of the pleasures of flow, and talked about the challenge of creating
a mental map. He often plays games for very long stretches at a time, partly in
response to that flow and partly because the mental investment in the map is
easier to maintain than resume. Similarly, he will get into the flow of a novel
and read for hours, so it is not just a gaming phenomenon with him.

Denise

Like Damian, Denise played *Black & White* much more briefly than the later
participants. Unlike Damian, she is not an experienced gamer (except on the
GameBoy handheld platform, a skill she attributes to hours spent in travelling
during her childhood). Unlike Drew in particular, she especially appreciated
the mix of plot and training at the beginning of *Black & White*.

Denise: At this point, like based on what's going on, I would probably just play with
            it myself because it seems to be just telling me how to do things and it's not,
            umh, it's not like your average game where they just sort of plop you in and
            say, "okay, go for it." They are actually telling you, "okay this is how you
            do this and this is how you want to do this and this is how you want to do
            this", so . . .
Margaret: Sounds like you appreciate that?
Denise: Yes. It makes getting into the game a little bit easier as opposed to, if you
            were just dropped in the middle and you have to figure how to get out of
            that first screen, then it takes you know, an hour to figure out how to get
            out of the first screen at which point you just say, "you know what, what's

the point?" So I find it, I'm finding this a little bit more user friendly than some of the games that I've encountered before.

Denise was quite clear, however, that user-friendliness was not enough.

Denise: To even have the world's most user friendly game, but if there's no plot or main line then there's really no . . . you're not going anywhere. Or you can have something that has so much plot, but you can never find it because there's, you can't figure out how to get to it, so.

Margaret: So the balance so far looks good?

Denise: Yeah, but there's enough, it seems as if there's enough going on. Like there's tasks that need to be accomplished and there's things you need to do and decisions to make and they're telling you, "This is how you go about making these decisions and this is how you go about doing things that you need to do."

Like Isaac, Denise is describing a case of appropriate balance between salience and ease of access, two factors that are significant elements in making a selection of a text (Mackey, 2002). It is interesting that Denise so explicitly drew on the importance of these two factors, given her evident lack of experience and of automatic manual skills with this game. Her GameBoy background did not give her particular exposure to complex digital stories, but she still recognized this good balance between significant content and manageable access. She did not, however, play this game long enough that I could place her approach into one of Bartle's categories.

Different Strategies and Approaches

The nine players were given options within the game: their search for the gatestones could be single-minded or half-hearted and distracted by the scenery and the inhabitants of the island; they could stop to practise or pursue the main story; they could choose one Creature or another; they could train their Creature as they chose; and so forth. But beyond the internal options of the game and consequent plot variations, these players also manifested quite different behaviours and strategies in how they moved into the game. More than one explicitly mentioned that if he were to play this game at home, he would run two games side by side, one for messing around and experimenting and one for achieving the perceived ends of the story. They commenced their interpretation of the game with a variety of strategies, as well as mentioning preferences for differing physical controls of the action (mouse controls, keyboard controls, joystick, trackball). They disagreed about the virtues of early instruction embedded in the diegetic world of the story or ring-fenced explicitly as instruction. This question of how they variously played themselves into a game is one to which I return in the final chapter.

In addition, the players found different aspects of the game to enjoy and value. While many of them paid tribute to the importance of an intelligent storyline, other sources of pleasure in the game seemed more diverse.

Revisiting the Maps

How do the theoretical perspectives outlined earlier in this chapter help us to look more closely at the players' games?

The Present Tense of the Game

All the players step into the fictional world of *Black & White* with every appearance of nonchalance. Taking this step into make-believe is something they are very accustomed to. After that common early stage, their instantiations of the game began almost at once to diverge. Some focused on assembling and assimilating as much background information as possible, raising the hope that the story could unfold with as little interference as possible from their own present-tense misunderstandings. Some simply forged ahead with game play, confidently or tentatively. We see a specific example of the present tense of the game at work in Seth's misplay; when he accidentally dropped his gatestone into the sea, he had no apparent way forward into the story. The story could not unfold without this step, and although the game prompted him to try again, he chose to abandon narrative progression for a kind of messing around in the territory, flinging sheep and peasants into the ocean.

Performing the Game

The players were united in attempting to align their physical responses to the needs of the game, but again that very basic starting point led to much breaking off into diverse approaches. Many players commented on the specificities of control, either in terms of the physical system (expressing a preference for a joystick or a trackball) or in terms of the hand actions needed to move the game ahead (complaining about the mouse movement needed to create forward motion, objecting to the difficulties of controlling the camera angle). Some players invested in practice time in order to render ways of making progress more fluent and transparent; others, such as Jocelyn, expressed an interest in the practice zone as an area where consequences of her actions might be reduced.

Players alluded to the necessity to perform the game in mental as well as physical terms, most often with reference to the need to create mental maps. It seemed clear overall that the need to *make the story happen* was part of the specific challenge and pleasure (with the ratio of one to the other varying with different players) of the game narrative.

Rules and Conventions

All the players demonstrated an implicit understanding that they would need to notice, signify and configure, in Rabinowitz's (1987) vocabulary. It was interesting to see Courtney at work; as Eskelinen and Tronstad (2003) and Elsaesser (1998) suggest may occur in games, she manifested something of an inversion of Rabinowitz's schema. In her game, the idea of "noticing" took on a tangible importance. Looking for "a rock with sparklies on top of it," she already knew something of its significance in the progression of the story, yet she had to physically notice it before she could pick it up and make the game move ahead.

Players varied in their capacity to notice, just as readers may do. But at some stages, no further progression through the story was possible until noticing took place, and players were all too aware that they had failed to notice correctly. The contrast with a print fiction, where the reader may proceed for pages and chapters, oblivious to the fact that a crucial component of the story has been overlooked, raises interesting questions about narrative.

Ludus and Paidea

The distinction between ludus and paidea was very helpful in terms of sorting player behaviours. Some, such as Damian and Drew, were highly ludic and goal-oriented in their approach; others, such as Courtney and Seth, were much more content with simply having a look around and perhaps finding playful potential in the territory. The transcripts do make some room for the idea of paidea as a default behaviour when aiming for objectives does not work or seems too difficult. Again, some players would be more satisfied with this approach than others; Drew, for example, specifically said that he would quit the game and start again with a view to making fewer mistakes rather than taking such a default option.

Player Types

Bartle's typology proved to be surprisingly robust in terms of categorizing this little set of players. Even if one makes all allowances for the fact that a player's stance will undoubtedly shift during the course of game, it was still clear that all four categories were represented among the players of Black & White. Denise did not get far enough into the game to be classifiable (her conversation focused on the importance of scaffolding for the novice player). The remaining eight players, however, could be readily labelled in Bartle's terms.

Damian and Jeremy, respectively, are easy to code as a killer and a socializer. To describe their games just in these terms would be reductive, but there is a strong bias in each case. Courtney and Seth are explorers, happy to spend time just moving around the island, listening to the birds and the waves, experimenting with possible actions either cooperatively or transgressively.

I labelled Jocelyn, Isaac, Ben, and Drew as achievers, but their interest in achieving manifested itself in different ways. Drew wanted to succeed on the game's terms. He was interested in exploring but his explorations were subordinated to a better understanding and higher achievement in relation to the game. He wanted as much as possible to be happening successfully in his game world. His preference, once his preliminary and error-prone exploration was completed to his satisfaction, would be to quit the game and start a new version with fewer mistakes.

Ben was committed, at least in the early stages of the game, to achieving an efficient understanding of the game's processes and procedures. Much of his initial sense of achievement appeared to be strategic in nature.

Jocelyn was interested in achieving an emotional connection to her game. Many of her comments on the game involve the achievement of such a link—to the guiding gods, to her Creature, to the little people on the ground. Her play was oriented towards making such connections.

Isaac wanted to achieve some kind of narrative shape—alone among these players in this aim. He spoke of the need to introduce some kind of mayhem into the situation, of the importance of avoiding complacency, of the necessity of understanding the role of entropy in the working out of the storyline.

Discussion

Our understanding of the literacies of game playing is still very tentative, and the testimonials to the plurality of the experience provided by these players serve as a reminder that any singular description of the process at least will be reductive and more probably will be actively misleading. The examples of these players at work do offer a glimpse of the complexities of interpreting this particular form of text. Physical alertness, strategic and symbolic attentiveness, and a capacity for grasping when to take action and when to let go of interpretive striving all play a role in how a player learns to make meaningful contact with a particular game. Individual predilections, acquired skills, and genre expectations contribute to the final achievement, as of course they do in all forms of interpretive behaviour.

· 5 ·

READING BEYOND THE WORDS:
WHAT THE MAPS SAY

Reading involves the interpretation of written words, but these words often function in relation to other sources of meaning. In this chapter, I will investigate what we can learn from theoretical approaches to polysemic or multi-channel reading. As Gunther Kress reminds us, we now often deal with texts in which

> language alone cannot give us access to the meaning of the multimodally constituted message; language and literacy now have to be seen as partial bearers of meaning only. The co-presence of other modes raises the question of their function: are they merely replicating what language does, are they ancillary or marginal, or do they play a full role, and if they do, is it the same role as that of writing or a different role? And if they play a different role, is that because of their constitution, their make-up, and their affordances (2003, 35)?

I will describe the kinds of understanding we have developed through study of picture books and graphic novels, and then take a brief look at the impact of music upon reading.

Words Plus: What the Maps Say

At first glance, the reading of print on paper would seem to have changed very little for centuries. Abstract ink marks on the page are simultaneously inspected and flooded with meaning by the competent reader. That meaning is a combination of conventional and personal understanding, as it has been since the invention of writing.

Yet there are changes both in uses of print and in how it conveys meaning. Many changes have been so long assimilated that we forget they were ever new: the convention of spaces between words, for example, or the related idea that a person can read silently rather than, or as well as, aloud (Fischer, 2003; Saenger, 1997). Other changes are more recent. I well remember my days as an undergraduate student journalist; when our printing company converted from linotype to offset printing, our options for—and our interest in—exciting layout possibilities suddenly expanded exponentially.

Design and layout are partners of print that are often taken for granted, but they make a great deal of difference to the reading experience. My great-grandfather's books of Presbyterian theology were undoubtedly forbidding in terms of what they actually had to say, but to me they were so repellent in their physical qualities that I never sampled the content. Large, heavy books in which three columns of small print in smudged lettering stare at you from every page—even today, I shudder to think of the discipline required to persevere with these tomes. In my own childhood, we acquired a set of the *Books of Knowledge*, 20 hardbacks, also large and heavy, with austere bindings. In a gesture to user-friendliness, as I recall, they presented double rather than triple columns and the print was a little larger and crisper than in the theology books; but the illustrations were rare, small, and dense to interpret, and anything in colour had to be a special insert. It is easy to forget how much has changed in what gets taken for granted, and how swiftly our most basic assumptions about what makes acceptable reading material have altered.

What happens to the printed word when it marries other media, and what happens to a reader who meets this word in such a context? We are in the initial stages of answering these questions. Probably the most extensive study until now has involved picture books, with observations on graphic novels catching up fast. Much interesting theory and research thus explicates the reading of words modified by their relationship with still images, often in the context of fiction. Scholars are also exploring the impact of non-fiction and information conveyed polysemically, and again the combination of words and still images is better understood than other arrangements, such as words and music, pictures and music, words and moving images, and so forth. The very differences between picture books and graphic novels offer some interesting insights into how words and images may interact.

The impact of printed words accompanied by moving images has been rather less thoroughly investigated. A lively example of this kind of work is David Macaulay's CD-ROM *The Way Things Work 2.0* (1998), which mixes words and animations that demonstrate, for example, how gears work. Undoubtedly the moving pictures make it easier to understand the principle of gears than any number of still images—I testify with feeling as someone who was baffled by physics homework on gears until my mother had the wit to get out an egg-beater and show me some gears in action. On the other hand, if I had learned about gears from repetition of Macaulay's little animation, I suspect that my understanding of their intricacies would have been considerably more robust but rather less articulate, as I would not have had to struggle with the abstraction of a verbal description—a gain or a loss? This kind of CD-ROM manifests something of the qualities of the fixed word (though the screen is not as stable as the page) with the pedagogical virtues of the equally unchanging replay. The animation can be perused over and over, referring back and forth to the words as seems most helpful.

The impact of mingling words and sound is perhaps even less well understood. Most of the studies that I am aware of deal with the combination of *oral* word and soundtrack, as in audiobooks (Cox, 1996; Varley, 2002), but digital media mean that electronically printed words may be attached to their own music or background sounds—one such text was used in this project. It is possible that the growing literature on the role of film soundtracks may offer some useful insights into this territory.

In other words, there is rich material to explore on the subject of words in association with other channels of meaning.

Words Alone

Before exploring these associations, it may be useful to take a brief look at some aspects of dealing with words on their own. Print offers many supple affordances. One of the most significant qualities of reading print is the power of a reader to control pace. A reader can spend days on a single phrase, or belt through a thick book as fast as eyes and brain will process the blur of words. Rereading is always an option, at any moment of the ongoing process or later.

Readers take advantage of this flexibility in different ways. In earlier work (Mackey 1995), I tracked the behaviours of a small group of teenagers reading a novel. A few of these individuals raced through the story; one particularly methodical reader refused to turn a page until he was convinced he understood every nuance of every word on that page; one reader lingered over passages that particularly resonated with her own reading history but read other chapters more quickly. There were other variations: one reader petered out towards the end of the book and had to force himself to finish; one read with a sharp eye for literary patterns while another made do with very rough-and-ready under-standings of elements in the story that were outside his daily experience. Our normal vocabulary does not account for these distinctions; all of these people would simply be described as reading that book.

The abstract quality of words on the page allows readers to infuse the story with images and emotional qualities invested from their own experien-tial and reading lives. The arbitrary outline of the letters of a word, the main physical quality that allows us to interpret it, provides almost nothing in the way of a brake on such personal infusions. Reading is thus tailored to the mental "shape" of the individual reader in very private and invisible ways.

The physicality of reading is often taken for granted in such a way that it is almost equally invisible until you stop to think about it. In general terms, all that is required is a surface for the print and some way of bringing this surface within focal distance of the eyes. In practice, at least when the print appears on paper or on the screen of a hand-held e-reader, the hand normally is the agent that organizes focal distance, either by holding the book at an appropriate distance from the face or by supporting the head above the page as it lies beneath the gaze. Our fingers are trained to turn pages with minimum disruption to the train of thought evoked by the words. At some level, our hands and eyes provide information to the brain about the left-right balance of the remaining pages, so that we know not to expect major complications to erupt when only a few pages remain on the right-hand, unread side of the book (or the reverse, of course, in some languages). Page-turning feels intui-tive to current readers, but the motions of control for manipulating a papyrus scroll might have seemed similarly transparent to earlier generations, and it certainly takes little time for fingers to re-train to forward-click an e-book screen with no disruption to thought. In such different ways, the spatial con-sequences of the organization of words ready for perusal are minimized and made unimportant to the process. Words "flow" forward under the eye, and it often feels like an undifferentiated stream as our attention is absorbed by the content and even chapter breaks may blur into one continuous telling of a story.

Words and Still Images

Picture Books

When words are coupled with images, some of these factors change. In picture books, for example, the spatial consequences of the page design are radically different. Pictures are spatial rather than sequential designs and they force some of their spatial affordances onto the words that accompany them. The position of the words on the page of a picture book is much more significant than the position of words in a novel, where, apart from chapter divisions, the main criterion for starting a new page of words is that the previous page is full. With a picture book, the page turn is not meant to serve as an invisible enabler of reading; instead it is part of the pacing and shaping of the story.

Although picture books are considered appropriate "reading" for the very small, they are, in fact, highly complex textual artefacts. David Lewis points out some of the elements of reading a picture book:

> The experience of reading picturebooks would suggest that as our eyes move from words to pictures and back again, far from leaving behind the meaning or effects of one medium as we enter the other, we carry with us something like semantic traces that colour or inflect what we read and what we see. . . . Although pictures and words in close proximity in the picturebook influence each other, the relationship is never entirely symmetrical. What the words do to the pictures is not the same as what the pictures do to the words. Roughly speaking, the words in a picturebook tend to draw attention to the parts of the pictures that we should attend to, whereas the pictures provide the words with a specificity—colour, shape and form—that they would otherwise lack. (2001, 35)

Lawrence Sipe refers to this duality as a form of synergy, suggesting that the combination of words and pictures creates a total effect that is greater than the sum of its parts.

> In a picture book, both the text and the illustration sequence would be incomplete without the other. They have a synergistic relationship in which the total effect depends not only on the union of the text and illustrations but also on the perceived interactions or transactions between these two parts. (1998b, 98–99)

Sipe suggests that words and images work together, but also, in a constructive way, work against each other—not merely in terms of the information they may convey, but also in terms of the kinds of interpretive behaviours they invite:

> The different ways in which we experience written language and visual art have important implications for the ways in which we try to relate the words and the pictures in a picture book. Because of the primarily spatial nature of the pictures and our drive to form "unified atemporal structures," our tendency is to gaze on, dwell upon, or contemplate them. In contrast the primarily temporal nature of the verbal narrative creates in us a tendency to keep on reading, to keep going ahead in what C.S. Lewis termed "narrative lust." There is thus a tension between our impulse to gaze at the pictures—to forget about time in creating an "atemporal structure"—and not to interrupt the temporal narrative flow. The verbal text drives us to read on in a linear way, where the illustrations seduce us into stopping to look.
>
> This tension results in the impulse to be recursive and reflexive in our reading of a picture book: to go backward and forward in order to relate an illustration to the one before or after it, and to relate the text on one page to an illustration on a previous or successive page; or to understand new ways in which the combination of the text and picture on one page relate to preceding or succeeding pages. Picture books have the effect of "loosening the tyranny of the one-way flow" of the purely verbal text. Therefore, picture books seem to demand rereading. (1998b, 100–101)

Another form of tension is the difference between verbal and visual telling in terms of tense. Philip Pullman observes that "pictures have a present-tense quality which anyone who has shared a picture book with a child will recognize" (1989, 167). The verbal storytelling lives in the past tense, even when camouflaged with superficially present-tense verbs. The moment of the telling comes *after* what is told, locking the narrative into the past. Readers must move between the pastness of the words and the presentness of the images as they interpret the full story.

Comics and Graphic Novels

A graphic novel is something like a grown-up comic, a larger incarnation of a popular method of telling stories through words and images. It is an oversimplification, but perhaps a useful one, to say that the primary unit of the picture book is the page, whereas the primary unit of the comic/graphic novel is the panel. David Carrier (2000, 4), in a study of comics, adds the presence of a speech balloon as another essential quality of a comic (a definition that rings truer in the United States and Canada than in Europe). The book used in this study, *The Three Pigs*, immediately puts the lie to both these distinctions, since it makes subtle use of speech balloons and takes our understanding of the organizing power of panels on the page as part of its plotline. However, for the purposes of discussion, I will incorporate questions of the panel and the speech balloon under this general heading of graphic novels.

Scott McCloud, in his discussion of comics, conducted in comic-book format, says that the sequential nature of a set of panels is at the very heart of what makes a comic distinctive. His definition involves "juxtaposed pictorial and other images in deliberate sequence, intended to convey information and/ or to produce an aesthetic response in the viewer" (1993, 20). In this definition, the role of the space between panels is crucial. "See that space between the panels?" says McCloud.

> That's what comics aficionados have named "the gutter." And despite its unceremonious title, the gutter plays host to much of the magic and mystery that are at the very heart of comics. Here in the limbo of the gutter, human imagination takes two separate images and transforms them into a single idea. Nothing is seen between the two panels but experience tells you something must be there. . . . Comics panels fracture both time and space, offering a jagged, staccato rhythm of unconnected moments. But closure allows us to connect these moments and mentally construct a continuous, unified reality. If visual iconography is the vocabulary of comics, closure is its grammar. And since our definition of comics hinges on the arrangement of elements—then in a very real sense, comics is closure! The closure of electronic media is continuous, largely involuntary and virtually imperceptive. But closure in comics is far from continuous and anything but involuntary. . . . From the tossing of a baseball to the death of a planet, the reader's deliberate, voluntary closure is comics' primary means of simulating time and motion. Closure in comics fosters an intimacy surpassed only by the written word, a silent, secret contract between creator and audience. How the creator honors that contract is a matter of both art and craft. (1993, 66–69)

Once we start attending to the panels as storytelling units, we realize that their power to break up our orderly progression through the page is a major feature of how we read graphic novels. Some panels read left to right, top to bottom, but many do not. Alan Purves suggests that our ability to deal with pages thus fragmented can lead us to better understanding of different forms of on-screen writing:

> Comics work by taking text out of the lockstep convention. They do so by adding space to text and most clearly by treating the text as but a part of the iconic complex. Traditional texts are framed in dimensions. They go across and down. . . . The reader and the writer are forced into a cross-linear pattern, and the pattern is generally rigid—left to right, top to bottom, and so on to the next page of the codex; recto, verso, recto, verso until we get to the thick cover and are let out.

Comics provide a chance to break and to understand this configuration. The gutters between the panels on the page form a hypertext configuration. That is to say that the reader (guided by the artist, of course) connects the panels in many different ways. The connections may be temporal or visual. The resultant pattern on the page may be horizontal-vertical or it may be circular, or (using arrows) a criss-cross or boustrophedon (the form of text that reverses itself at each line like the movement of an ox pulling a plow). . . .

In their great variety, comics help us to understand the ways in which hypertext and writing on the screen work. (1998, 239–240)

These links between comics/graphic novels and hypertext and digital games are highly suggestive. I suspect that one prime factor in these relationships is that comics, graphic novels, and indeed picture books, have pushed readers to develop skills in reading both polysemically and spatially. Because they are printed on paper, these formats offer the stability of the page as part of the experience. It is at least plausible that this combination of stability and flux in the page design provides some kind of "training wheels" for readers who must deal with similar issues on the screen in a context of evanescence, often with no options for replay or rereading.

One final element of the picture page that deserves some attention is the speech balloon. David Carrier pays close attention to the impact of the speech balloon:

Speech balloons . . . are visible to the reader but do not lie within the picture space containing the depicted characters. . . . The speech balloon is a great philosophical discovery, a method of representing thought and words. Almost unknown before being exploited by comic artists, the speech balloon defines comics as neither a purely verbal nor a strictly visual art form, but as something radically new. . . . Comics, in my view, are essentially a composite art: when they are successful, they have verbal and visual elements seamlessly combined. (2000, 4)

Carrier is interesting on the place of the speech balloon in the narrative context of the story:

Words in balloons . . . are neither entirely within the picture space nor outside it. . . . Awareness not just of the words balloons contain but also of their purely visual qualities is part of our experience of comics. We treat the balloons neither purely as holes in the picture nor as things depicted. (2000, 29)

He even raises the question of tense: "Words in a balloon usually are in the present tense, like dialogue in a novel" (2000, 33).

Once multiple channels of meaning are opened, it is remarkable how many ways they can be played with and how readily readers learn to navigate between different channels, making sense of the overall story and enjoying the flexibility and suppleness of the patterning potential. Philip Pullman, who also draws attention to the paradoxical ontology of the speech balloon with its non-space in the story, claims that this plurality is the chief contribution of "the complexity of interplay between picture-meaning and text-meaning" (1989, 171). He refers to "the greatest storytelling discovery of the twentieth century: namely counterpoint," and continues,

> Because once the full range of caption, speech balloon, thought bubble and sound effect had been developed, the comic strip could do what words alone had never succeeded in doing before: it could show different things happening at the same time. We could see characters saying one thing while doing something else. This revolution (and it was nothing less than that) had nothing to do with technical developments in printing. . . . In a comic strip we can see several things happening together, and it doesn't matter which we read first. In the frame of the comic strip, the stream of time breaks up into little local eddies—and this loosening of the tyranny of the one-way flow makes counterpoint possible, releasing the most extraordinary virtuosity in storytelling. (1989, 171–172)

Ironically, young readers are learning how to manage sophisticated forms of data-handling and interpretation from sources that have regularly been perceived as humble at best, pernicious at worst.

Words and Music

It is possible also to read polysemically with words and music, though it is an activity that currently involves rather more in the way of individual experimentation than pre-set artistic control. Drew, for example, described an idiosyncratic habit: when he reads a book, he selects one music CD and sets it to repeat over and over again, providing a kind of soundtrack to his reading. That music is then forever associated with that book in his mind.

Not many readers are as committed to the idea of linking their reading so strictly with one particular piece of music as Drew is, but many readers are happy to combine their reading with background music of some rather more miscellaneous kind. Occasionally a publisher will issue a book alongside a CD of appropriate or related music (and Drew mentioned *Shadows of the Empire* [McNeely, 1996], a *Star Wars* CD explicitly created to be the soundtrack for the book of the same title), but for the most part the two items are separable. As electronic forms of reading take hold, however, it will become easier and more commonplace to find reading and music or sound effects more closely linked, and readers may have to disable the sound if they object to the combination. Even today, we are beginning to see new forms of association between books and music: the fascinating wordless picture book *Yellow Umbrella* (Jae Soo Liu, 2003) comes with its own CD, and, instead of pictures and words, the book/CD package offers pictures and piano music written expressly to accompany those pictures. It is a surprisingly powerful and pleasing combination, evoking the many pleasures of a rainy day in sensually provocative ways.

We do, of course, have an ancient tradition of associating words with music that is rooted more deeply in our culture than even the act of writing. That tradition is the creation of songs. Although a song marries words and music in rather different ways than the combinations we will be discussing here, there are still things we can learn about reading from considering how songs work.

Songs by their very nature routinely interfere with a reader's capacity to decide on autonomous pacing in the reading of the lyrics, since the music, rather than the reader, establishes the parameters of rhythm and timing. Music is also somewhat less interruptible; the imperative to move to the end is very strong. Also, our minds remember music differently; observe how few notes, heard just in passing, it takes to revive the complete song in the mind. Often a single chord will establish the identity of the entire piece.

I am not really talking about songs in this section, but the issue of how music establishes pace and cadence will be an important question nevertheless. As Tia DeNora expresses it, "Music has power. It is implicated in every dimension of social agency" (2000, 16). DeNora raises a further point of great interest when she says, "Music may influence how people compose their bodies, how they conduct themselves, how they experience the passage of time, how they feel—in terms of energy and emotion—about themselves, about others, and about situations" (2000, 17).

Susan Douglas also speaks of our bodily reaction to sound, and contrasts the group effect with the solitary aspects of reading.

[O]rality generates a powerful participatory mystique. Because the act of listening simultaneously to spoken words forms hearers into a group (while reading turns people in on themselves), orality fosters a strong collective sensibility. People listening to a common voice, or to the same music, act and react at the same time. They become an aggregate entity—an audience—and whether or not they all agree with or like what they hear, they are unified around that common experience. So even though the visual system of the brain is larger and much more extensive than its auditory system, it seems that hearing's immediate and transitory quality is what gives it such power. The fact that we hear not only with our ears but also with our entire bodies—our bones, our innards vibrate, too, to sounds, and certainly to music—means that we are actually feeling similar sensations in our bodies at exactly the same time when we listen as a group.

In part because of this physical response, listening often imparts a sense of emotion stronger than that imparted by looking. (1999, 29–30)

One major effect of music upon words is that the words enter the time of the music. Just as words inflect pictures and pictures inflect words, so paired words and music impinge upon each other in the experience of the reader/listener. Courtney made this link explicit; talking about reading to music she said, "So it's kind of like, you know, umh, read this quickly—or this slowly— because, you know, here's the music, so follow along." Unlike Drew, she found this an unpleasant intrusion on her reading and chose not to play background music when she read.

In this specific project, I will be talking about a reading experience in which an online poem is accompanied by music and images—which sounds rarefied. But young children are often put in a situation where their screen reading in particular (whether on television or on the computer screen) is musically charged. *Sesame Street* and a variety of educational CD-ROMs have long capitalized on the powers of music as a matter of routine. And the idea of music as a mnemonic is surely not new; how many children over many generations have managed to keep track of the alphabet by singing it? The impact of the holistic memory for music is undoubtedly part of the effect here; although it is easy for our memory for words to run out after a few lines, the memory pursues the complete work of music and the words may be carried as passengers.

Music may be synergistic with words or images, and it may also subvert print, just as it may subvert images in a film. David Morgan discusses how the polysemic associations of film music may channel different information from what is being conveyed by the pictures and voices.

While most cinema is literal—what we see is usually what we get—film music by its very nature allows a filmmaker to expand the scope of a film by introducing nonliteral elements: emotions not evident on the faces of actors, memories of events long gone and undramatized, or contradictory commentary on the action of characters. When an audience sees an adorable, innocent little boy but hears a hellish, swirling mass chanting praise to Satan, they understand that they are not to believe what they see. Conversely, if we watch a boxer being pummeled and losing a prizefight, but the soundtrack blares a triumphant horn passage, we are being reminded that "victory" and "loss" are not so easily defined. Audiences can be challenged to rethink what they experience, and thus film music can make a film deeper and more resonant than it might otherwise be. (2000, xi–xii)

The music accompanying the online poem read by the participants in this study does not really attempt anything even at the relatively simplistic level of subversion described here by Morgan—but more than one reader in this project expressed opinions about its role in the reading process.

· 6 ·

READING BEYOND THE WORDS:
WHAT THE TRAVELLERS SAY

In the course of this project, the participants looked at many different kinds of reading. Two operations involved print on paper alone: the nine subjects inspected photocopied opening pages of selected novels and then browsed through the novels to decide whether their interest was caught. They also chose one out of a selection of three photocopied short stories and read it through from beginning to end.

In terms of looking at words with pictures, the participants read one picture book from beginning to end (*The Three Pigs* by David Wiesner) and browsed through a variety of graphic novels, picking one to read more extensively (but not for long enough to finish it). They also read onscreen material from a CD-ROM supplying background for one of the graphic novels on offer (*Maus* by Art Spiegelman).

The participants read several electronic texts. They experimented with *Victory Garden*, a hypertext novel by Stuart Moulthrop. They looked at two renditions of another hypertext novel, *253* by Geoff Ryman. (These two versions are different in format—one displayed on the screen with hyperlinked "pages" and one in paperback book form with the pages bound together—but otherwise identical in content.) And they read an online poem, which features mobile text, background images and music, and a designer-determined pace of reading.

In this section, I will report on those examples that seem most illuminating. I will not linger long, for example, on the participants' work with *Victory Garden*, which they largely disliked and were baffled by. Nor will I spend much time talking about their responses to *McSweeney* #6, the literary magazine with accompanying CD soundtrack. More or less universally, the readers thought there might be some future for such reading/audio links but they did not find this example a successful one and their comments were brief.

It is not surprising to discover that where they were startled and then intrigued and sometimes delighted, the participants were far more articulate and perspicacious. So it is not out of incipient Pollyanna-ism that I concentrate on those texts that pleased the participants; it is because they had so much more to say, and because so much of what they had to say was so interesting.

In these accounts of actual reading responses, I will explore participants' reactions to three texts, starting with the online poem, "Designing a Bird from Memory in Jack's Skin Kitchen," and moving on to consideration of the picture book and the graphic novels.

"Designing a Bird from Memory in Jack's Skin Kitchen"

This online poem is difficult to describe with any justice, and readers should look it up for themselves (at http://www.bornmagazine.org/projects/designing/begin.html). Below I supply a transcription of this poem, but stable words on paper can represent only part of the experience of reading this piece. The words slide onto the screen, a few at a time. The measured pace, the ambiguity of some sentence fragments, which change meaning as later words join them on the screen, the swirling images behind the words, the sombre background guitar and sound effects of a hollow wind all affect the impact of this work.

Designing a Bird from Memory in Jack's Skin Kitchen
By Eliot Khalil Wilson
Design by Rick Mullarky

We hated everything below us,
We'd come to hate the ground itself,

to dread the heavy ropes of gravity
drawing us down from blue
to a brooding green

which would billow in tan dust
like waves of fistic clouds.

We'd come to kill
the afternoons, to evade
the blanket heat by flying out of rifle reach

and dropping mortar rounds through the clouds and trees,
our demented resentment
entirely non-personal.

I would come to forget Isaac
our Arab gunman with his shell carton filled with baklava

and just how mixed he was
bearded, but awash in after-shave,

dropping incendiary bombs and Hershey bars at the same time,
Viet S'mores we called it.

How he could shoot his .50 caliber, stoned on hash,
as accurate as fate itself.

How he'd shoot children and dogs,
but not women or birds. *Bad luck,*
he said, *Even when they are dead,*
women and birds remember.

I would forget how we found him later in Song Ngan Valley mixed with the ground
    and chopper,

repatriated, tangled like a lover,
his broken hand up and open
as if feeling for rain,
or patiently expecting some small gratuity.

The visor of his helmet shining the same
blue-black iridescence
as the glass of the Chartes cathedral.

Right here, I tell the tattoo man
giving him my arm,

A blue bird, that certain blue, with black eyes
and rising.

This is a partial transcription of an Internet poem onto paper: the words are complete but the other effects are missing. Online, the words of this poem fly in, spinning, and settle against the background of pictures, which are a mixture of still, rotating, and animated images (the element of animation is a flying bird that appears on every screen). The visuals include many kinds of sky scene, often also featuring the uppermost corner of a building; in addition, there are roads, puddles, perforated metal, and other gritty urban images. The effect is relatively abstract, often grey.

I have transcribed the lines according to the following rules: each set of words that flies in together is written as a single line. Each set of lines that occupies a single screen is written as a stanza. Punctuation and capitalization are kept as in the original form (as is the spelling of "Chartes" cathedral).

The subdued background music, a desultory guitar plucking against the sound of a strong wind, is not represented in this transcription in any way.

To move from one screen to the next, the reader clicks on a +sign located somewhere on the border of the square image; the location of the +sign changes from one screen to another. It is also possible to move backwards by clicking on a −sign, which returns the reader to the previous screen.

This poem appeared online in *Born Magazine*, which describes itself as "an experimental venue marrying literary arts and interactive media. Original projects are brought to life every three months through creative collaboration between writers and artists" (http://www.bornmagazine.org/, accessed April 5, 2004). The *Electronic Literature Directory* lists this poem and describes its target audience as "literary" (http://directory.eliterature.org/expand.php?rectype=work&eid=3d66a27191127, accessed April 5, 2004).

Author Eliot Khalil Wilson, interviewed for *Scene 360*, an online magazine for film and the arts, commented on the poem. Interviewer Ariana-Sophia Kartsonis compared the setting of the poem to a film in her question:

> I loved the way that your poem, "**Designing a Bird from Memory in Jack's Skin Kitchen**" worked out in **Born Magazine** and the way they made of it, a short film of sorts. What was it like to see your poem literally set in motion that way? How much did you work with the computer graphics artist, Rick Mullarky and how does the final product capture the (for lack of a better word) "essence" of your sense of the poem?

Wilson's reply was interesting; it sounds as if the writing came first and the online setting was a follow-up operation, a kind of performance or even adaptation:

> It was creepy in much the same way that hearing someone read your work is creepy. There are different accents and phrasings that you hear and don't like for being different. I worked with Rick only in setting up what we didn't want the piece to do. We didn't want it to be a war video. He was in Berlin at the time and had access to great and stark industrial images that were, in their own way, the stuff of war and loss. He got the essence of the poem. (http://www.scene360.com/STORYboard_interview_eliot.html, accessed April 5, 2004)

This relationship sounds similar to that of an author-illustrator team in a picture book or graphic novel; it also raises the kinds of questions that arise in the adaptation of a print text to film.

Inside the Online Poem

After many readings of this poem (both alone and alongside the participants as each read it twice), I find it very difficult to reconstruct my first reaction to it. It is telling to say that I am still not tired of it. I find the different elements work together very powerfully. The images swimming behind the letters, the droning of the background music, the rotating and unsettled words—all contribute to my feeling a hazy, weighty sensation that is connected in my own mind to the atmosphere of the kind of threatening summer afternoon when it is hot and humid and the thunder lurks just out of earshot. In part, I suspect this feeling is augmented by the forced pace of the reading, slow indeed by my impatient standards.

This slow, heavy feeling seems appropriate to the Vietnam connection, both in climatic terms and also in the oppressive connotations of being swamped in a nightmare that any recollection of that war brings to my mind. It was interesting to observe how my own reactions to the poem changed, or at least heightened, in the final official session in which it was read for this project. Seth was the participant, and, in the short interval between the time when I read it with Jocelyn and this particular session with Seth, the 2003 war in Iraq had begun. My recollections of television coverage of Vietnam, which had always shadowed my reading of this poem, were suddenly sharpened by new TV images from the nights preceding this session—and the sense of fearfulness, mitigated in the case of Vietnam by time and knowledge of the outcome, were suddenly new and raw again.

The inter-connectedness of the different elements of this piece is fascinating. The words have a spatial component in that they enter the screen spinning, and settle in a particular part of the screenscape, but their essential forward thrust remains sequential. Many of the images are constantly in motion, but that motion is circular. The bird moves from one screen to the next. The music goes nowhere at all, consisting of repeated guitar notes that have little melodic organization.

To me, the impact of the words is powerful both despite and because of the swirling background images, the stagnating music, the haunting wind that goes round and round. In the teeth of so much going-nowhere, I never lost the impulse to see where the words were heading. The words remain the driving force of this multimodal production for me, and the background images and music resemble nothing so much as "our demented resentment" in being almost "entirely non-personal."

My feeling during the participant sessions was that the hypnotic effect of the swirling words and droning music often united all of us in the room (participant, research assistants, and me) in some of the ways that Susan Douglas (1999) described in her account of listening collectively. We were all "audience" together. Frequently the research assistants commented on the impact of the online poem as we packed up the equipment at the end of the session.

"Designing a Bird from Memory" is startling in its own right, and it bore little connection to the other materials the participants were exploring, except in its multimodal novelty. I was very interested to see how they would respond.

The Online Poem: What the Travellers Say

"Designing a Bird from Memory in Jack's Skin Kitchen" is a serious literary and multimedia enterprise. I think it is fair to say that of the seven participants (I did not find out about this poem in time to show it to Denise and Damian), only Courtney would (possibly) describe herself as a literary reader. The others read popular materials mainly or only. This text compounds its complex and powerful literary content with images, music, and visual controls on pace. I was curious about how the readers in my set would respond.

The readers all looked at this poem in the context of exploring a variety of electronic texts. Before reading this example, they had all been fairly perplexed by *Victory Garden*, the hypertext novel, and relieved to find that *253*, a different kind of hypertext fiction, made greater intuitive sense to them. Thus by the time they came to look at "Designing a Bird from Memory," they were at least accustomed to the idea of electronic novelty.

Drew

Of all the readers, Drew was the most hostile. At an earlier session, he had described himself as a Zionist. The word "Arab" triggered a strong reaction, and he drew on the paratextual information of the website address to reach quick conclusions.

Drew:	The first time I read it, this is probably going to sound bad, but the first time I read it I was kind of [*hesitates*] angry I guess, because one of the frames has the word *Arab* in it. And I can be very prejudicial I guess, so at that point it seems as if this was going to be some sort of requiem for a friend who had been Arabic, and that made me think it was, one of the first thoughts that I had when I saw that was that this was probably made by, because it is *born.magazine.org*, it is some project that is probably made by some Palestinian boy who is mourning the loss of his brother because brother stepped on some bus and blew it up. So I really—took a negative opinion after that frame, of it.
Margaret:	Do you still think that is what it is about?
Drew:	It is not that violent, no. But I still feel a certain umh—to me I feel that that is what it is about. It is a requiem for a friend who died, and now that they are truly free, and it seems to follow that cycle with the backgrounds, because it starts with sky. And ends up with a lot of chrome, so I don't know, the dangers of Western industry and then back to the sky—.
Margaret:	So, in a way you are saying your personal response flooded your reaction to what was going on, on the screen, is that a fair description?
Drew:	Yeah, I just—I put up a barrier and I just refused to feel any, anything positive out of it because of what I expected it to be.

It was not just the content (both verbal and visual) that bothered Drew, however; he also reacted to the form as something arty. I asked him what he thought of it as a way of reading or presenting something.

Drew:	[*pause*] It is not one that I am particularly keen on. Umh, it's poetic, but it's—I find myself just naturally fighting against it because it's something I see as fine art. So it is not something that I can really readily agree with because I just don't understand it and I just understand the views and it's very liberal, and it is just, I guess it makes me feel claustrophobic or something.
Margaret:	Yeah. So would hostile be too strong a word to describe your reaction?
Drew:	No.

Jeremy

Jeremy found the poem very challenging: "It's really interesting, the way it's laid out. Umh, I'm still not sure that I understand what the story is." He read it a second time and said,

Having it in separate chunks, when they're flying in, it's a little difficult to keep the flow going. But I like the background imagery and the subtle music, which adds to the tone without needing to write anything descriptive. But as for the actual reading, I found it pretty difficult. I'm still not sure what's going on.

The pacing of the flying words, Jeremy said, challenged him to pay attention in a different way. "I think maybe it would push me to take a little longer to read each individual section, to try and remember it. Because once I've gone forwards, it's not as easy to jump back for a quick reference."

Isaac

Isaac, who often focused on the visual elements of a text, was annoyed by the choice of illustrations.

> For what you—this—story was talking about, like, if you would have stuck in some relevant pictures, it would have made it more interesting to read and I would [pause] probably have felt better for having taken the time to read it than this just kind of felt like a waste of my time and I wouldn't continue if I had a choice.

Isaac spoke several times of the importance of illustrations and concluded,

> I think for something like this, ah—the pictures would have—have added so much to it. Umh, because it is, it is a powerful little thing, but it's also got this just abstract [pause] yugh [transcriber's note: "??"] stuck in. It's almost an annoyance. . . . All it's about is the bird, according to the pictures, it's not, and yet the story is about all this other stuff that is relating to or leading up to or symbolizing the bird. Whatever. Umh [pause] I just think there could have been such powerful pictures added for what was written and I'm disappointed that there weren't.

Jocelyn

Jocelyn, with her instantaneous acceptance or rejection of any text, chose to accept this one, though with only moderate enthusiasm to begin with.

> Mm—it's okay. Like, I don't hate it, it's different so I think it's okay and it's kind of neat. Like, I kind of like the pictures behind, but it's a little bit confusing, like you kind of have to read you know, really read the words. You know, it's neat actually. It's not too bad.

We talked about the forced slow pace of reading—words cannot be read until they appear on the screen. Jocelyn was a bit surprised that she was not irritated by this phenomenon.

Jocelyn:	No I wasn't actually, for some odd reason, because I don't usually like something like this, but I did like it.
Margaret:	It's kind of like a poem isn't it?
Jocelyn:	Yeah it's neat. I like the—I don't know—I just like the way it was, it's really neat because I know sometimes with some PowerPoint presentations you know, sometimes when they come in, it drives me crazy, I'm like, c-o-m-e ooonnn, come on, come on, but this didn't because I think because there things for me to look at and I really liked the layout, it was just kind of, I don't know—I just really liked it.

Jocelyn initially paid little attention to the music, but as she began to think about it, she said, "It's kind of weird, that music there was kind of strange." Reflecting further, she observed, "I think that if it didn't have music I think it would be a little strange too. The silence would be a little strange. I don't know if I would choose this kind of music though." Her personal choice would be for something more classical.

Jocelyn's reference to PowerPoint is a useful reminder of the broad range of screen reading now relatively commonplace in our society. The idea of words as manipulable in space has taken serious hold on our imaginations, though I doubt many of us often have cause to elide the idea of PowerPoint with concepts of artistic consciousness. Nevertheless, it is helpful to keep in mind that screen words have many different kinds of resonances with readers nowadays.

Seth

Seth also found the poem "kind of neat." His reaction to his first reading was that he suspected there might be more than one story in the text. His response to the forced pace of the flying words was, "I guess that's a stall tactic so you can see what you're looking at here before the words come in. I don't know if they pertain to the story, like I was going back and forth and you've got to look where to click. Like I said, there's a lot going on."

Seth wondered if the fact that some words were black and some were white meant that they were telling two different stories—a reading that respects the semiotic potential of design decisions. I asked him what he thought Jack's skin kitchen might be, and he said, "I wonder if that's I don't know, something to do with the war they're talking about. You've got ah—a human grocery store, bodies lying on the—"

Seth's reading experience differed from everyone else's in one contextual particular: he was the only participant who read this poem during a time of war.

Whether this increased his sensitivity to the image of the "human grocery store" is not a question that can ever be answered. He read the poem on only one occasion so would not have felt the sense of contrast and added intensity that struck me so strongly.

Ben

Ben observed many details about this text, but also had some broader comments to make. His opening remark was, "Some of the pictures in the background really mess with your head." Invited to expand on this remark, he said, "There was the one of a foot and the world was spinning around reasonably fast similar to the way it is now, but it really messes with you when you're trying to read and the background is spinning."

Ben commented on the "interesting colours, the change of text from black to white, the fact that the bird is always the same in every screen . . . kind of interesting," he said. He was positive about the floating words: "Well, if they're not placed in an organized fashion, then it would kind of mess up the story, so the fact that they're not placed, they're directly from the start that it floats in makes it better, so that you know where to read." In other words, the sequential arrival of each line plays a role in directing reader attention, somewhat like the arrow from one panel to another that may organize reading order on a non-linear comic-book page.

He looked at the line "We'd come to kill" and said, "That's a very powerful starting line." I commented on the change in meaning when the second line, ". . . the afternoons," flies in and he said, "But they don't let you read that part, they just—*we'd come to kill!*"

Ben preferred the online version to a hypothetical paper transcript. He thought the graphics were meaningful and said it would be a loss if things like the different colours for the type were gone—"simple text wouldn't convey that nearly as well." Also he thought that losing the forced pace would be significant: "They want you to really like, take your time on it and make sure." His comments about the music were damning, however: "I don't know if the music means much. Just sounds like it's one of those CDs that put you to sleep—but it may have its own meaning in itself too."

Courtney

Courtney was the most positive and perhaps the most eloquent of all the participants. Reading the poem and commenting at intervals, she said,

It's more like poetry. Very visual, quite beautiful. The way the text comes out and then organizes itself. I couldn't imagine this in a book form. You would lose everything that it intends. Very strange, a little bit, but umh, it's so beautiful and yet it's talking about such dark things. It's a little bit dizzying. It's very much geared for children of this generation that need things moving all the time. Umh, a little bit distracting.

Courtney identified the Vietnam War as a major subject of the poem, and was clear about the role of the tattoo in the overall impact of the poem.

> Umh, I read it rather quickly and as far as I can tell, umh, it's about the Vietnam War and he was talking to one of the vets and they were talking about the—well, they did some talking about what good luck and bad luck and you know, superstitions, I guess, and there's some about his memory, a little bit how you lose it. I think that the images kind of compound the words. They're very descriptive, they're very poetic, there's some really deliberate language. And then when he gets his tattoo, it's like he's trying to package all that up into, you know, all that feeling into something that's significant.

Courtney also had an interesting take on Jack's Skin Kitchen:

> I think "Designing a Bird from Memory" . . . so he's talking about a tattoo. . . . "in Jack's Skin Kitchen"—umh, that's himself. That he is his Skin Kitchen. And that he is designing something, kind of like a decorative thing for his Skin Kitchen, which is himself. Umh, to put on from memory so he's remembering back to Vietnam.

She was also astute about the forced pace:

> It's kind of like, it creates some tension between, umh, reading one line and then hav- ing to wait for the next line, so it gives you time to think about it. Umh, but at this point it's, unless you're reading it again for the second or third time, then you know, it becomes less, less so. It's still [inaudible] very effective writing.

Asked about the impact of reading it for a second time, Courtney was still positive.

> Courtney: It's much more [inaudible]. Because in the first reading you're so over-
> whelmed with you know, the design of it, the beauty of the graphics,
> the way they're put together, you know, the artfulness of how the lan-
> guage comes up. And the language itself is amazing, you know it can
> be so much, and so that's a total distraction from the message, so you
> have to like read it three or four times in order to really appreciate the
> nuances.
>
> Margaret: What would happen if you just took the words and put them on paper
> as a poem?

Courtney: It would still be a nice poem, but it would certainly lack the impact. Because you shouldn't read a poem like this in a minute.
Margaret: Right.
Courtney: Really quickly, just scan scan scan and that's it, you're done. Because you wouldn't have to wait, there's no tension, you wouldn't have to wait for the next line. You wouldn't have to wait to see, you know, what the next graphic is or how it interacts on the page. Umh, and how some words come more quickly and some words more slowly, just like a gap in the timing. I think that it would still be beautiful, I mean the words, you know, would stand by themselves quite nicely, but you just wouldn't have the same impact.

Discussion

We do need to remember that these participants came to this poem in a context of looking at varied forms of electronic text, so they were in a way perhaps a little "softened up" for taking this text in stride. Nevertheless, take it in their stride they all did. Drew objected to the politics and was hostile to the format; Jeremy struggled with interpreting the content; Seth was lukewarm about the poem and then apologized for his lingering flu that was making him feel tepid about everything that day; Isaac was cross about the images used. But no one was baffled by the concept of a sophisticated multimodal text; no one was in a position of making no sense of the presentation. Furthermore, the objections and problems they expressed were not specific to this text. Drew had objected to a different text's potential for anti-Zionism at another stage in the project; Jeremy struggled with coming to terms with the irony in his short story in a way very similar to his problems here; Seth's lingering flu symptoms inflected everything he looked at in the fourth session; Isaac was fussy about the use of images throughout the whole project. There was nothing in their responses to this particular text that stood out as unique.

I strongly suspect that they would have reacted with considerably less interest to the same poem in the paper version I have given above. Some participants say as much, directly, and it can be inferred from most of the responses. Their attention was caught and then fostered by the form of presentation. Their responses to the content varied from "beautiful" (Courtney) to "powerful" (Isaac, Ben) to "interesting" (Jeremy) to "neat" (Jocelyn, Seth) to "poetic" (Courtney, Drew—with caveats!). With the exception of Drew, whose main reaction was anger and then hostility, all the others gave every indication of being intrigued even if they were sometimes a bit puzzled by the content.

Clearly, novelty value played its part in these responses. But the reactions of the participants were subtler than simply saying, "How unusual"—even if most of them did say some version of that phrase somewhere along the way.

It is also worth mentioning that this poem was almost the only text that was read twice. It was rare enough in this project to encounter a text that they could read completely rather than merely sampling a fragment. With this poem, I deliberately asked everyone to read it for a second time, and the forced pace of the word display made it quite difficult for them to skip through it (it could be argued that they gave the picture book a kind of second read in their retelling of their reactions to it, but skipping clearly could and did happen on that occasion). Most of them found that a second reading clarified their understanding, and it may be that their articulated responses are correspondingly more acute.

In their responses, the participants mentioned all the polysemic components of this production: the words, the images, the design features, the use of colour, the music, the sound effects. It was clear that their meaning-making processes took account of many channels of information, and they were able to articulate what they found novel and what they found meaningful in this arrangement. The poem offered a new kind of experience to many of them, but they were clearly all comfortable with the scaffolding provided in the production itself and in their own multimodal background experience.

The Three Pigs

A simplistic argument would make the case that all these readers should naturally be expected to make ready sense of a picture book. These are adults, competent readers, experienced processors of images. But anyone who is familiar with contemporary picture books knows that they can be more sophisticated than many so-called adult texts. In this case, the book I gave the participants, *The Three Pigs* by David Wiesner (2001), challenged many of their expectations. Many of them had not looked at a picture book for years; some were indeed rather surprised to be offered such a thing at all and initially looked at it only out of politeness.

Nevertheless, *The Three Pigs* generally caught their attention in highly interesting and informative ways. The overall reaction was one of surprise, and in some cases it would not be too strong to say, delight. The set of responses is universally articulate, extensive, and full of different kinds of insight. It is probably the point of the project where reactions most closely approached unanimity.

In part, this is because *The Three Pigs* is such a clever and funny book, and so successfully captures the contemporary convention of taking well-known stories and inverting them in ingenious ways. As was not always the case with the texts I offered them, these readers clearly came to this story with all the necessary repertoire to enjoy it—not without effort, because they certainly had to think about it, but without strain. It is obvious from their responses that the requirement to think was actually part of the enjoyment.

Inside *The Three Pigs*

The Three Pigs begins conventionally enough with the wolf attacking the home of the first pig. The words say that he huffed and puffed, blew the house down, and ate the pig. However, the pictures show us that the pig made a get-away, *out of the picture itself*. He is blown right out of the story, as his speech bubble makes plain; he escapes into the white space between the picture panels, and heads for the next page. Carrier's observations about the special narrative space of the speech balloon clearly hold true in this book. The conventional narrative of the wolf huffing and puffing appears indubitably in the past tense of the narration, while the speech balloons of the runaway pigs provide a present-tense contradiction that factors into our understanding of the story.

The second pig is under threat from the wolf when the first pig beckons him from outside the frame of the panel. After they attract the attention of the third pig, they decide to use the picture panels present on this page to make paper airplanes for sailing off into the white space created by the removal of the pictures. When they eventually land, after several pages of flying through white space, they are outside the world of *Hey Diddle Diddle*. The graphics of this world are quite distinctive, very pastel and cartoon-like, and as the pigs push into that world, their own depiction changes to match. The edge of the picture is a distinct ontological boundary in the qualities of "pigness" portrayed.

The pigs linger only briefly in this pastel world. The cat with the fiddle decides to escape with them, and the four go hunting further. They discover a dragon in imminent danger of being slain by a prince (again with his own distinctive pictorial qualities which the pigs adopt visually as they move into his picture) and rescue him too. But at this point, they discover a set of picture panels hanging in a row. The panels include some images from their own story, so the five companions smooth out the paper airplane pictures and go back to the pigs' own world. The cat and the dragon squeeze with the pigs into the little house made of bricks. The wolf can be seen on a faraway hillside but the five friends are last seen making soup—possibly alphabet soup out of the letters of the story, which are still dancing round the page, not all lined up in a row—and living happily ever after.

Pleasure in the intelligently ridiculous is a difficult emotion to describe in rational terms. "Delightful" is a shop-worn adjective, as likely to close down further thinking as to expand on it. However, in my own reading of this book, I did indeed find Wiesner's wit and imagination in this anarchic romp through very familiar territory to be delightful—engaging, funny, and appealingly combining wildness with coherence. As with "Designing a Bird from Memory," I found that reiterations of the story in the company of different participants enhanced rather than reduced my enjoyment of the book.

I had the advantage over many of the participants in that I knew before I began reading that a picture book can be a very sophisticated exercise indeed. Few of the subjects of this study were expecting the twists and turns of Wiesner's metafictional games, so their reading was heightened by a kind of surprise I can now only observe and not expect to experience for myself. I do think it is fair to say that astonishment did not slow them down for long, and they were just as capable of being delighted.

The Picture Book: What the Travellers Say

Verbal and visual jokes abound in this foolish story, and the transcripts record a great deal of amazement and laughter. The word most commonly used by the participants to describe *The Three Pigs* was "cute" (Courtney—many times, Drew, Isaac, Jocelyn—many times, Damian, Denise, and Seth). However, for the most part, the readers went beyond ideas of cuteness and explored many other aspects of this demanding picture book.

Drew

Drew, often laconic, was amused but not gripped. Most of his comments came as he was reading the book for the first time, rather than retrospectively, and it is possible almost to hear his thinking:

Margaret: So what's going on?
Drew: At this point there's really just a some—it's no longer really a story of you'd be used to as The *Three Pigs* are, ah—blew, basically, the

story apart or the storybook apart, so they're standing on ah—some of
the cartoon drawings and they're going, "hey let's go and explore this
place." Lots of white space—and—now I'm no longer—I mean, ever
since that I'm not really sure where the story is leading anymore, so—it
has my attention.

The book he said, was "strange, but okay, not something that you would have
expected."

Jeremy

Jeremy was also terse but positive. "Well, I liked the pictures for one. It just
seemed like typical children's story for the first little while until the story
changed, really. Once you saw the pigs outside of the pages, that struck me
as different and pretty funny." The book is "introducing some different fairy
tales and mixing them up with [*pause*] the same sort of idea. Just exploring the
different fairy tales."

Ben

All the others were much more extensive in their comments than Drew and
Jeremy. Ben was very taken with the idea of the pigs "knocking over the pages
and goofing off," and commented that the pages containing the flight scenes
are "white probably simply because they have knocked over all the pages." He
commented on the change of picture style as the pigs cross story boundaries,
and drew connections between the pigs' story and the dragon's story. "They
go and decide to enter a comic strip with the dragon and a knight but they
decide to save the dragon instead of letting the story go. Kind of like they
saved themselves from the wolf." He also commented on the return home of
the five new friends:

> They don't just go home themselves, they take their new friends with them and they're
> having their friends help putting the story back together so that they can actually
> go home and that's *really* got to go and mess with the wolf's head [*laughter*], having a
> dragon's head pop out the door rather than huffing and puffing and blowing it, but he
> was never supposed to succeed in blowing the brick house down anyway. And since
> they've messed with the pages, you can see letters falling and they're trying to catch
> them all in the basket. They still haven't put the story completely properly together,
> so they're still working on it. . . . It's still a work in progress.

Ben drew on a comparison with DVD conventions to summarize this book: "It's quite a humorous little outtake on the original story."

Damian

Damian and Denise, in the pilot study, were actually asked to read the book aloud, an idea I dropped later.

Damian was pleasantly surprised by *The Three Pigs*. "It's kind of a step outside of the book. It's a book within a book. Then bringing in just different concepts, trying to be cute and ah, kind of amalgamating them all and putting them back into first framework." As he read much of it aloud, he omitted the words in the speech bubbles at the outset. I asked him about this omission. He said, "Yes, because it's a different format and I guess it's intentionally meant to like, trip you up because you can't jump from one to the other you have to break away from the story to go into it."

As we discussed the book, Damian's analysis became more philosophical.

Margaret:	What about those white pages?
Damian:	I think he was just, he was trying to give you the big departure, beat you over the head with the freedom of the storyline. It like the, it's a big break for the reader to say, "this is really completely different now!" Now for something completely different. Yeah.
Margaret:	It's a big break for pigs too isn't it?
Damian:	The whole operation, that's when they break out and find their way. Take control over their own destinies. Searching around for the big dragon. I like one of these books to have a mean angry dragon. They're all nice and friendly, just like the pigs, here we go! Oh yeah, you want to see if the, the real or more real cat [that is, the cat after he escaped from the cartoon picture of *Hey Diddle Diddle* into the more realistically drawn world of the pigs] could hold the fiddle, but he has the bow. [*laughter*]
Margaret:	That's a very good question. I like that question.
Damian:	But not nearly as much as in the cartoon. The cat was holding it right up. Oh no, back in the cartoon so you can do it. The cat obeys more real life physics, laws, anatomy.
Margaret:	They are more substantial when they make their getaway aren't they? What about the broken up words?
Damian:	No, that's the, kind of just the, changing of the ah, fairy tale. They brought a new force into it and destroyed the status quo. Here's the little wolfie, trying to follow his lines and everything is going fine. [*laughter*]

Margaret:	Well, part of his line is to lose in the long run isn't it?
Damian:	Yeah. He was even robbed of that. [*laughter*] Of his dignity. [*pause*] The pigs jumped in and out at will now.
Margaret:	Yeah, they cracked it now by the end, hadn't they? [*pause*] Could you imagine any or all of your adult friends enjoying this book or would they just have to be a real novelty value thing?
Damian:	How many drinks are involved? [*laughter*] Umh, well it's interesting. It certainly wouldn't be, you know, "read this book!" If it was lying on the doctor's table or something it would be more interesting than a normal *Three Little Pigs*.

Damian's take on the ontological changes of the pigs crossing borderlines of different illustrations introduced a fascinating parallel question of modality: how much of a cartoon cat do you have to be to hold a fiddle in a plausible way? It is clear that the "rules of the game" are a source of pleasure to him.

Denise

Denise also read the story aloud, but interspersed her reading with substantial comments. She interpreted the plot:

> It looks like they are pulling the pages away—oooohhh okay, this is interesting. Now they've built, this is interesting! Hee hee, sneaky little piggy, [*inaudible*], mmmm, now they want to explore, they are riding a paper aeroplane, that's the funniest little faces, the pig with the smile. Now this is a very interesting twist on this book. Mm—the little piggies, now they are going to crash into something aren't they? It's a paper aeroplane so they have to crash into something eventually.

She also commented on the stylistic/ontological shifts:

> As they are walking into the picture they're becoming cartoons and as they are leaving again they're becoming their normal, well their other selves again. So they are becoming more like the original drawings. It's interesting!

Like Damian, Denise omitted many of the words in the speech bubbles as she read aloud. Asked about it, she said, "To me the speech bubbles need to be related to something. Like, you can't just have random sentences thrown in, or in terms of the story, it doesn't make sense. So if I was reading this book to a small child, I would leave the little speech bubbles out."

Margaret:	Would you paraphrase them, would you say what they're saying?
Denise:	I would—term it in more of, "oh look, this little piggy is trying to

> do this and all of this is what he's trying to do" as opposed to, "this is what he's saying" because to me that is more for, you look at it and it's just side commentary. It has very little to do with the actual meat of what's happening and for a picture book, it's all explained in the picture anyway.

Margaret: Do you think some of it is just that you're used to reading stories in sentences and the speech bubbles don't come into their own sentences.

Denise: Yeah, they don't seem to fit in to me as well, so.

Margaret: It's hard to incorporate them into the rhythm of the book.

Denise: Yeah, especially when it's a story that you knew, well at least started off knowing. Like you have an idea of how it is supposed to go and the sort of feel of it and all of a sudden it just doesn't fit in so.

Both Denise and Damian seem to register the point made by Pullman (1989) and Carrier (2000) that the speech bubbles do not exactly belong either to the picture plane or to the story zone. The speech bubbles in this story, in my view, contribute more to the telling than Denise is prepared to acknowledge, but her response and Damian's to the formal qualities of the text make considerable sense. Many people who have tried to read a comic or graphic novel aloud will recognize Denise's complaint that the speech bubbles don't really fit with "the sort of feel of it."

Interestingly, the "big conversation" that runs constantly in Denise's head as she attempts to make sense of the opening pages of this book also raises questions of modality: "the other two have straw strapped to their backs and I suppose if they don't have hands, but if they don't have hands why are they building a house?"

Courtney

Courtney was entertained by register changes in the narrative and dialogue of the book. "Their conversation is not of the diction of the story book, you know, it's more colloquial," she said, citing examples such as *Come on!* and *Oops!* and *Uh-oh!* The dragon, she observed, "kind of slithers out of the story—the old-fashioned *O brave and noble swine*, he says. *Don't mention it!* you know. [*laughter*]"

Courtney was also pleased with the way the pigs changed visually as they moved into other stories (equally a register change), but was a bit surprised that it was not the dish (already running away with the spoon) who chose to leave with them. She was perceptive about many details in the picture, but said she thought all the white pages might make a child reader anxious—"about all the white space, well, what's happening, what's going on, you know, and page after page, it still doesn't really end." She did like how the audience was brought into the book by asides from the different characters. And she was very taken with the idea of alphabet soup rather than wolf soup to finish the story.

Isaac

Isaac liked the artwork very much and mentioned it several times. He spoke of different levels of reality as a way of describing the book.

> So, but it just went along normally, good artwork though. And here is an indication of something odd . . . different. He blew me out of the story as opposed to he ate the pig up, but he's looking. Okay. So, there he is again. Hey wait you know, exit the story, and so there's the wolf all confused because, umh, so in a sense it's like reality and non-reality. They're stepping out of what is supposed to be their reality and then they just grab the third one and in the meanwhile the wolf is kind of locked into it and then they have a bunch of fun, kind of at his expense because they—umh, folding up and flying in the one [the picture panel] that's him [the wolf]. So, and then the story, just like they've left the story, they've left reality. So it's like, cool, okay, while, uh, I was expecting a whole bunch of just blank pages for the rest of the book, but then okay, they crashed. [chuckling] So, cool, what are they going to do because obviously their reality is gone and then they brought me in [pause] and this is kind of well, okay but it is an interesting, I guess, starting point for showing that they're crossing realities.

Later he said, "It's almost like the, ah, umh, *Star Trek* ah, time paradox that, you've heard there's so many different versions of that, that, umh, these are all the same reality, it's just different choices or something, and so, they, well they decide to go back to theirs." He called it "smart parody" because "the story has been disrupted and so they've got, but they got still, the, the, the, the dialogue of the story." He too commented on the alphabet soup: "Soup's on, alphabet soup even though they don't say that anywhere, it's just cleverly in there."

Isaac said this book would be a good coffee table book. "I think every friend of mine who would come over and pick this up would finish it before they would put it down."

Jocelyn

Jocelyn was also positive about the book. She recognized quickly that the book was not going to be "normal" but did not initially see what kind of "pattern" was being laid out. "I thought something was going to happen but I wasn't sure what." She expanded on this point more than once.

Jocelyn:	Well I knew it was going to be different and I didn't know what was going to happen and I had no idea that it was going to end in different fairy tales and they were going to rescue other creatures and stuff, but here I just thought, "Okay, they are going to rescue each other" and I didn't know what they were going to do after that.
Margaret:	Right.
Jocelyn:	And then I just thought this was cute when they started you know, flying on the paper airplanes, I thought that was pretty cute. I like this picture a lot [pigs on paper plane].
Margaret:	What appeals to you in that picture?
Jocelyn:	It reminds me of my dog [*much laughter, Jocelyn points to pig on right*] just because his ears are—.

Later she said, "I kind of thought that they were just going to go back to their land, but they weren't, and then obviously when I saw this [the *Hey Diddle Diddle* page] I knew what was going to happen. There was going to be a couple of fairy tales, but I still didn't think that they were going to rescue anybody else until this happened, that surprised me." And Jocelyn likes surprises; she was utterly consistent in this trait throughout the entire project.

Jocelyn was also the participant who most consistently made personal and emotional connections to the material we offered her; here she connected the pig to her dog.

Seth

Seth, in some ways, produced the most surprising reading, in part because the frame of reference he brought to bear was so unexpected. Initially the book "threw me for a loop," he said, but he went on to explore in some detail the complexities of the different worlds involved.

Seth drew on comparisons, mostly from films, to help him sort out a confusing story. His one print reference was to say that the opening sequences made him think of the story of the Prodigal Son in the Bible. I reproduce an extensive extract from his conversation because it is illuminating in a variety of ways.

Seth:	This is back to the regular story and then it pans over here to ah . . . *come on—it's safe out here.*
Margaret:	So where is it safe, where is this pig?

Seth: In the real world?

Margaret: Uhuh. [*laughter*]

Seth: Which, I don't know—sometimes we want to be in fantasies and fairy tales and the people in the stories want to be where we are. It's always greener on the other side, or the grass is always greener on the other side.

Margaret: Well I think if you were in a story where the wolf ate you up, you would be categorically feeling safer somewhere else.

Seth: Yeah, but I don't understand it. I mean, I can sit here and be all, "Well if he ate the wolf or if he ate the pig, why is he still there?" It doesn't make sense.

Margaret: How do you make sense of it?

Seth: Well basically, I mean he's—he's just been taken out of the story, out of the pictures, but, I mean, it doesn't mean he doesn't exist or didn't exist.

Margaret: Right, but he has escaped from the story.

Seth: Yeah. I guess (pause) this almost sounds like umh, I don't know, this is a really obscure comparison, like a *Nightmare on Elm Street* kind of thing.

Margaret: Right. [*laughter*]

Seth: You know, where the wolf is Freddy and you know, I don't know—like, do you know what I mean?

Margaret: I do. No, it makes sense.

Seth: Yeah, so that's sad to think that *The Three Little Pigs* would remind us of that, heh? [*laughter*] What kind of scary-ass childhood did I have? [*laughter*]. . . . I don't know, like it's very different. I've never seen anything like this before in this form of story telling. It's not the traditional tale that I grew up with.

Margaret: No, well that's why I gave it to you to see what you make of it . . . .

Seth: I don't know, it just seems like—like, when you're dreaming, myself personally, sometimes I [*inaudible*] I have nightmares and stuff and I think, "You know, if there's a way that I can—it's my dream, why can't I take control, why do I have to be scared or why do I have to be naked?" or—do you know what I mean?

Margaret: Right.

Seth: I don't know, it just seems like these guys—I don't know—like they take control, they're not going to feel belittled or intimidated, which is you know, it's really cool! Umh—yeah—so what we perceive as being dreams, this is their life and how they chose to deal with it, so I think things are possible if you just put your mind to it and ah—I don't know—maybe things aren't always as they seem just because somebody was eaten in the story doesn't necessarily mean they're actually dead. Ah—maybe it's—I don't know, what would be the word, a metaphor?

Margaret: Mm, yeah it works for me.

Seth: To something in life you know—umh—and then I don't know—you see the three of them here doing their own thing, they stick together, they're having fun. I don't know, they must be brothers or something.

Margaret: Yeah, they usually are, aren't they?

Seth: There's safety in numbers and comfort in the family. [*laughter*] And then they're flying their little plane here, it crashes—it makes you think, "Boys will be boys." I'm assuming they're boys because they're pigs, that's what my mom called me, so I don't know, it's a cute little book.

Margaret: So what's happening on this page [*Hey Diddle Diddle*]?

Seth: [*pause—inaudible*] I don't know, it makes me think of ah, *X Files*, I think someone's up there. Everything around us, what we perceive to be, the all and be all of our lives, that's only in our view, our perspective—I mean, we're not, maybe we're not the only—life in this universe or in this galaxy or whatever, but I see here they're even drawn differently.

Margaret: Yeah, it's a different story world.

Seth: Different perceptions yeah, and when they come back again, all I can think of is *Nightmare on Elm Street* you know, where he jumped back through the TV or something, so—and this little guy escapes. He wants to go and see what's going on in the real world I guess and—I don't recall this story with the dragon, I don't know—

Margaret: I don't know if it's a specific story here or if it's a general dragon story. I don't know the specific reference.

Seth: Now, I don't know, now it seems that we're getting into a—where there's all of them here, the wolf bullied the pigs and they went out for backup like *Boys in the 'Hood*, they got shot up in a drive by, so now they're going back. [*laughter*] I lead a sad life.

Margaret: I think you're doing very well here.

Seth: So yeah basically what happens is you know, they have the odds stacked in their favour, so they're going back to their, I don't know, their crib I guess and ah—yeah I guess they just—the look on his face is priceless. I like the way the author scrambled up the letters there and stuff, made it part of the story and these guys are all like, "Oh yeah!" Yeah, I don't know, it just looks like they all stuck together to beat the odds.

Seth's intertextual references, to scary films and television programs, may seem a little idiosyncratic at first glance, but they actually lead him to a full evocation of the emotional pull of this odd little book. In his comments about being helpless in his dreams, he provides a fascinating counterpoint to the characters of conventional fictions, who are tied to their printed or filmic destinies; in his admiration for the pigs taking matters into their own hands, he expresses a wistfulness about a life that might be fairer. Although he mocks his own references, he makes use of them to his advantage.

Discussion

I think it is fair to say that none of these readers expected *The Three Pigs* to be the kind of book it is. All of them were lulled by the conventional nature of the opening, and the moment when the first pig was blown out of the story forced each of them to reconsider their stance to the book. It is a measure of our culture that this shift of stance seemed to be a source of pleasure more than confusion for them—they all knew how to respond to the challenge. It might be reasonable to say that adults reading a picture book should naturally have no problem, but I think things are more complex than that. Adults, very often, expect the words to tell the story but the words are often less significant than the images in this book, and on the third page (the book is unpaginated), readers must make a quick decision to trust the illustrations and the speech bubbles more than the linear words.

"Designing a Bird from Memory" and *The Three Pigs* share a robust bossiness towards the implied reader. Both disrupt the kind of automatic processes that slide from a standard prediction to a safe conclusion. The readers may have expected disruption in the online text—at the least, they knew that they were not quite sure what to expect. With the picture book, the surprise was more complete because the opening was so deceptive. Yet finding a metaphor to describe the moment that a reader realized he or she had to read differently is quite difficult. A flick of an inaudible switch is perhaps one possible comparison. Whatever description is used, it should include two elements: (1) there was a moment of definite change, (2) but that shift was very smooth and practised—a kind of "Oh! Okay" moment. The turning point was sometimes marked by an exclamation or by laughter, and it was clear from the comments that readers enjoyed being "bounced" into a new stance by the text.

"Bouncing," of course, is not new. Jokes have traded on bouncing readers and listeners for many centuries. But the ability to reconsider original decisions about reading stance is both essential and sophisticated. These responses to two different but equally unexpected texts offer us a window into one interesting but often ignored aspect of successful reading behaviours. "Designing a Bird from Memory" obliged readers to be tentative right from the start. They knew immediately that they were in unfamiliar reading territory, and attended to the text accordingly. With *The Three Pigs*, it seems certain that many of these readers began in a spirit that was anything but tentative—they recognized the words, they glanced at a suitable picture, and they began to read more or less on autopilot. The third page took them by surprise but they shifted to a more tentative approach at once, as smoothly as an experienced driver switches off the cruise control button when the traffic suddenly becomes busier. What I find intriguing in the transcripts for *The Three Pigs* is the insight they give into a transition from automaticity to a more alert attention—more commonly, we expect to slide the other way, from a tentative beginning to an automatic and transparent immersion into the story world. With the reverse switch of *The Three Pigs*, readers commented on this moment, mostly with pleasure—they were pleased to be challenged, at least by humour, and they enjoyed the surprise.

At the same time, and equally smoothly, the readers stopped simply glancing at the pictures and realized that they had to read more polysemically. To continue the automotive metaphor, they not only switched off the cruise control, but also reached for the gearstick, taking conscious control of the interpretive processes by attending more closely to the information in both pictures and words and exploring the imaginative space created by the contradictions between the print and the illustrations.

Making sense of a picture book is often regarded as a simple kind of reading, but the sophisticated transitions in the disposition of their attention made by all of these readers would probably strike us as miraculous if they were more visible. The kind of "slow-motion" observation made possible by video record and transcript allows us to apply a kind of magnifying effect to the ease and swiftness of the interpretive decision-making that occurred during the readings of this deceptive little book.

The Graphic Novels

With the game of *Black & White*, the online poem, and the picture book, all the participants encountered the same text. At various points in the project, however, they were given a selection and invited to pass judgement on whether they would like to keep going with a particular text. In the case of the graphic novels, there was a set of a dozen different books, as dissimilar in content and style as I could make them. They ranged from Raymond Briggs's biography of his parents, *Ethel and Ernest: A True Story*, to *Maus: A Survivor's Tale*, Art Spiegelman's prize-winning account of *his* parents in Auschwitz; from *The Tale of One Bad Rat*, Bryan Talbot's riff on Beatrix Potter and homelessness, to *Mort: A Discworld Big Comic*, an adaptation of Terry Pratchett's fantasy novel; from *Gemma Bovary*, Posy Simmonds's suburban parody, to *The Watchman* by Alan Moore, Dave Gibbons, and John Higgins. The complete list is in the appendix. Participants were asked to look carefully at each book and choose one for further reading.

The participants did not duplicate each other at all in their selections. It is, of course, impossible to say to what extent the style of drawing and the nature of the storyline affected what they had to say about how they read. I found, in fact, a striking similarity in many of their comments, no matter what book they were reading.

A number of participants commented on the adult nature of some of the books (most especially *David Boring* by Daniel Clowes). As it happened, none of them was a committed reader of graphic novels in the regular run of things. Asked about their background in this kind of reading, they referred to *Archie* comics; *Calvin & Hobbes*, the daily newspaper comic strip, now gathered into anthologies; and Marvel Comics—but of those, only *Calvin & Hobbes* appeared to play any role in anyone's adult life. The limited and somewhat fluffy repertoire that they developed through reading short versions of the format may well have contributed to how they read the graphic novels I offered them. They also differed in how enthusiastic they were about this material, with a full spectrum of response running from Jocelyn, who did not like any of them, to Seth, who would have taken them all home if I had given him the chance. Denise deliberately chose to read a book that she could bring herself to put down after a few minutes, rejecting *Maus* because she thought she would get too quickly involved in the story. Most of the others, however, did not seem troubled by the idea of a sample reading—by this stage in the project they had already done quite a bit of sampling.

I offered a choice between full-colour and black-and-white stories, and some readers cared more about this distinction than others. Density of information on the page seemed to be a stronger signal to some of them.

But before I move into more detailed accounts of the participants and their approaches to these graphic novels, I will, as usual, turn first to my own reactions.

Inside the Graphic Novels

I find that most graphic novels throw an unflattering light on my normal— and normally invisible—reading preferences. When I hit the road-block of a graphic novel, I suddenly discover the enormous extent to which I prefer my reading processes to be speedy and automatic. Graphic novels slow me down and they interfere in very serious ways with my automaticity. I am a very experienced reader, but a graphic novel, more than almost any other kind of text, will bring me to the not very happy conclusion that I do not actually like being a flexible reader.

Habit is a powerful force, and my reading habits have been set in place for years. Automaticity leads me to read more and further and faster, and I have to take conscious action to interfere with that long-standing reaction. In reading a graphic novel, I will often find that I have reached the end of a two-page opening and forgotten to look at the pictures. If the opening includes a number of panels, I have some serious backtracking to do before I can carry on with the page turn. As a reader with a strong preference for sorting out misunderstandings by reading further forward rather than looking back (though I will resort to re-checking if absolutely forced to it by a state of total bafflement), I find this constant re-working of my interpretation to be entirely tedious. It does not help that I know at all times that it is my own failing as a reader that causes all this trouble. A lifetime of my kind of constant reading has actually equipped me very poorly for this particular challenge.

I am happy to linger over the illustrations of a picture book, assuming that there are only a few to each page. When there are numerous little panels, my lingering tendencies evaporate and must be coaxed back into service by deliberate action.

In short, reading a graphic novel generally calls for a great quantity of reiterated resolution from me. My automatic speed-reading tendencies have to be quelled over and over again—it is just too simple to *forget* that I am supposed to be reading carefully and attentively and polysemically.

If this self-flagellation were merely indulgent, I would not bother with it here. I do think it is important to keep reminding ourselves of the many and varied kinds of demands that reading makes and of the many forms of response that are differentially available to readers. My inadequacies as a reader of graphic novels serve as a reminder of the individuality of the process.

They also serve as a reminder of the limited value of exhortation, even self-exhortation. I know perfectly well how to become a better graphic novel reader. I should simply read more of them, more often. I should re-read the ones that I like. I should maintain awareness that slow and careful is a legitimate form of progress. But that will not be enough. Realistically, I am never going to be a successful slow and careful reader, however determined my intentions, so I need to find ways of speeding up my progress through the panels while not losing the thread of the information in the pictures. I even know that if I invest this kind of effort, the rewards will be substantial, since there are so many intriguing and exciting graphic novels to be read. Some day I may actually get round to it.

In the meantime, I will simply report on the responses of the readers in this project to the set of graphic novels made available.

The Graphic Novels: What the Travellers Say

Each participant was asked to look through a pile of graphic novels, choosing one to read for a longer period of time and describing why that one was chosen and why the others were rejected. After they had spent 15 minutes or so with their preferred title, I asked them to describe their reading processes. The answers were general and related to the specific title only in connection with small details. In fact, many of the answers had far more in common with each other than otherwise.

Here are some examples.

Ben: [choosing *Watchman*] The way I go about it, like I kinda scan the page and I like, take note of those and then kinda read what they're saying and stuff.

Margaret: Now in this panel, would you have read the words first or looked at the picture first?

Ben: A little bit of both.

Margaret: Uhuh, so you kind of move back and forth between them?

Ben: Yeah.

Margaret: So your eyes are actually fairly busy?

Ben: Reasonably yeah . . . .

Margaret: How much attention do you pay to the details as you go?

Ben: Umh—ow—I'd like to say I pay a lot of attention to the details, but I don't. Sometimes I still have to go back and read just to clarify everything.

Courtney: [choosing *Jimmy Corrigan*] It's kind of got umh, an interesting script, not too much that it, you know, overwhelms the reader but there is enough going on that you kind of can get an idea of the story just by kind of flipping through it. . . . I like that there is an interesting way you know, that they have changed, you know, the text sometimes goes one way then switches the other way.

Courtney: [looking at *Maus*] Umh, it's not that I wouldn't read it because you know, it did catch my attention that there was quite a lot of text, which would be a very big draw for me. There is enough of a read that you don't have to rely heavily on the pictures to tell the story. You could just get away with reading the text and still get the full gamut of what they are trying to tell you. Umh—but it would have to be a particular time and a particular place. It's not like light reading, you just drag along with you and just flip open or whatever.

Margaret: Can I ask you just a little bit about the experience of reading a story told that way? Do you look at the pictures first or the words first or do you switch back and forth between them? Can you recreate it?

Damian: Ah—

Margaret: The page [of *Maus*] is very dense, isn't it?

Damian: I read it first, then looked at it.

Margaret: Uhuh. So how far do you read before you check the pictures, is it panel by panel?

Damian: Yeah pretty much.

Margaret: Does that slow down your reading or do you get into the rhythm of it reasonably easily?

Damian: It's, yeah it seems to work.

Margaret: Umh, can you just tell me a little bit about reading that [*Ethel and Ernest*]? About how the words and the pictures work, the kind of work that you have to do as a reader to make sense of that?

Denise: Umh, it doesn't umh, it strikes me for the most part as being something that you don't necessarily need the speech, but like the words to be able to figure out the story that you can see that this is happening and it's like, in the beginning you can see that she's a maid, he's riding by and eventually you know, they keep seeing each other, they keep seeing each other and then eventually he comes and brings her flowers and then they go out, and it doesn't necessarily require a lot of reading other than to actually get details about the story. So if you say handed this someone who didn't read English they'd probably be able to get the gist of what was going on.

Margaret: Uhuh. Now, do the words serve as kind of pointers to what you should be paying attention to in the pictures?

Denise: Yeah. And they give you a little bit more detail as to about who they are and what they're, umh, who they are and what they're looking at. I don't quite know how to put it. [*pause*] It's just giving more specific details as to their characters and stuff and the life they're trying to live and the time that they're living in.

Margaret: Do you find that this is slower to read than continuous print or faster?

Denise: Umh, I would say faster because you can—mmm—I would say faster because you can sort of absorb a lot of it from a picture and then the words are sort of just dressing it up and making it a little bit more specific.

Margaret:	Do you think that would be the case of all of these that you looked at?
Denise:	Probably not.

Drew:	[choosing *Fax from Sarajevo*] I guess I look at—I get an image. I look at the picture first. And then I read the text, but I don't actually like, look and take in the picture, I just kind of—glance at it and then read the text.
Margaret:	And then do you go back and look at the pictures?
Drew:	No, I go on to the next one.
Margaret:	Okay. So it's just an impression from the pictures?
Drew:	Well of—basically yeah.
Margaret:	And then you get the story from the words?
Drew:	Mmm.
Margaret:	Right, so that kind of quite verbal, that tactic works reasonably well then?
Drew:	[*Pause*] I guess so.
Margaret:	If you were puzzled, would you go back and check the pictures further or would you try and make the sense from the words?
Drew:	If I was puzzled—usually if I get confused reading a comic, I generally read the words as opposed to look at the picture because generally a lot of the pictures don't tell you much, it's just two people with faces and two people talking.

Margaret:	Can I just ask you a little bit about reading a graphic novel? Do you read the words first or look at the pictures first? What would you do there, with one you have never seen before?
Isaac:	Depends what the picture is. Umh, I had this [*Mort*]. I looked first.
Margaret:	That's quite a complicated page.
Isaac:	Yeah, and then I find them down in the corner, but I'm, I'm also then making sure that there's nothing else I need to be aware of anywhere. . . . Here Death almost has a little bit of an impish grin. And then his hand is like, well if you don't want it [*laughing*], it's umh it, actually this is drawn very well. Here he is angry, angry again, and here he's . . . cutesy and pleasant because he is playing with the kittens.

Margaret:	I want to just ask you a little bit about how you read it [*The Tale of One Bad Rat*]. Do you read the words first and then look at the pictures?
Jeremy:	Yes.
Margaret:	Do you go down the page reading the words or do you read the words for one picture and then look at the picture?
Jeremy:	Yeah, I read the words for one picture then look at the picture and then move on.
Margaret:	So, you're doing it panel by panel basically?

Jeremy:	Yes.
Margaret:	And do you have a look at the page to see how the panels are organized before you start or is it all straightforward?
Jeremy:	It's all pretty much all straightforward. . . . I don't know, I just looked at the pictures after that. After I read these three.
Margaret:	So it's definitely words first?
Jeremy:	Yeah.
Margaret:	Do you find you read more slowly when you're trying to check out the pictures as well as the words or does it just feel the same way?
Jeremy:	I tend to read a little more slowly.
Margaret:	Uhuh, and is that a problem or is it just something that goes with the territory?
Jeremy:	It's not really a problem because you have the pictures as well, adding information, so I might be looking at the pictures, but it's not like I'm sort of half reading the book.
Margaret:	Right. So you're not wasting time?
Jeremy:	Yeah.
Jocelyn:	I'd get bored with this real fast.
Margaret:	Okay.
Jocelyn:	I find myself just skimming. I'm just looking at pictures now [laughing].
Margaret:	So this is not your kind of reading.
Jocelyn:	No. I'm not into this.
Margaret:	Yeah, I just want to ask you about how you actually read it [*Watchman*]? Do you read the words first or the pictures first or switch back and forth? How do you process it?
Seth:	Umh—yeah I never really thought about it. I think—
Margaret:	Find a page that you have actually read and see if you can recreate it . . . .
Seth:	I think what happens is that I notice the drawings, but not for the reasons you would think, like to see what's happening. Umh, when I look at a comic book or you know, a comic novel or something umh, I appreciate what goes into it because I—like I say, I'd guess I'd give anything to be able to do something like this and I appreciate what goes into it. The detail, ah—just you know, those types of things, they way it's drawn, the characters, their umh—I guess the best way to explain it would be to ah—compare it to that movie *Unbreakable*, Bruce Willis, Samuel Jackson, have you seen that one?
Margaret:	No.
Seth:	Anyways, Samuel L. Jackson plays a character who as a child you know, was reading comics and he grew up and later he has some sort of gallery, a museum of classic comic book, pictures, and stuff. Just the way

he depicts or describes the pictures of the way the artists depicted you know, noticed the villain's abnormal head to his body, the hero's strong jaw line, like that. Just the things like that, that really—the detail that goes into it that you can really appreciate and then from there and like, that happens instantaneously, you just look and then it's like, "oh yeah, there's a story here" and then you read what's happening. It's kinda like when you used to watch the old silent films and sit there and the little subtitles thing would come up.

Margaret: Okay, I'm just going to stop you now on that page where you were [in *David Boring*], this is a good example, you've got no colour, you've got a ton more writing than the rest of the book, how did that affect the experience of reading this one?

Seth: Umh, it's a novel with pictures I would think. Ah . . . I think you get the best of both worlds. A real book and a comic book as my parents would have put it.

Discussion

All these readers knew that they would not get the chance to immerse themselves deeply in the graphic novel they had chosen. Even in making allowances for this fact, however, it is striking how impressionistic their reading processes sound as they describe them. The vocabulary is consistent for many readers: "I kinda scan. . . . I [don't] pay a lot of attention to the details" (Ben); "you don't have to rely heavily on the pictures to tell the story—you could just get away with reading the text and still get the full gamut of what they are trying to tell you" (Courtney); "I read it first, then looked at it . . . pretty much [panel by panel]" (Damian); "you can sort of absorb a lot of it from a picture and then the words are just sort of dressing it up and making it a little bit more specific" (Denise); "I get an image. I look at the picture first. And then I read the text, but I don't actually, like, look and take in the picture, I just kind of—glance at it and then read the text" (Drew); "something like this, I read this first and then I go to the picture" (Isaac); "I read the words for one picture, then look at the picture and then move on" (Jeremy); "I find myself skimming. I'm just looking at pictures now" (Jocelyn); "I notice the drawings, but not for the reasons you would think, like to see what's happening . . . I appreciate what goes into it . . . the detail that goes into it that you can really appreciate and then from there and, like, that happens instantaneously, you just look and then it's like, 'Oh yeah, there's a story here' and then you read what's happening" (Seth).

In my earlier work with adolescents reading a complete novel (Mackey, 1995), I discussed a phenomenon I labelled "good-enough reading." Good-enough reading involves finding a personal balance between momentum and accountability to the text. I would describe my own reading of graphic novels as generally *not* good-enough because I keep being trapped between the need to make progress through the text and the need actually to be aware of the information on offer. A good-enough reading would balance that trade-off in a more functional and ongoing way.

In slightly different ways, most of these readers are describing forms of good-enough reading. Jocelyn, who never faked an interest she did not feel, was not interested in the graphic novels at all and did not make any pretence at accountability to the information on the page in front of her. All the others seem, at least in this relatively fleeting contact with their chosen graphic novel, to be finding ways of making good-enough progress. Ben could not say whether he looked first at words or pictures; his eyes move back and forth between them. Courtney, Damian, Isaac, and Jeremy look at the words first and then glance at the pictures. Denise, Drew, and Seth start with the pictures. Drew glances at a picture before reading the words; Denise and Seth appear to draw rather more information from the pictures than the words.

I would describe all of these readers (with the partial exception of Jocelyn) as perfectly comfortable with their reading capacities in connection with these graphic novels. They were interested; they were articulate about what they did and did not like; they were enthusiastic (with the total exception of Jocelyn). Seth, as usual, wanted to read them all, and I think many of the participants would have taken one or two home with them, given the option. But it is quite noticeable how their descriptions of their reading behaviours contrast with the complex theoretical discussions provided earlier of what might be called an ideal reading of this format. Jocelyn expressed a complete lack of interest. Denise and Seth spoke quite casually about the limited impact of the words, as did Isaac, though he did look at the words first. All the others were equally casual about the pictures.

In part, I suspect this response has to do with their backgrounds in this kind of reading. Different participants mentioned Marvel Comics, *Archie*, *Calvin and Hobbes*—all material with a strong base in the short unit. They were certainly aware of the graphic novel as a format, but their experience of extended reading in this format was clearly limited. There was little discussion about any kind of equal partnership of words and pictures; by and large these readers privileged one channel and subordinated the other. I do not think it would be stretching the evidence to say that overall there was a strong bias towards momentum, with rather less interest in accountability. Even Denise and Isaac, who were more interested in pictures than words, mainly looked at the pictures for information that would contribute to the progress of the story. And Isaac was actually hostile to the idea of too many words: "Umh, *this*, too much, uh, reading to do with it. Umh, I might as well read a book. Umh, that would be like having a narrator talk throughout the whole movie—no thanks." Only Seth expressed an interest in lingering on the pictures for the pleasure of it—coming to, with a bit of a start, to remember, "Oh, yeah, there's a story here."

It may be that their reading histories, largely confined to the daily comics in the newspaper and comic books from childhood, predisposed these readers to think that good-enough was plenty for this format. I am more inclined to think that good-enough is very often a default position in all kinds of reading and viewing, and perhaps playing as well. And in a world where mutation of textual formats is constant, a strategy of finding the point of good-enough is actually a reasonable survival strategy.Um num ipsummodiam, suscin hendips uscilisim vulla corting endreet ummodo eum in heniat incillan vullamet diat wis aute magnismod diamcom moloborperat in veriustie minisis delissed tiscipsustie ent auguero od dolore magnit exeraessim il incilisi.

Velessed dolor ad dolor auguero ea commy numsandipsum quis ea coreet prat, commy nit lobore consenim dio od dunt lor sis nim eugait luptat. Esto cor atue dunt ad enibh ea autat ationul lumsandreet lorerat vel ulla auguerat, conse facip exer accum dolobor sum duis amconsecte modo cor alit at velisi tionse do od molortio del dolore tionum niat. Odolore tissim dolore delessi sciliquat. Ipsusto dunt wis alit, velessim esequisi.

Ud dolore veliquat. Ecte molorpe riustismolor atet amet, suscipisi te ex ea feugait pratum acidunt augait am, quisis nulpute velessi tatetummod esse exerill andions equatincil utat prationsed tatio odolore dio odigna con venibh el ea at. Iriustie tationu llaore dunt praesse quatum digna faccum nos at wis eugiam zzrit vulla feu feugait do dolor iriusci eum ipsum dignis nissit aci tat nim iliquisl eugue tem duis ametum zzrilit am, quatin hendrer aesequis do dio do consed tin ulputat wissi.

Accum qui blan eros accum doloreet velestrud molorem velesecte tat volortie faccumsan henit in exer si.

Xerit alit estrud mod dolor irilit laorper sequat atem nit augait aliqui tie veliquipit venim ing eugue dolorperatie min ut alisl exero endre doloreet wissim zzrit at, qui blandrem in vullandiat ut praesequam dolor sed mod magna

DEPARTURE POINTS:
MAKING SELECTIONS

Selection is the invisible enabler of reading, viewing, or playing. Lack of ability to make satisfying selections is often a major ingredient in reading fall-off. Many people who think of themselves as poor or reluctant readers are perfectly competent readers who are poor choosers. Making the move from one general stage of reading (early series books, to take a very common category) to a broader or more challenging stage often throws up a barrier that stops people from reading altogether, or greatly diminishes their satisfaction in this activity. Yet we devote very little educational time to issues of selection; it is generally perceived, when thought of at all, as just one of those things that readers know how to do.

Librarians who do readers' advisory work—talking with readers about how to locate that satisfying next read—know how important their job is, but it is not always a job that is given major consideration in the overall structure of a public library. For teacher-librarians, this role is perhaps even more important, as they are in a position to reach those non-readers who never enter a public library, and who are often not so much bad readers as poor choosers.

I emphasize reading as there is more anxiety about non-reading than about non-viewing and non-playing. However, I believe many adults flinch from digital games for equivalent reasons; they are ill-equipped to select games that might appeal to them and enable them to strengthen their skills. Paradoxically, poor viewing selection skills may sometimes lead to more viewing rather than less, leading to those desultory hours spent by many people watching anything that comes along on the box, an activity that often provides little satisfaction.

· 7 ·

MAKING A CHOICE

In this chapter, I look at what we know theoretically about selection strategies, and then discuss two different ways in which participants told me about their own powers of selection: as they talked about their own choices, and as they responded to various texts supplied by me in terms of two simple questions: if you could, would you keep going with this text? And why? To extend my landscape metaphor, in this section, I also explore some particular landmarks, as it were, investigating what we may learn about readers from looking at some of the texts they select for their own enjoyment.

Making a Choice: What the Maps Say

Anyone who has tried to pick the perfect book for a friend in hospital knows that it can be very hard to read someone else's mind about what makes a title work for a reader—or a viewer or a player for that matter. People select and reject titles for what seem to outsiders like very arbitrary and incomprehensible reasons. Like the participants in this study, most people can explain why they vote yes or no on a particular title, but the explanations may sometimes seem to pivot on very small issues indeed.

Selection is the secret ingredient of being a successful user of texts. Knowing how to find what you like, knowing whose advice will work for you, knowing how to browse and how to sample—these are significant skills in the creation of a happy reader/film-goer/television viewer/game player.

Anyone who has worked with reluctant young readers knows how quickly they can pick up a book, give it a perfunctory glance, and reject it. Slowing down the rejection process sometimes is really all it takes to lead to the occasional acceptance. Achieving that slow-down without simultaneously putting pressure on the unwilling reader is the hard part.

Frank Hatt makes a telling argument that selecting a title is part of the reading experience, a part too often overlooked in studies of reading:

> Even the more thorough of the models of the reading process take the coming together of the text and the reader as "given," and locate the commencement of the reading act at the point where the reader starts to perceive the words on the page. This is hardly satisfactory. If we accept that a reader's mental "set" is a key factor in reading performance, then it would seem that the approach route to the text is crucial. If what the reader gets from the text depends on the questions he addresses to it, then these questions derive initially from expectations which are roused before he encounters the text. In effect, a reading act, extended to include the "finding" of the text, can be seen as a series of questions which the reader puts to a store of messages. At the beginning of the reading act, the questions may be vague and amorphous—"What should I perhaps be doing about my garden?"—and the store is the whole world out there. As the reading act proceeds, the questions become more specific and the store narrows to a text—the gardening manual—which in turn narrows to a chapter, then a paragraph, then a sentence, which might answer a question so specific as to be meaningless without the context supplied by the fining-down process which has gone before—a question like "how deep shall I plant it?" If we present the reading act in these terms, then the central skill may be that of asking the store the right questions so as to frame subsequent questions for putting to the messages. (1976, 66–67)

Hatt is discussing non-fiction selection here, but many of the same issues arise with fictional choices also, although the questions are more likely to involve emotional criteria such as mood and curiosity. In any case, the process of winnowing down possible choices from the original set of "all the books in the world" or "all the books in this library/bookshop/friend's shelf" remains a significant part of the reading act as Hatt describes it.

The art of finding a satisfying text in any medium is a frequently overlooked (and seldom taught) element of successful interpretive practices. Catherine Sheldrick Ross, who has devoted considerable attention to this challenge, conducted a study of 194 experienced and enthusiastic readers. She reports, "Being able to choose successfully among materials is an important skill that is never directly taught but is learned by readers who teach themselves, beginning in childhood" (2001, 9). Her account of what the readers in her study have told her is illuminating:

> Most of the 194 readers have taught themselves strategies for choosing enjoyable books that less practiced readers may never discover. When asked how they go about choosing a book to read for pleasure, most interviewees launched into an elaborate description, involving many interrelated considerations, often starting with their own mood at the time of reading and going on variously to how they find new authors or what clues they look for on the book itself. (2001, 9)

According to Ross, selection does not simply happen at the point of contact between book and potential reader:

> Notably the systems they described for choosing books usually depended on considerable previous experience and knowledge of authors, publisher, cover art, and conventions for promoting books and sometimes depended on a social network of family or friends who recommended and lent books. We can consider this to be "behind the eyes" knowledge that the reader can draw upon when considering for selection or rejection any particular book that comes to hand. Past experiences with books and remembered information from reviews or from word of mouth are carried in the reader's head and available to be called upon when the reader is browsing in a bookstore or library. In order to be alerted to the existence of new books that will provide the reading experience they want, committed readers typically put out antennae that scan their everyday environments for clues. (2001, 11–12)

The Emotions of Selection

The kind of ongoing information-gleaning behaviour that these readers describe is important, but at the moment of choice it takes a back seat to something much more immediate, says Ross: "The bedrock for choice is the reader's mood: What do I feel like reading now? What will I want to read in the future (that I should borrow or buy now to have on hand)? Readers overwhelmingly reported that they choose books according to their mood and what else is going on in their lives" (2001, 13).

Greg Smith, writing about film rather than books, is helpful in unpacking the idea of "mood" in a way that may shed light on selection processes in a variety of media, including books:

> The primary set of orienting emotion states is mood. A mood is a preparatory state in which one is seeking an opportunity to express a particular emotion or emotion set.

> Moods are expectancies that we are about to have a particular emotion, that we will encounter cues that will elicit particular emotions. These expectancies orient us toward our situation, encouraging us to evaluate the environment in mood-congruent fashion. . . . Moods act as the emotion system's equivalent of attention, focusing us on certain stimuli and not others. (2003, 38)

Smith discusses what he calls "the mood-cue" (2003, 43) approach to film, pointing out how emotion markers may be part of the content or be formal or stylistic in nature. He suggests that many forms of mood-cue are genre specific:

> Genres are composed of narrative and iconographic patterns, but they also specify patterns of emotional address, providing the viewer with scripts to use in interpreting a genre film. . . .
> The most significant genre scripts with relation to emotion are not the broad expectations for the overall shape and form of a film, but genre microscripts, intertextual expectation sets for sequences and scenes. (2003, 48)

Recognition of "patterns of emotional address" may be one strong element in books and games as well as films; it is certainly worth scanning the responses of the readers to their selection challenges to see whether this phenomenon arises.

Knowing Where Not to Look

Readers do not make a choice out of the entire universe of books, or even from the entire set of books on offer in a particular library or shop. They eliminate entire categories before they start. Ross's readers were quite clear that there were books that need not trouble their attention. "The interviewed readers were emphatic about what they *don't* like in a book, and used cues on the book itself as a warning" (2001, 16, emphasis in original).

Todd Gitlin suggests that knowing where not to pay attention is a vital skill in an overcrowded information universe. To cope with the glut of words and images that surround us every day, he says,

> it takes not only principles of selection but stratagems of inattention. . . . Coping, in other words, demands a willed myopia. Everyone learns not only to see but not to see—to tune out and turn away.
> But tactics of inattention are hardly enough. We need navigational strategies as well. . . . To live comfortably with [the torrent of mass-produced images and sounds that surround us] we gravitate to our favorites, classify the parts, get our minds around segments while doing our best to ignore the rest. (2001, 118)

Writing more than a decade ago, Stephen Heppell used the then unfamiliar territory of the computer game to draw attention to the problems of being overwhelmed by data in selection choices:

> When we adults observe children playing computer games, what we see is coloured by our own experience. Our experience does not usually include computer games in any depth. We find a cacophony of sound, an anarchic blur of vision and action. We see children reacting to this, absorbed in their activity, but we under-value what is happening because we don't see what they see. They see sophisticated cues and clues. They see categories of visual information. They have expectations about the behaviour of objects of the screen, and within this environment they see challenges and solve problems that their parents and teachers are not even aware of.
>
> This is no different to the way in which a sophisticated reader sees books differently from a non-reader. To a non-reader, a library is a confusion of books, unstructured, chaotic. For teachers and parents, with a long history of familiarity with books and libraries, the same shelves hold past memories: Fiction, Romance, Reference, Travel and so on. The books are familiar friends and they can be referred to in conversation with other literate adults. (1993, 3)

I find the two-way nature of this analogy to be very helpful, shedding light on both book selection and game interpretation. Previous experience and what the reader or player has stored "behind the eyes," in Ross's lively term, are invisible to the outsider. Eliminating certain categories or genres is one way of reducing selection to something manageable. Knowledgeable readers do their best to eliminate categories that are unlikely to appeal to whatever mood they bring to bear on the selection of a particular moment.

This combination of the very personal nature of mood and the broader-based background that enables readers to gravitate towards or avoid large categories of materials creates a fluid and shifting dynamic. Other factors, of course, also impinge. Clearly in this study, participants considered books, films, games, and graphic novels that they would not have looked at on their own—but a recommendation from a trusted friend may have the same impact, opening a reader/viewer/player to a world that might not otherwise be considered, and even shifting mood as the interpreter engages with the new text.

Taste and Growth

Relying on previous experience and momentary mood may lead to very conservative reading habits, and certainly some of the participants in this study were extreme in this regard. Isaac and Ben effectively read only one author each.

Isaac, having chosen the very prolific Piers Anthony, was unlikely to run out of reading material any time soon, but Ben had periods of reading drought as he waited for the appearance of each new title in his preferred series, *Sword of Truth* by Terry Goodkind. In each case, it is tempting to speculate that their strikingly singular approach to books may be based either on restricted background experience in making broad choices or on the association of a very particular kind of mood with the whole experience of reading—or on some combination of the two.

Many cultural influences might reinforce such conservative tendencies, not least the idea of the kind of total loyalty expressed in the concept of "branding." But there are other pressures, some of which may lead to more expansive sampling of texts. Todd Babiak, in an interesting commentary on youth and culture that appeared in my local newspaper as I was working on this material, speaks of market research companies and their "focus groupthink divisions that promise to capture 18–34-year-olds for their clients" (2004, C1). Decrying Hollywood's trend of wooing kids by pandering to them with dumb jokes, sexy innuendo, and what purports to be kids' own language, he describes himself between 18 and 24 as a contrast:

> I didn't want to hear every sentence oiled with cuss words and "like" or watch my peers ride skateboards and take bong hits all day long. If I wanted to hear, see or experience my culture, all I had to do was open the back door. Instead, I pretended to understand stories in the international sections of newspapers and magazines. I pretended to know a lot about European cinema of the 1950s and I bought tickets to the theatre because that's what real adults did. Yes, I was a pretentious jackass but I can't take a time machine back to 1991 and slap myself smart. (2004, C1)

Babiak quotes the artistic director of Edmonton's Citadel Theatre, Bob Baker: "[A]t a certain age, in your twenties, you want to read up and think up. You want to be given the dignity of intelligence and full adulthood" (Babiak, 2004, C3).

Reading up and thinking up call for a certain kind of energy. I think it is possible to underestimate the significance of such energy by dismissing it as externally driven anxiety about the acquisition and display of "cultural capital" (Bourdieu, 1984/1979, 53). What Babiak describes, and what emerges from time to time in my transcripts, is rather an urge well described by Beverly Cleary's character Ramona, who yearns to feel herself "winning at growing up" (Cleary, 1984, 182). How these participants responded in generally positive—though not necessarily sophisticated—ways to the book and game versions of *Sophie's World* does indicate that they were not averse to "thinking up." And many of the participants referred to times they have consciously set out to find out more about a topic, or to extend their textual range.

Salience and Fluency

In this project, I showed participants opening pages of novels, opening credits of movies, and opening scenes of computer games. I asked them to browse through graphic novels and console games. I used many of these tactics in an earlier study with younger readers (Mackey, 2002), and at that time I determined that selection processes often rested on establishing a satisfactory balance between questions of personal salience and issues of fluency, or ease of access. Greater salience often meant that fluency was a less important issue, and vice versa. This meta-strategy was media-neutral, applicable to books, films, and games equally.

The older participants in this current study also discussed questions of salience and fluency in relation to all the media I showed them. But when I looked for patterns of personal response, I could not establish any regularity either in personal or medium-related response. In general, people talked more about fluency in relation to games and graphic novels than they did with novels and films. This response is not really surprising; experienced readers and film-viewers would expect a certain amount of transparency with these formats. In a number of cases, the issue of ease of access in movie-watching was mentioned at all only because I rigged the set of films, pressing the issue of fluency with *Memento, Time Code,* and to a certain extent *Moulin Rouge.*

Signature Responses

When I say that every person in this project mentioned issues of salience and issues of fluency with regard to every medium I proffered to them, I come to the end of the commonalities. What came across much more strongly was a sense of the individual attitude to texts, what Lawrence Sipe has helpfully identified as the "signature response" (1998a, 87), an individual response style that manifests itself in reaction to a variety of texts.

Ross talked about the knowledge and skills located "behind the eyes" of her experienced readers. Certainly my participants manifested many of these tacit skills and they were quite definitive about knowing what appealed to them and what did not. But there was a larger sense of individuality residing "behind" even these specific and text-oriented attributes. Jocelyn was constantly on the alert for an immediate emotional connection. Drew was always interested in the larger fictional world. Isaac regularly paid particular attention to visual information. Seth invariably made intertextual references.

If I had to group the responses according to a larger rubric, I believe Bartle's (1996) rough-and-ready categorization of the MUD players (explorers, achievers, killers, socializers) would actually serve a useful function. Moods come and go, and certainly feature in many selection decisions (as Ross's readers identified), but a more general stance towards text might well be invisible to these readers because it is much more likely to remain the same.

So let us revisit these categories for a moment. (It is perhaps worth noting here that the *Black & White* session was the last of the five, so it did not affect any of the selection sub-projects, which all preceded the extensive playing of that game. In other words, participants were not cued into killing, achieving, or whatever, as a result of just having played *Black & White*.)

Making a Choice: What the Travellers Say

Drew

I talked about Drew's game of *Black & White* being oriented towards achievement, particularly the achievement of control. Drew's taste for control manifested itself in many different guises as he looked at the wide assortment of texts I offered him. If it was some form of control of a big world, so much the better. He was consistent in this preference over many sessions. For example, he spoke of *Civilization* (either II or III) as his favourite computer game: "It's got a replay value that you never see in other games. It's essentially, you manage your own empire, you build your own civilization, you compete with others, and there's a number of ways you can win the game." The books he has re-read most often are Hickman's *Dragonlance*—"not the chronicles, the legends. I probably read them somewhere between 40 and 50 times. I'm very repetitive." Challenged by the four-way-split screen of the film *Time Code*, he said he would keep on watching, "just because I've almost got it figured out. I have no idea [what is going on], but I kinda, I'm trying to understand how the little cells work together. . . . It's one of those movies, I think, you have to watch six or seven times before you actually understand what's going on." With the graphic novels, he raised many points about ease of access, but his predilection for expansive detail led him to say he thought he would enjoy *Gemma Bovary*, Posy Simmonds's suburban comedy of contemporary middle-class *mores*. At first glance this might seem an unlikely choice, but his rationale fit plausibly into his general set of textual attitudes and preferences. "I'm really taken to the style or the layout of this book, it's presented in, and the fact that the artwork is done basically all grey scale, all in pencil. . . . And in some of the pages, actually in a number of pages, you could actually go into more detail if you so choose. For instance, the page I just was on, there was a bunch of letters that you know, as part of the picture, you don't need to read but you can if you choose." Mastering the territory of any given fictional world seems important to Drew, no matter which medium is involved.

Isaac

In my account of *Black & White*, I described Isaac as an achiever with an interest in the achievement of a plot. His interest in plot came through with other media as well, as did his strong interest in visuals. He rejected *Moulin Rouge* on plot evaluation terms: "Nothing's happened yet. There's nothing. . . . It was just a whole lot of *nothing* with a teeny little bit of set-up, but it's not the set-up that interested me." Similarly, he dismissed *The Purple Rose of Cairo*: "Nothing's happening. It's a Woody Allen movie. It's a thinker, so there's not enough—there's no comedy happening yet, and even if there is it's going to be really deep or it's going to be there and then gone. Um, and there's no, nothing interesting happened yet. So just too much background." His more positive comment on *Memento* was also plot-related: "You want to know what led up to that because obviously the way, like, that's a concluding kind of thing. They went in reverse so now what's going on with that?" Isaac's response to *The Sims* presaged his later reaction to *Black & White*: "A Pro-social world would get totally boring after a while. You've got to throw in a little mix and see how that affects them." He was positive about *American McGee's Alice* because, "I get to do something. Umh, but I also have to read and think to understand some stuff. . . . It takes a while to get somewhere but you want to complete something. You don't just want to just run around for half an hour then just stop because you're out of time. You want to go till you've completed a level or whatever task, follow the rabbit. Got to get in the hole." He liked the look of the book *Monster*, saying: "There's a lot of narration to it and a lot of explanation for what people are thinking behind what they do." The quest for finding the story element, for registering the disruption that makes a story begin, comes through in many of his comments.

Jeremy

Jeremy was a socializer, and this preference came through strongly in many different discussions. Talking about game choices, he said, "I tend to rely a lot on other people's opinions." His real enthusiasm for *Half-Life* lay in the online social world surrounding that game: "I ended up meeting a lot of people over the Internet playing these games." He said, "I spend more time talking to them than actually playing." With his real-world friends, he went to the movies, usually to the cheap theatres. He went with whoever was around and willing to go, and said it did not matter much what the movie was: "probably going out is worth it." He rented DVDs, but rarely bought one; his criterion for purchase also had a social edge to it: "It would have to be something that I *really* loved. That I can show off to my friends as well." His criteria for choosing novels and graphic novels were more personal and internal, based on whether he found the story appealing, but he expressed more interest in which ones had won prizes (also a social criterion) than almost any other participant. Jeremy spoke of socially scaffolded reading, viewing, and playing on many different occasions.

Seth

Seth was an explorer in his playing of *Black & White* and, in his very non-judgemental approach to all texts, seemed to be an explorer across different media as well. To him, it was important not to reject very much. Of the set of graphic novels, he said: "If these were at home, I'd probably go through all of them anyways." Looking at the films, he said, "I'm not too picky." Responding to the novels, he observed: "Whether it's books or movies, I just take them for what they're worth, an escape from reality. So unless it really sucks, yeah, I'm not hard to please, but I'll keep my hands on anything for the most part." "It has to be something really crappy," he said, before he would say no. But he turned down *Sophie's World* because he did not find it intriguing enough. "The reason why I'm reading a book is, for, you know, entertainment. I want to see what they're throwing at me. . . . You know, and you just can't wait to turn the page, so—is Timmy going to get away, kind of thing." And it was no surprise when he said of the computer games: "I play all kinds. Like, I don't have a certain type that I'm partial to." He did prefer good graphics, "something you enjoy watching as well as playing." This capacity to accept and develop interest in almost any text is a feature of Seth's approach to all media.

Damian

The one killer in this set of participants was Damian, and he was the one exception to the general observation that these tendencies veered towards media-neutrality. Damian undoubtedly played killer in all the computer games we gave him. His comments put together read: "Is it wrong to cheer for the bad guys? . . . Start talking about dismembering someone. . . . Games are much more fun when you're shooting stuff. . . . [The appeal is] pointless distraction, just running through killing things, big guns, big explosions. . . . As long as you're killing things it's okay. . . . I'm going to try to cause as much havoc as possible [in *The Sims*]. . . . Hah! [of *Alice*] a psychotic girl in a cute uniform running around killing things. *What's not to love?*" Yet this killer instinct did not seem to cross media, and indeed, when pressed to explore the appeal of certain games he was as likely to talk about the pleasures of mental mapping and flow as of death and dismemberment. He spoke of the pleasure of the flow in the training at the start of *Alice*, and went on to say, "The main thing is having a real, well not real, but a developed character and personality." He was explicit that flow was an appealing quality in novels as well. His criteria for choosing a movie to watch were nowhere near as bloodthirsty as his comments on games: "The big, I do like the big special effects. [*inaudible*] Umh, other than that, that it's well written. There's some terrible, terrible movies out there. Ah—mostly it's just word of mouth. If it's actually entertaining." At the time of our session he was reading *The Grapes of Wrath* for his English class, and the most recent novel he had read for his own enjoyment was *The Lord of the Rings* (the first film had just premiered). *The Hobbit* was the "first real novel" he had ever read, he said, and he had read the trilogy "many times." He had also recently read *American Psycho*, finding it "a little slow to progress really, but it was good." (This was the only reference to a non-game text involving killing on a broad scale unless *The Lord of the Rings* is taken as a book about killing.) Generally he read action/adventure, Top 40 kinds of books—he mentioned Grisham—but he said his reading was varied. "It's a pretty good smattering actually. Generally it's like, if somebody hands me a book and says, it's pretty good, I'll read it." He seldom left a book unfinished, and read in big stints rather than small dribs and drabs (back to that flow again). Flow was really one of his driving selection issues; the issue of "killing" did largely seem to be confined to the interactive texts.

Discussion

I am not making any great claim for the robustness of the particular categories I have just outlined; in fact I think they are rather rough-and-ready. What I do want to argue is that there seems to be a bigger factor than simple mood at work in the kinds of choices made by these participants. Many of them mentioned mood from time to time, but fleetingly. I actually did a search of all the transcripts for mention of the word mood, and the results were interesting. Ben did not use the word at all. Damian, Denise, and Jocelyn mentioned it only once each. Courtney and Isaac referred to the idea most often, four times each. Altogether the participants mentioned the word a total of 19 times, in a total of 90 hours of transcripts. Four of these mentions were broad-sweep in nature, talking about the need to be in the right mood to opt for one medium or another: a macro-choice of game, movie, or book. Three talked about the need to be in the right mood to "get into" a story in one medium or another; if they were in the wrong mood they might not be prepared to make the necessary effort. Only six mentions of the word "mood" involved the selection of one particular text from a range within a single medium, and all the remainder involved issues of a text setting a mood, by dint of humour or background music.

Of the six remarks about selecting the right text to meet a particular mood, four were made by Courtney, who was much the most inclined to use mood as a qualifying factor. Her comments crossed media; she talked about the importance of matching her mood with regard to books, movies, websites, and short stories. It is possible to speculate that Courtney, as one of the most committed readers of this group and probably the most literary, came closest to matching the specifications of Ross's pool of avid readers. It is also possible to wonder whether gender might be a factor. My data-set is far too small to make any judgement on these issues, but I leave them as questions.

So, while the idea of mood was present to a limited extent, it did not appear to be a determining factor in many of the decisions described. One reason is undoubtedly that all the participants shared a "research-project-participation" mood at the time of the sessions; they were simulating selection rather than making real choices, and the nuances of their own moods were a secondary consideration. At the same time, I think it is reasonable to suggest that, especially in their comments about making choices in their own time, a larger kind of "interpretant identity" could be said to be at work. I do not think it is entirely surprising that Ross's readers mentioned the dynamic elements of book selection but overlooked the larger, more static qualities of their own being that also govern choice; it is something like the case of the goldfish being unaware of the nature of water but able to talk about the specific items of changing scenery inside the bowl.

Sipe's idea of the signature response is useful here, though it might need to be adapted to include the idea of a kind of "signature selection" that takes effect before any kind of response can kick in. I tried many different ways of analysing people's criteria for saying yes or no to a particular text. In the end it was clear to me that all forms of inter-personal comparison were random and confusing in contrast to the relative clarity of the intra-personal consistency displayed by many of these participants. Issues of salience and fluency were discussed by all of them, without exception, but the larger question of "what makes something salient" was a highly personal one, and one that could be identified throughout their responses in many cases. Norman Holland speaks of "that ineffable effect of personality on perception" (1975, 4).

Gitlin describes how we build up experience of selecting and rejecting to create something that amounts to a personal style: "To manage the unmanageable, we cultivate navigational strategies, which, when they firm up and become habitual, deserve to be called styles" (2001, 119). Holland says much the same thing but ascribes a more psychological origin:

> [R]eaders respond to literature in terms of their own "lifestyle" (or "character" or "personality" or "identity"). By such terms, psychoanalytic writers mean an individual's characteristic way of dealing with the demands of outer and inner reality. Such a style will have grown through time from earliest infancy. It will also be what the individual brings with him to any new experience, including the experience of literature. Each new experience develops the style, while the pre-existing style shapes each new experience. (1975, 8)

In this project, I may have access to a certain quotient of individual style, but I am certainly not privy to how these participants deal with the demands of their own inner reality. The once-over-lightly utility of Bartle's categories of stance is suggestive of the notion that deeper issues of personal style and signature response may be relevant in these questions of selection, but it would take a very different kind of study to tease out the deep motivations at work.

It does, however, seem reasonable to suggest that the issue of mood is the second stage of selection, and that it arises from a more profound *given* of personal style and stance.

Making a Choice: What the Selected Texts Say

Selection is an under-studied element of recreational text use, but it is clear that much of what occurs at the time of choice is deeply personal, subtly nuanced, and often almost completely tacit. What makes a text capture one person's attention and repel another's is one of the mysteries of how we make a commitment to a particular fiction. As part of my attempt to probe this obscure aspect of our textual pleasure, after the interviews were complete I acquired some of the texts mentioned by participants as particularly appealing. I was interested to see whether a perusal of this material would shed new light on the process.

Almost at once, I ran into a methodological problem: with the best will in the world, I could not reproduce participants' pleasure in these titles; their tastes are significantly not my tastes and, in many cases, reading or watching or playing became pure labour. My access to the source of the appeal was radically faulty. Nevertheless, it was not a worthless exercise, although on another occasion I would acquire these texts sooner and ask participants to comment directly on what made them so attractive. At the least, some of the examples offered reinforcement of of the concept of the signature response.

Take, for example, Jocelyn and Drew. Jocelyn favoured quick absorption; she wanted to be hooked immediately and not to look up from the story. Drew preferred an elaboration of a fictional universe and the opportunity to master complex detail. Here are two examples of their preferred reading.

One Door Away from Heaven

The example for Jocelyn that I chose to look at was Dean Koontz's *One Door Away from Heaven*, which was this author's most recent mass market paperback at the time of my interviews with Jocelyn (early spring 2003). Koontz is Jocelyn's favourite author and one of a very small number indeed that she might contemplate re-reading.

Here is a typical example of Koontz's shock and horror: 9-year-old Leilani's mother (who seems inexplicably hostile to the child) keeps a snake which has surprised the girl into attacking it with a hollow steel pole snatched from her mother's closet. Leilani has poked and jabbed it into silence under the chest of drawers, and now assumes it is dead but she is too tense to let go of the pole.

> Leilani . . . was saved only because she met her mother's eyes and saw where they were focused. Not on her daughter. On the nearest end of the makeshift cudgel, just behind Leilani's two-handed grip.
> The tubular-steel rod was hollow, two inches in diameter. The snake, not dead after all, seeking refuge when the battering stopped had squirmed inside the pole. By this pipeline, it traveled unseen from beneath the chest of drawers to Leilani's exposed back, where it now slowly extruded on the floor behind her like the finished product of a snake-making machine. (2002/2001, 188)

This passage offers one of Koontz's trademark ingredients: having lulled readers into believing the battle with the snake was over, he creates a second surprise from the same ingredients. The combination of surprise and fear clearly appealed to Jocelyn and she spoke highly of materials that offer this kind of jolt. Koontz's writing, while pedestrian, offers no stylistic impediment to following the chain of events, which would also appeal to Jocelyn, who liked to move quickly into an emotional connection with her chosen texts. In short, this sample of text confirms Jocelyn's self-description and lends itself to the style of interpretation that she demonstrated whenever she could during the research sessions.

The Dark Elf Trilogy

Drew mentioned the writing of R.A. Salvatore as among his favourites. Here is an example of Salvatore's descriptive scene-setting from *The Dark Elf Trilogy*, a *Forgotten Realms* story.

> Beyond Tier Breche, through the ornate stalagmite columns that marked the entrance to the Academy, the cavern dropped away quickly and spread wide, going far beyond Dinin's line of vision to either side and farther back than his keen eyes could possibly see. The colors of Menzoberranzan were threefold to the sensitive eyes of the drow. Heat patterns from various fissures and hot springs swirled about the entire cavern. Purple and red, bright yellow and subtle blue, crossed and merged, climbed the walls and stalagmite mounds, or ran off singularly in cutting lines against the backdrop of dim gray stone. More confined than these generalized and natural gradations of color in the infrared spectrum were the regions of intense magic, like the spiders Dinin had walked between, virtually glowing with energy. Finally there were the actual lights of the city, faerie fire and highlighted sculptures on the houses. The drow were proud of the beauty of their designs, and especially ornate columns or perfectly crafted gargoyles were almost always limned in permanent magical lights. (2000/1998, 7)

This description offers much more detail than can be of any possible significance to the plot, and occurs at a very early point in the story where it might put off those readers looking to be hooked by plot or character. The kind of invitation to readers that is being offered here is made explicit from the very beginning: the detail of the setting is an important part of the nature of the story and pausing to look around at that detail is an essential component of the narrative style. The goodness of fit with Drew's expressed and demonstrated preference for elaborate world building is quite manifest. Again, the selected text reinforces the description of a reader already being compiled.

Comparing and Contrasting

I initially selected these quotations from Koontz and Salvatore simply with a view to providing typical examples of their writing. However, when we look closely at these small quotations, it is noticeable that they contain a point of comparison that leads usefully to further thought about the kinds of literacy practices involved. Each sample of text offers an observation on the importance of what is achieved in the story by a character's line of sight. In the Koontz extract, Leilani's eyes catch those of her mother, a connection that led her to observe the immediate and unexpected peril of the snake, suddenly confronting her for the second time. Her line of vision is held strictly within the story and actually forwards the plot. In the *Forgotten Realms* story, on the other hand, Dinin, despite his "keen" and "sensitive" vision, explicitly cannot see the limits of the world in which he is walking; it extends "far beyond" what he can behold. These two ways of seeing within these two stories serve as a metaphor for a distinction in reading practices that I have found helpful in contemplating the different ways in which Jocelyn and Drew chose to read.

Jocelyn liked to be completely committed to her story, oblivious to the outside world, open to overwhelming shock and surprise when her story took an unexpected turn. Drew enjoyed being absorbed in a story but he was much more likely to take account of a world broader than the explicit events of his fiction. In fact, the compositional steps that are necessary to create that fictional world appealed to his imagination sometimes more than the events that take place within that world.

It is not surprising that Jocelyn and Drew mentioned favourite materials that seem to reinforce predilections that they both described and manifested in other parts of the project. This kind of reinforcement does add a small block of evidence to the idea that factors more permanent than transitory mood play a significant role in making selections. I am not attempting to dismiss the importance of mood; obviously the question "What do I feel like reading (watching, playing) today?" plays a major role in choosing. Nevertheless, it plays out against a background of more stable tendencies.

SECTION IV
CONTOUR LINES

· 8 ·

MAPPING THE MAIN CONTOURS:
A CHANGING LANDSCAPE

The participants in this study moved between and across media in diverse ways, yet it was possible to discern some elements in common, some patterns of activity. In this penultimate chapter of the book, I attempt to sketch some of these larger patterns and explore what they may offer to how we understand contemporary literacies.

Five headings organize this section: "thick" play, immersion and engagement, big worlds, reading outside the book, and questions of ownership, mastery, and control.

"Thick" Play

In many ways, the participants were distinct in their tastes and behaviours. Yet larger patterns of response could often be discerned among the idiosyncrasies of the participants, and the variation in detail made these patterns even more fascinating.

One example of such a pattern lies in the propensity of many participants to immerse themselves in a particular textual experience in very great depth.

Examples of such behaviour are commonplace among the participants and occur in and/or across a wide range of media:

- Isaac collected music CDs. If he found a group to his taste, he set out to acquire every recording ever made by that group. He was not at all interested in downloading music online, but he used the Internet to research band histories and to locate hard-to-find materials. He also used his computer to index his collection, which amounted to 2,200 CDs at the time of our meeting.

- Jeremy also collected music, but he downloaded it from the Internet and stored it in a big cache on his computer. On a few occasions, he and his friends presented their own online radio station, selecting, introducing, and playing music from their collections in an organized way.

- Ben was a *Spider-Man* fan and was delighted when the DVD was released partway through our time working together, although he had already watched the film in the theatre. He bought the deluxe DVD version on the morning of its release, took it into college that same day, and resorted to the ruse of defragging his computer in order to clear some (illegitimate) time to watch it straight away. He intended to watch it enough times that he would effectively be able to recite the dialogue from beginning to end; he had already mastered *Batman Forever* in this way and took pride in being able to astound his friends with his extensive quotations.

- Courtney maintained an elaborate network of online correspondents, and wrote both to them and to a larger public in a variety of web formats, including chat rooms, online diaries, and web publishing. Her correspondent groups included local real-life friends, other young mothers whom she had never met in person, and a variety of writing support groups. Courtney and Drew shared a single computer and their computer time was carefully rationed between them; Courtney spent a good deal of her screen time in writing to these different audiences, and posting pictures and descriptions to record the life of her baby.

- Jeremy spent the summer before our sessions intensively playing the massively multi-player online role-playing game *Half-Life*. At the time of our meetings, he had recently decided to quit the game cold turkey because it was consuming his spare time to an overwhelming degree. In describing the appeal of the game, he spoke not only of the fictional enticements of the story but also of the social appeal of the game-playing chat that was part of the world of *Half-Life*. He had indeed met some gaming correspondents in person and spoke of them as a potential social network in his new life as a university student.

- Drew was a game master of a *Forgotten Realms* fantasy gaming group that met every Monday evening to play out the newest stages of their ongoing story. As game master, he researched possibilities, planned moves, made maps, created scenarios, and was sometimes frustrated by the quality of commitment to the game shown by his fellow gamers.

- Ben read novels in a selective kind of way, and was very committed to a series by Terry Goodkind called *The Sword of Truth*. A paperback version of *The Pillars of Creation*, the seventh volume in that series, was published during the course of my time with Ben and I thought he would be as pleased as he had been over the release of *Spider-Man*. However, he had already purchased and read the hardback edition, and was waiting impatiently for the appearance of the next title in the series, which he would probably also buy in hardback.

At one level, these are very different stories: different media, different actions, different responses. Yet it is possible to discern an overarching pattern of intense commitment, of extensive time and energy devoted to particular forms of text and particular narratives, and of the development of ease and expertise in relation to particular content. In some cases, it seems that part of the pleasure involved bringing many forms of attention to bear on a single project.

During my early reflections on this study, the outlines of this particular pattern of response began to clarify, as an image takes shape in the development tray in a darkroom. At this time, I was in the throes of considering my contribution to a panel on new directions in research in media and online literacy for the International Reading Association (Hagood et al., 2003). In the course of writing that piece, I talked about the well-tried tool of "thick" description (Geertz, 1975), and moved on to discuss the importance of "thick" analysis. Thick analysis, to me, means taking account of the huge complexity of factors at work in a situation; thus, for example, in the case under consideration, a thick analysis would make it impossible to look at reading

without taking account of all the other forms of textual interpretative experience in different media that readers bring to bear on a print text.

These terms were knocking about in my head as I began to take a preliminary look at some of the early participants in the study. I may thus have been
predisposed to see a connection that I rapidly came to describe as "thick" play.
I am not entirely satisfied with this term, especially as the word "thick" has
derogatory implications in many parts of the English-speaking world. However, in the Geertzian context of "thickness," the idea of thick play provides
a very useful starting point for looking at many of the behaviours described by
participants.

I therefore define thick play as extensive in terms of time and whole-heart-
ed in terms of imaginative and/or mental commitment. It may often entail a
growing mastery over many kinds of detail. It need not involve engagement
with fiction or narrative, as Isaac and Jeremy's musical ventures illustrate. Nor
is electronic technology an inherent ingredient; Ben's engagement with the
Sword of Truth novels is pretty low-tech, and one of the most intense examples
of thick play I can recall in my own life involved my brother, who spent an
entire winter when he was 9 or 10 exploring all the maps in our complete set
of *The Books of Knowledge*, absorbed and oblivious to the world around him.
Lego-builders are often very thick players; so are car enthusiasts; so too may
be opera aficionados and Janeites.

Thick play often involves what Mihaly Csikszentmihalyi describes as
"flow" experiences, where actions seem effortless and automatized and attention focuses on content rather than on process (1997, 29). Csikszentmihalyi's
description of flow speaks eloquently to some of the attractions of thick play:
"When goals are clear, feedback relevant, and challenges and skills are in
balance, attention becomes ordered and fully invested" (1997, 31). Such a
description can apply to many forms of activity: for example, reading, playing a computer game, playing a physical game, performing music, engaging in
extended web surfing, managing a complicated chat sequence where questions
and answers occur in real time but slightly out of sync with each other. The
absorbed attitude, the pleasure in developing mastery and acquiring new detail,
the inattention to time—these, rather than media specifications, are the elements that compose what I am calling thick play. But thick play may precede
the experience of flow, and indeed is sometimes a precursor to the development
of automaticity. Consider the early stages of playing a new digital game, for
example; the investment of commitment precedes the intense absorption of
flow play. Frustration and impatience with failure are the hallmarks of many

cases of early game play; later flow play may be seen as the reward for early and relatively thick investment.

One of the requirements for being able to develop pleasure in thick play is, of course, time. Perhaps it is ironic that the very economic uncertainty that pervaded the lives of so many of these participants allowed them the kind of "dawdling time" that we so often lose when that secure, full-time employment finally occurs. It may be no more than coincidence but neither Jocelyn nor Seth, both working full-time, manifested many spontaneous examples of thick play operating in their lives.

However, it is important to remember that not everyone necessarily wants to engage in thick play at every stage of his or her life. There may be other good reasons why Seth and Jocelyn stood out from other participants. Jocelyn was clearly impatient and visceral in her response to every form of text: she liked to be jolted, she looked for a *frisson* of genuine novelty. This is not a taste easily satisfied in thick play. Seth, in contrast, was a very open-minded and accepting consumer of texts. He would read anything, watch anything, play anything—with perhaps a concomitant reduction of commitment to any particular textual world.

It seems very likely that some adults will pursue forms of thick play through their working lives (sports fans are one large and obvious group of thick players, with their ongoing detailed attention to particular teams and standings and statistics). Others will diminish their devotion to vast textual experiences as time pressures increase, and will turn to singular examples of engagement rather than the sprawling, extensive commitment of thick play. Still others may be impervious to the attractions of thick play throughout their lives.

Virtues and Drawbacks of Thick Play

Thick play is a pleasurable road to expertise. It is a form of thick play, very often, that turns children who are merely able to decode print into children whom we recognize as real readers. Stephen Krashen (2005/1993) has assembled a wealth of evidence about the importance of free voluntary reading (FVR) as a route to reading success; such reading is a form of thick play.

> FVR means reading because you want to. For school-age children, FVR means no book report, no questions at the end of the chapter, and no looking up every vocabulary word. FVR means putting down a book you don't like and choosing another one instead. It is the kind of reading highly literate people do obsessively all the time. (1993, x)

Free voluntary reading is not a guaranteed solution to reading problems, Krashen says, but, "free readers have a chance. . . . [T]hose who do not develop the pleasure reading habit simply don't have a chance—they will have a very difficult time reading and writing at a level high enough to deal with the demands of today's world" (1993, x)

In addition to featuring in stories of reading success, the idea of thick play helps to explain the frustration of many adults with different aspects of computer use. To generalize a little bit (but not much), thick play is often the most productive route into understanding computers. Those adolescents who famously have the time and commitment to mess around with their computers—whether gaming, programming, messaging, or surfing—very often wind up becoming the users with most confidence and skill. Those adults who approach the computer with a particular and singular problem they want solved, preferably before lunchtime, often wind up frustrated and demoralized. As with reading, computer expertise very often flourishes in conditions of thick play.

It is not hard to multiply examples of cultural engagements that are fostered by thick play. Developing an understanding of jazz or opera or any other form of complex music, becoming comfortably familiar with the details of a particular historical period, assembling a knowledgeable framework for any number of hobbies, all these activities are more likely to be successful if thick play is part of the picture. It can be a very potent learning tool.

On the other hand, the shadows of obsessiveness do lurk around the borders of many forms of thick play. Jeremy's abrupt departure from the seductions of the world of *Half-Life* is a testimonial to how some kinds of thick engagement can become a sink in which the rest of normal life simply disappears. Even reading, for all its positive aura, can become obsessive, as many parents of avid readers will attest. The very potency of thick play can become a problem. Thickness may morph into inertia and the possibility of simply becoming mired in a long-standing habit of engagement sometimes offers a road to futility and frustration.

How it Works

What is it that makes thick play such a powerful force? Frank Smith suggests that "making an effort is an inefficient way to learn" (1998, vii). But this seems too sweeping a statement to explain aspects of the commitment described by some participants in this study.

Michael Smith and Jeffrey Wilhelm (2002) have made powerful use of the concept of "flow" in their account of the literate lives of 49 young American men. They do not speak of the elimination of effort, rather of effort focused in particular ways. Their paraphrasing of Csikszentmihalyi is helpful:

> The *sine qua non* of flow experiences is that people are so focused on what they are doing they lose awareness of anything outside the activity. Csikszentmihalyi (1990a) speaks of this quality in a number of ways: the merging of action and awareness, concentration on the task at hand, the loss of self-consciousness, and the transformation of time. . . .
>
> The young men in our study. . . . valued their favorite activities for the enjoyment they took from the immediate engagement in those activities, not for their instrumental value. (2002, 41)

It is perhaps the focus on "instrumental value" that Frank Smith disdains in his sweeping remark above.

Where I may part company with Frank Smith about the *efficiency* of this kind of learning experience is that such thick play does indeed take time. Thick play can be effective without necessarily being efficient as well. There may be times when the inefficiencies of "making an effort" are actually a more flexible and useful response to a particular short-term demand. However, it seems clear that the tacit gains of thick play, of flow experiences, can be significant and long-lasting.

Immersion and Engagement

Most readers, viewers, and players are familiar with two associated phenomena. One is the sensation of being completely absorbed in a fictional world. A different form of involvement includes the capacity to move in and out of that absorbed attention in order to consider wider questions about the fiction, yet without entirely leaving the "fiction zone."

An example I have used before is that of a conversation I had with my daughter after a harrowing episode of *ER*, the medical TV drama series. Main characters Carter and Lucy had been stabbed by a psychotic patient and were bleeding on the hospital floor as the credits rolled. I talked about which, if either, of them would survive; my daughter, though clearly still wrapped up in the high emotions of the episode, was able to tell me that the contract of the actor playing Lucy had not been renewed, and so it was reasonable to think of that character as doomed. While not completely inside the world of the story, at that point, she was clearly still in the broader zone of the show.

Gamers spend a great deal of time in a zone wider than that created by the internal specifics of the fictional game world. They deal with issues of strategy rather more than questions of "insider" information about actor contracts, but it is commonplace to see them step outside the story world to discuss their options for making progress, and then reinsert themselves into the internal world of the story once more.

Readers are perhaps less likely to verbalize their movement out of the fictional world into the broader zone of the story, but they have strategic questions of their own. Hugh Crago (1982) has produced a stimulating analysis of a reader's differential absorption in a story from the early stages where much is mystifying, to the engrossed middle section, to the wrap-up questions that draw the reader out of the trance once more. In his account of his own reading of *The Chance Child* by Jill Paton Walsh, he provides a temporal guide to his own changing involvement in the story.

> As I read these first pages, I'm intensely aware (the intensity will fade later) of the *physical* book that I hold in my hand. Is it simply because I'm a 'visual' person . . . that I'm so aware of the wide white margins, of the *neatness* of the narrow-seeming columns of type? And, in some way I don't articulate until now, these visual impressions are helping to form my attitude to the story, just as the dust jacket did when I first picked the book up. Indeed, the appearance of the physical page is now fusing in my mind with those associations of coolness, control, elegance, which were touched off in me by the jacket's design and colour scheme. By a process I don't fully understand, I seem to *transfer* some of these associations to the narrative. (1982, 174–175)

Janet Murray suggests that much reader energy and creativity may be involved in developing commitment to a fictional world.

> The pleasurable surrender of the mind to an imaginative world is often described, in Coleridge's phrase, as "the willing suspension of disbelief." But this is too passive a formulation even for traditional media. When we enter a fictional world, we do not merely "suspend" a critical faculty; we also exercise a creative faculty. We do not suspend disbelief so much as we actively *create belief*. Because of our desire to experience immersion, we focus our attention on the enveloping world, and we use our intelligence to reinforce rather than to question the reality of the experience. (1997, 110)

Marie-Laure Ryan reminds us that readers render the face of the text transparent by their actions.

> [T]he construction of a textual world of message is an active process through which the reader provides as much material as he derives from the text. But the inherently

interactive nature of the reading experience has been obscured by the reader's pro-
ficiency in performing the necessary world-building operations. We are so used
to reading classic narrative texts—those with a well-formed plot, a setting we can
visualize, and characters who act out of familiar logic—that we do not notice the
mental processes that enable us to convert the temporal flow of language into a global
image that exists all at once in the mind. (2001, 16–17)

A Working Vocabulary

We need language to describe that feeling of being completely absorbed in the
"global image" of the story world, and its counterpart, the feeling of shifting
between our own surroundings and those of the story. Douglas and Hargadon
(2001) have supplied a useful pair of terms. *Immersion*, according to their
account, involves being fully committed to the world inside the text; *engagement* involves moving inside and outside of the text world.

> When immersed in a text, reader's perceptions, reactions, and interactions all take
> place within the text's frame, which itself usually suggests a single schema and a few
> definite scripts for highly directed interaction. Conversely, in what we might term the
> "engaged affective experience", contradictory schemas or elements that defy conven-
> tional schemas tend to disrupt readers' immersion in the text, obliging them to assume
> an extra-textual perspective on the text, as well as on the schemas that have shaped
> it and the scripts operating within it. (2001, 156)

Immersion is the transparent experience, occurring entirely within the diegetic
world, that is, the narrated world of the fiction. Engagement involves movement in and out of that world, but in Douglas and Hargadon's sense it may
involve more than just reflection on the terms of creation of the textual world.
Their concept of conflicting schemas seems to me to be somewhat broader.
We may use the word "engagement" to involve the idea of moving in and out
of the story world, perhaps to regain awareness of the text as a physical object,
aesthetically created, but perhaps also (or instead) to regroup, to consider new
strategies for making progress, to draw on information external but relevant
to the story world (such as the state of Lucy's contract), to confer with fellow
viewers or gamers or (perhaps less often) readers.

Both terms, of course, are defined variably by different scholars. Alison
McMahan (2003, 68–69), for example, suggests that we may have immersion
in the diegetic world but that there is also such a thing as immersion at a non-
diegetic level, in terms of strategy and deep background knowledge. I believe

it is exactly this kind of non-diegetic commitment that is encompassed by Douglas and Hargadon's term "engagement," and that this form of engagement deserves closer inspection. In many cases, the participants in my study referred to forms of engagement with text in addition to their immersive experiences, but these engaged connections to expert knowledge, to strategy, to background information seemed often to be dedicated to increasing and intensifying the experience of submission to a text rather than to an informed and critical aesthetic of how the surface of the text is constructed to be an artifice. To return to Murray's phrase, readers are using "intelligence to *reinforce* rather than to question the reality of the experience" (1997, 110, emphasis added).

The issue of engagement is substantially complicated when an engaged or multi-faceted, multi-schematic reading is actually a cooperative reading, when the author *intends* readers to draw on multiple schemas and struggle with the surface of the story. For example, it is probably impossible to read the entire novel *If on a Winter's Night a Traveler* (Calvino, 1981) in a transparent, immersed way (though it is perfectly possible to be immersed in any single chapter, and such immersion also seems to me to be a cooperative reading at the level of the chapter). Being bounced back to the surface of the text by the inter-chapters is also part of the authorial reading, however, and this form of engagement is clearly part of the authorial intention.

I do not think it is much of a stretch to suggest that many games are designed to be played in an engaged rather than completely immersed fashion, and that therefore it may be reasonable in some cases to regard engagement as a route to greater submission to the game experience. In such cases, the sense of manipulating schemas is actually part of the designed, authorial experience. The implicit notion of engagement as containing a more critical and reflective component does not necessarily apply in such a scenario.

Murray's (1997) idea of engagement as reinforcement is a useful concept to apply to a world of complex and layered texts. This kind of response frequently occurs on the pages of my transcripts.

Thick Play with Immersion and Engagement

Thick play occurs in a variety of fields and the concepts of immersion and engagement are not necessarily relevant to all of them. However, in many cases of textual thick play, it seems to me that these concepts enable us to look more subtly at questions of flow, especially in terms of contemporary popular culture.

Immersion often feeds off momentum and drives the reader, viewer, or player just to *keep going,* to get to the end (while paradoxically striving to stay in the story world as long as possible, a contradiction most readers are familiar with). Engagement, however, offers ways of lingering, of revisiting, of reworking and re-enjoying the story world in different ways.

Preliminary immersion followed later by engagement is a cultural pattern that shows up in many forms and is strongly supported by many commercial enterprises. When a new *Harry Potter* book is released, for example, buyers rush to take the book home and to sink into the world of Hogwarts for as long as it takes to get to the end of the story. At that point, the re-reading, the comparison of different books in the series, the trivia games, and the souvenirs begin to take priority, and attention shifts to a more engaged form. When a new *Harry Potter* movie comes out, however, although immersion is also a strong feature as viewers watch it for the first time, the inevitable comparison with the books means that fans are rather less likely to be absorbed into the workings of a single schema. In a sense, watching a film adaptation of a well-loved book is always already an engaged experience. It is for many people one of their earliest experiences of an engaged connection with a text.

How do the concepts of immersion and engagement mesh with Barthes's dichotomy between the readerly and the writerly text? According to Barthes, a writerly text calls for more than mere reception, calls for the reader to be "no longer a consumer, but a producer of the text" (1974/1970, 4). Douglas and Hargadon's distinction between the immersed and the engaged interpreter deals with some of the same territory, but they place the emphasis on the stance of the interpreter rather than on the text. The *Harry Potter* example shows that an engaged stance towards a readerly text (one designed for relatively passive reception) is not only feasible but also more and more commonplace as stories expand multimodally. The role of immersion in writerly texts is a more complex question but one worth considering as our textual worlds expand and become more sophisticated.

Signature Responses Again

Some participants in this study provided clear evidence of a preference for immersion or for engagement. Let us return briefly to Jocelyn and Drew, whose reading tastes were contrasted in the previous chapter. Jocelyn clearly preferred immersion on almost every occasion. Her pleasure in the writings of Dean Koontz reflected this preference; Koontz's work makes every effort to keep readers entranced inside the story world. Drew, on the other hand, found ways to develop an engaged response to many of the texts that came his way. Even when there was a single schema at work inside the story, he layered soundtracks, maps, and other outside information.

If Margaret Meek (1988) is right and texts teach what readers learn, we may see here these two readers not simply responding in the first instance to the text in hand (readerly or writerly as it may be) but also drawing on repertoires developed from previous encounters with enjoyable texts—and on accumulated experiences with "text bundles" such as the *Harry Potter* set above. For a reader with a taste for engagement, it is clear that a writerly repertoire can be developed from an interlocked set of readerly texts. It might be argued that a preference for singular immersion is sometimes more difficult to sustain in contemporary culture. (Jocelyn's vigorous rejection of potentially boring texts may be a defensive tactic against too much engagement and a striving for purely immersive experiences.)

Big Worlds

A number of the participants in this project expressed a preference for some kind of enlarged fictional universe that expanded beyond the limits of a single title. Especially after the pilot work with Damian and Denise was over, I made a point of asking for examples of favourite titles, and participants also made incidental reference to stories that gripped them in one way or another. A surprising number of the titles that came up in these ways involved the phenomenon that I have labelled the "big world."

A big world may be constructed in many different ways. Once again, *The Lord of the Rings*, which dominated popular culture during the time of my sessions with these participants, may serve as a paradigmatic example. J.R.R. Tolkien deliberately created a fictional universe that is much larger than the limits of any single title. At the most basic level, the three books of the trilogy relate to each other, and knowledge of *The Hobbit* expands a reader's understanding still further. Tolkien, of course, was famous for his in-filling exploits: he invented complex languages for his different races to speak; he wrote back stories, histories, and legends about Middle Earth in *The Silmarillion*; he provided a complex geography complete with maps.

So far the creation of this big world was fuelled by Tolkien's perhaps eccentric imagination and passion for complete detail. However, what makes this example so useful for the purposes of this discussion is what happened subsequently. Fans took the basic ideas of *The Fellowship of the Ring* and developed elaborate *Dungeons and Dragons* role-playing games, first played in person and then later also converted to digital formats (King & Borland, 2003). Drew's commitment to the *Forgotten Realms* fantasy game represents a late flowering of this particular line of descent.

Readers of *The Silmarillion* might assume that it would be impossible to render Tolkien's fictional world any bigger, but when other media became involved, the expansions became exponential. Ralph Bakshi's animated version of *The Lord of the Rings* (1978) was, by common consent, not very successful, but Peter Jackson's ambitious filming of the three books in the late 1990s and early 2000s added many layers to the Tolkien world. At one level, the films, like almost any film of almost any novel, were smaller and shorter than the books; on the other hand, the meticulous visual detail of the settings, the costumes, the weapons, and the atmosphere created a palpably large universe.

The theatrical showings of the movie were just one part of the expansion of this world, however; the phenomenon clearly moved onto yet another plane with the release of the deluxe DVD versions of the films. With many hours of incredibly detailed background information about every element of the movie-making process, these DVDs, like many others of their ilk, made the craft of the fictional production part of viewers' wider understanding of the fictional universe. This sense of knowing what alternatives might have been part of the story is a different aspect of the "big world" from knowing the insider details of the fictional universe itself, but one that is very real and very significant for many contemporary interpreters of media. Not only DVD contributes to this broader understanding of how a fictional world is put together; television, specialist magazines of all kinds, and the Internet also feature vast amounts of background information (see Mackey 2001, 1999). Viewers can become experts on two levels instead of one, on the processes of creation and development as well as the content of the story.

The big-world attributes of the DVD are beginning to cross media boundaries. It is very interesting to see DVD "extras" having an impact on print publishing as well; in November 2003 the online notices from *The Bookseller* included the information that HarperCollins' paperback imprint Harper Perennial had decided

> to introduce additional content into its titles. A final section, called P.S., will carry about 15 pages of author CVs and interviews, critical opinion, newly commissioned

articles, notes on cover choices and recommendations for further reading. . . . HC said it had been inspired by the film industry which adds value to releases in DVD format with fresh content such as documentaries, trailers, and unseen footage.

(http://www.thebookseller.com/?pic=4&did=9639, accessed November 14, 2003)

Drew's comments on *The Lord of the Rings* draw attention to other aspects of the "big world" phenomenon. Drew had not actually read the books (he tried but found them "too wordy"), but, at the time of our sessions, he had seen *The Two Towers* once in the movie theatre, and had watched *The Fellowship of the Ring* "fifteen to twenty" times on DVD. Expanding the perimeters of the big world still further, he also listened obsessively to the soundtracks of *The Fellowship of the Ring* and *The Two Towers* and commented that, as a matter of routine for a fiction in which he was this interested, he had read every word of the liner notes that accompany the CDs. In our conversation he referred to the role of the Norwegian fiddle as an example of information that appealed to him. I tracked this reference to the liner notes for *The Two Towers*, which provide an example of the kind of detail that animates some big worlds:

> Howard has made use of a range of culturally specific instruments to evoke the many different worlds of Middle-earth. Dermot Crehan plays the signature sound of Rohan on the Norwegian fiddle called a hardinger. More familiar to you will be the North African reed instrument the Rhalta, played by Jan Hendrickse which forms part of the Mordor theme. Mixed in with all of this you can hear the sound of the ciambalon, which plays directly to Gollum, the dilruba, log drums, wood xylophones, to name but a few of the extraordinary sounds which feature in the score. (Broucek, 2002, liner notes)

Both Drew and Tolkien himself could perhaps be described as having an extreme case of "big world" syndrome. Drew mentioned more "big world" texts than anyone else, and clearly has a taste for elaboration and extension. To supplement his description of the *Forgotten Realms* world, for example, he emailed me a map of Faerun, "the proper name for the continent on which the setting of the Forgotten Realms takes place."

But Drew, though perhaps an extreme case, was far from being an exception in this little set of participants. In their discussions of their own personal tastes, Jeremy, Ben, Isaac, Seth, and Courtney also mentioned big world texts.

- Jeremy had just withdrawn from one of the biggest fictional worlds currently available: the massively multi-player online role-playing game *Half-Life*. He also spoke of picking up a book by Terry Brooks and going on to read the whole series.

- Ben's pursuit of Terry Goodkind's print series *The Sword of Truth* was a big-world commitment. In his keen attachment to *Spider-Man*, he also demonstrated the power of insider information to increase the sense of inhabiting a world bigger than the singular story.
- Isaac read only the novels of Piers Anthony and it was clear from talking to him that the attractions of the big world were a serious element in the appeal of these stories. Of all the materials he looked at, it was the novel (*The Light Fantastic*) and the graphic novel (*Mort*) from Terry Pratchett's very elaborate Discworld universe that he spoke of exploring further in his own time; the intricacies of that large universe clearly appealed to him, as did Pratchett's mordant humour.
- Seth was a big fan of *The Sopranos* and read a variety of background material, both online and on paper.
- Courtney was a broader reader than some of the other participants, but again her favourite novels encompassed a universe comprising many worlds and three titles: the series *His Dark Materials* by Philip Pullman.

The Phenomenon of the Big World

The big world is not new, nor is it confined to print or to fantasy, despite the dominance of print fantasies in the list above. For more than a century, Sherlock Holmes has inhabited a big world, both in terms of expanding beyond a single set of covers and in terms of being reworked in a variety of different media.

Today, an interesting big world belongs to Seth's favourite TV program, *The Sopranos*, whose complex personal and social history has layered and palimpsested over several seasons of television programs. The story of this family has also moved outside the limits of the Home Box Office channel to a plethora of websites and to a print back story told in a stunning variety of textual formats. *The Sopranos: A Family History* (Rucker, 2003) is a coffee-table book, complete with police records, email correspondence, chatroom conversations, school projects, family trees, cashflow diagrams, photographs, credit card bills, and many other documents. It also expands with the expansion of the world of *The Sopranos*; new editions have been released with several new seasons of the show. The Soprano family's location in the very real geography of New Jersey has added another scale of engagement (see Strate, 2002 for a very interesting discussion of the phenomenon of the overlap of fictional and actual geography). Big worlds that have a fictional life and a real geographical referent, even at the second level (for example, the New Zealand settings of the films of *The Lord of the Rings*, now a tourist attraction) offer their own distinctive and enlarging appeal.

As digital equipment shrinks to domestic scale, and digital expertise expands, young people have more opportunities to create mediated big worlds of their own. In a very different cultural zone from *The Lord of the Rings* or *The Sopranos*, Barbie recognizably occupies a big world with dolls and clothes and accessories, books, movies, CD-ROMs, websites, and a sweep of dashing lifestyles. You can purchase a Barbie video camera (pink, of course) for children to record their own activities and create their own stories. Lego has taken the toy universe one step further, and offers a film camera plus a digital editing suite for young Lego-masters to make their own digital videos of their creations, which can be mounted on the Internet. (Barbie and Lego also provide a springboard for mentioning, just in passing, the paradoxical appeal of the miniature big world, which can be very captivating indeed.)

Lego also offers a glimpse of ways in which big worlds can become nested in contemporary culture. You can buy Lego sets of *Harry Potter* to build and then play your own version of this big world. In addition, you can now also buy a computer game of *Lego Harry Potter*, which involves the following layers:

- a digitized version
- of a Lego version
- of the film version
- of the novel version
- of a fictional world.

Spelled out in this way, it is quite breathtaking in its complex layering; on the screen, all these layers may be taken completely for granted by a child interpreter of this game, though they may well also be learning more about parody than the Lego manufacturers anticipated.

Big worlds abound in popular culture today for a variety of cultural, commercial, and technological reasons. A fictional universe that can be reiterated in a variety of formats means marketing opportunities; at the same time the Internet all by itself plays a major role as a kind of "world enlarger," supplying a plethora of background information, commentary, correspondence, and fan fiction. Beyond such material enablers, however, there would also seem to be a contemporary cultural taste for big worlds. An exploration of the political, social, and psychological appeal of this phenomenon would be intriguing but is beyond the scope of this particular project.

The Pleasures of a Big World

A fictional universe can be expanded through a variety of dimensions. It can be a *geographic* space, larger than whichever corners of it may feature in a single story but well mapped and charted and understood by readers and players. For example, Terry Pratchett's Discworld setting is huge. Particular books are located in one city or one area of the countryside, and extensive information about Pratchett's complete world is available in print and online—or it may simply be mentally assembled by alert readers. For such readers, the background geography is a component of their understanding of any particular book in the series.

Expansion may also be *chronological*, layering up the history of the world itself or of the protagonists of the story. One frequent feature of a big world scenario involves the infilling of past details, reshaping the perception of a world through the addition of extra historical information. This activity has acquired its own entry in *The Jargon Dictionary*; "retcon" is the shorthand label for *retroactive continuity*, which is defined thus:

> [T]he common situation in pulp fiction (esp. comics or soap operas) where a new story "reveals" things about events in previous stories, usually leaving the "facts" the same (thus preserving continuity) while completely changing their interpretation. For example, revealing that a whole season of "Dallas" was a dream was a retcon.
> (http://info.astrian.net/jargon/terms/r/retcon.html, accessed November 17, 2003)

The Jargon Dictionary's definition describes a formal reworking, and prequels may provide another form of retconning at work. Retroactive continuity can also be a more informal kind of activity when readers, viewers, or gamers encounter elements of a big world story out of sequence and have to recast their understanding and appreciation of the overall story in light of previously unknown prior data. The intellectual and affective charm of this kind of narrative work on the part of an interpreter can easily be underestimated; many readers and viewers seem to find it a very beguiling procedure. The recasting of current understanding in the light of new information may just be done mentally, but some readers will return to the entire series for re-reading/viewing/playing in canonical order.

A third dimension of expanding a fictional world can involve increasing understanding of the *craft* that created it. DVDs have particularly fostered this approach, but television, magazines, and the Internet also provide significant background information. This form of world-enhancement uses aspects of engagement to enlarge on the original immersion. But as Drew pointed out, this particular route to expansion is not without risks. Talking about the background information for *The Fellowship of the Ring*, he offered this warning:

> I don't know, it makes it a more complete experience but at the same time there's sacrifices for that. For instance, if you haven't seen the documentary on the extra 6-hour, 6 ½-hour documentary, on the making of *The Fellowship of the Ring*, don't watch the one on—they show you how they make hobbits so small and then when you watch it through the next time, you pick it up. . . . It can interfere, and in that case, it does, which is disappointing.

Asked whether this interference was permanent, he used some interesting vocabulary in his reply:

> Mmmm—it might be permanent. It has gotten to the point now, it's been a while since I've watched that segment and now it is more . . . distant than when I watched it, so it's getting better. As to the degree of the healing, how much it will get better, I don't know.

Drew here points out the risk of destroying the fiction by too much big-world exploration of the crafting of that fiction—but at the same time, he provides a terrific example of the lust for world-expansion that grips some people. When I asked him whether it was worth the risk, he had the grace to point to his own predilection for totality:

> Margaret: Was it worth the risk, or are you sorry you did it?
>
> Drew: I guess I am sorry I did it, but on the other hand, it's worth the risk, so you know, had I known beforehand I could have watched everything else except for that one. Just skip that one over.
>
> Margaret: Yes, that's hard to know. Would you have the strength of character to resist if somebody told you?
>
> Drew: No, because I wouldn't trust their judgement. That is what it boils down to.

Fan fiction is a fourth route to enlarging a universe. Take already-established characters and setting and create your own adventures for them. The Internet again plays a major role, this time providing an outlet for publication; and fans can read each other's enlargements as well as enjoying their own.

Crossovers, where a character or idea from one fictional world makes an appearance in another, provide another, surprisingly common form of world-expansion. Jess Nevins (n.d.), in an online essay, suggests that an ancient precedent for crossovers came when Jason recruited the Argonauts from a variety of other stories (http://ratmmjess.tripod.com/crossovers.html, accessed January 14, 2005). Malory in the 15th century, and Balzac and Verne in the 19th, provide more recent examples. Series books for children throughout the 20th century often made use of crossover characters. Combining Nancy Drew with the Hardy Boys is an idea that has manifested itself in different formats, ranging in style from an anodyne television series to pornographic fan fiction. In North America, the sweeps months of November, February, and May are when viewing figures are aggregated for the purposes of making decisions about programming and advertising; producers will sometimes attempt to augment audiences by means of crossover shows where the hero of one series appears in a different program. And comic books, of course, are famous for their crossover extravaganzas. Part gimmick, part creative challenge, the crossover expands one fiction through the associations of a second, in a wide variety of media.

Big Worlds and the Extension of Reading Experience

Big worlds are often encountered on the plane of engagement, where readers (or viewers or players) take time out from the experience of being inside the story to move outside, or to dodge back and forth across the narrative boundary (see Mackey 2003 for further discussion of this topic).

Readers who stop to draw maps, make family trees, look up background details, or write further adventures of the same characters are expanding the narrative world both outside its fictional borders and also, in many cases, outside its traditional linear prose. Users of the Barbie and Lego cameras develop and expand fictional universes using different media, but the general idea is often the same, as child film-makers create new stories for Barbie or the Lego people.

Clearly there is pleasure both in the entirely imagined universe (such as the Discworld) and in the fictional world that overlaps with real-life geography (such as the New Jersey landscape inhabited by the Soprano family). It does indeed seem as if the ontology of such pleasure can be complicated to further degrees; New Zealand is building a substantial tourist industry around the settings for the Jackson films of *The Lord of the Rings*, and Great Britain has established *Harry Potter* tours that take in many different locations that were edited together to make a single setting for the movies. These hybrid sites, mixing fiction and real-life geography, suggest that our pleasure in big worlds can be extremely robust.

One possible appeal of the big world story lies in its potential for the development of distributed narrative. Assembling the primary story from multiple sources is an exercise that offers numerous intellectual and emotional satisfactions.

Reading Outside the Book

Adults, especially teachers, parents, and librarians, often associate the idea of reading very tightly with the idea of books. Magazines and newspapers sometimes get a look-in, but are often considered inferior. In fact, reading, even more than ever before, occurs in many guises and formats. I will explore three different cases where reading involves media other than print on paper: reading that occurs as one element of a multimedia collection of activities, reading that draws on narrative experience in a variety of media to assist in comprehending an unfamiliar story, and reading that is located completely online.

Reading as a Single Element Among Many Media Activities

Seth read novels all the time—but his reading was also associated with movies, games, television shows, and the Internet. Here is a partial list of some items Seth mentioned in relation to reading:

- He bought picture books and how-to books about movies.
- He owned an art book of the making of *Star Wars*.
- He also owned a screenplay of *Star Wars* but it was more "something to have" than something to read for its own sake.
- He would buy a "philosophy of" book if he liked the movie well enough. "Part of the fantasy is to escape that reality to become what you . . . what you are in tune with. Like what you're infatuated with," he said.
- He started watching the film *Memento* (which tells the story backwards in time) on a digital cable receiver. "I went 'What's that about?' so

you hit 'Info' and it gives you a brief description and that sounds a bit cool." What he read on the "Info" button enabled him to follow the backward narrative intelligently.

- He had done considerable background reading as a fan of *The Sopranos*. "I've gone to HBO on the Web and everything and I've looked up, like, the family tree, the FBI files and all that kind of stuff. It's really neat." He had read a couple of *MAD Magazine* spoofs of the program. He owned an entertainment magazine with the series recaps, published before the start of the fourth season, but found he remembered enough that he did not really need it. Given the chance, he also read sneak previews of episodes online.
- When logging on to the Internet, he always went straight to Yahoo. He checked his Hotmail and played Yahoo games.
- He looked at car audio websites sometimes but was more inclined to read magazines on that topic. Online he looked at all brands of electronics.
- He used the web to check movie listings and watch previews and trailers.
- He played Psychobabble, a game of phrases and sentences, online.

There are other examples, but this list gives some sense of how reading is part of a larger media experience in Seth's life.

Drew's encounters with *The Lord of the Rings*, already mentioned, also featured reading as one ingredient in a multimedia fictional experience. Drew had not read Tolkien's books (finding them "too wordy" for his taste), but he had seen the movies and read background information for the movies, including the liner notes for the soundtracks. Interestingly, he had read some of Tolkien's appendices to *The Lord of the Rings* and also a history of Middle Earth. He read many books, such as novels by R.A. Salvatore, that fed into his fantasy games, which themselves reflected many aspects of *The Lord of the Rings*. He read background material for these games, and created maps and charts. His experience of Tolkien and Tolkien-related fictions was multi-faceted and intense; reading was but one component of this engagement.

As it happens, neither of these men rejected reading a free-standing novel; Seth in particular was an inveterate book reader. Yet much of their narrative experience involved reading as only one small ingredient in a broad encounter with many facets of a particular fiction. Such reading was sometimes co-ordinate with other experience of a fiction; sometimes (as, for example, with Seth's checking of sneak previews of *The Sopranos*) it was subordinate to that main experience.

In some picture books, the primary role of the words is to draw attention to particular aspects of the pictures. Some of Seth's reading fell into this role: his "Info" check certainly told him how to watch *Memento*.

For many vigilant adults who worry that the young people in their charge are "not" reading, such co-ordinate and subordinate reading is often invisible. The prestige of the stand-alone novel may blind such adults to the fact that this other kind of supplementary reading may serve as a single prong in a larger encounter with a complex fiction. There is a good deal of muddled thinking, in fact, about what it is that we actually value about reading. We want our young people to develop clarity of thought, sensitive qualities of empathy, well-stocked imaginations—but it may be a category error to assume that these virtues are hot-wired to print reading alone. Reading in conjunction with other media will sometimes enrich those media, sometimes focus the experience of those media, and vice versa. To ignore such reading is to misunderstand one element of contemporary culture.

Repertoires of Narrative Assumptions

Readers use their assumptions about narrative to help them read, and this is true whether their assumptions are borne out or confronted by a particular story. Contemporary readers build up a repertoire of narrative assumptions from exposure to a wide variety of media. Seth provided a paradigmatic example of a repertoire gleaned from film and television and then applied to a print narrative. Reading *The Three Pigs* by David Wiesner (2001), a post-modern spoof of the traditional story, he drew on references to horror movies (*Nightmare on Elm Street*), sinister television programs (*The X-Files*), and a contemporary story of violence and solidarity (*Boys from the 'Hood*) to interpret the strange goings-on in this children's story.

Much contemporary writing, of course, consciously acknowledges and makes use of the fact that readers have multimodal repertoires—not simply in terms of content but also in terms of style and composition.

Online Writing and Reading

Other kinds of reading often pass under the radar of concern about print literacy. Courtney was an avid novel reader, but a huge amount of her daily reading and writing occurred outside the covers of her books. Producing and reading online diaries and blogs and chat was a significant feature of her life. She was not alone though there is considerable debate over the current scale of the blogosphere. The *Blog Herald* in November 2006 estimated a world total of 34.5 million blogs in existence (http://www.blogherald.com/2005/01/10/blog-numbers-are-closer-to-345-million-wordwide/, accessed November 8, 2006), but *Wired Magazine* offered a cautionary note on the scale of such figures:

> More than 10 million of the 12.9 million profiles on Blogger surveyed by splog [spam blog] researcher Vasa in June were inactive, either because the bloggers had stopped blogging or because they never got started. (The huge mass of dead blogs is one reason to maintain a healthy skepticism toward the frequently heard claims about the vast growth of the blogosphere.) (Mann, 2006, 112)

However blogs are counted, Courtney, at the age of 26, clearly has many peers. On the other hand, Mann's scepticism about the scale of the blogosphere is perhaps reflected in a minor way by the fact that I had to make a special effort to recruit Courtney, that the volunteer participants in my study were not all that interested in online writing. The experimenters are making headlines and featuring in research studies, and this is as it should be; it is important, nevertheless, to keep in mind that there is a large group of the adult population moving more slowly and idiosyncratically towards the productive end of the communications spectrum.

That Courtney kept a diary was utterly unremarkable, given her enthusiasm about writing. But an online diary is a public as well as a private document, and people responded to her entries. Courtney commented,

> Umh, it's interesting, when I first started to have writing and then to have all the responses. When it was the full diary, say, and then at the bottom after typing you get different people who can leave things in your diary and then you can click on them if they had a diary and it would take you their diary. And—then you can see whether people would follow you through the nuances of your life or whatever.

Courtney also read and occasionally wrote to an online site for mothers whose children were born in June 2002. These mothers were spread throughout the world, she said.

Margaret: Do you think of them as your friends or do you think of them as your Internet friends or do you think of them as supportive nebulous acquaintance—how do you think of them—as colleagues?

Courtney: Before my wedding I had a lot of time—I spent a lot of time on this site and—getting to know them every day, like, I would check in every day

and see what they were doing and how they were doing and what their
babies were like and how their babies were growing and they got to be
more than just a nebulous glob of people.

Margaret: Right.

Courtney: That I just kind of knew about. I could have probably told you, you
know, that this person has three sons, what their names were and all
that and how they were doing at any given point.

A rich thread of her literate life was thus paper-free and interactive—and
invisible to those whose idea of literacy automatically includes the concept of
paper. Courtney's concept of literacy would seem rather to include the idea of
interlocutors as part of the literate experience, with a consequent shift in her
sense of personal privacy. As Emily Nussbaum has observed, "For many in the
generation that have grown up online, the solution is not to fight this technological loss of privacy, but to give in and embrace it: to stop worrying and learn
to love the Web. It's a generational shift that has multiple roots" (2004, n.p.)

Courtney's online literacy was independent of her encounters with other
media, rather than supplementary as in the examples provided by Seth and
Drew. Its reference points were her own life and opinions. The interactivity
enabled by the Internet publication added a feature that she clearly valued
very highly.

Since all three of these participants happen to be relatively keen book
readers (Drew rather more spasmodically than the other two), it is clear that
such examples of reading certainly do not preclude the particularities of book
literacy. But there are undoubtedly young people for whom such subordinate
or exclusively online reading is the major reading that they do. If the adults
who sit in judgement on their literate lives fail to notice such activity, they
may well consider these young people to be non-readers, an unfortunate and
unfair over-simplification. Indeed, the young people themselves may imbibe
this attitude and think of themselves as not being readers. But reading today is
multi-headed and can occur in the context of many different frameworks.

One Conceptual Plane

Lev Manovich, discussing how new and old media draw on each other, suggests
that print, film, and human-computer interfaces are manifested, as it were, on
the same playing field:

Today, as media is [sic] being "liberated" from traditional physical storage media—
paper, film, stone, glass, magnetic tape—elements of the printed word interface and

the cinema interface that previously were hardwired to content become "liberated" as well. A digital designer can freely mix pages and virtual cameras, tables of content and screens, bookmarks and points of view. No longer embedded within particular texts and films, these organizational strategies are now free floating in our culture, available for use in new contexts. In this respect, the printed word and cinema have indeed become interfaces—rich sets of metaphors, ways of navigating through content, ways of accessing and storing data. For a computer user, both conceptually and psychologically, their elements exist on the same plane as radio buttons, pull-down menus, command line calls, and other elements of the standard human-computer interface. (2002/2001, 73)

Manovich speaks of media as being "liberated"; readers, intent on engaging with a story in dynamic ways, also seem to be less bound to a particular medium or interface as they composite meaning and satisfaction from many sources. A focus on the plane of the *story* effectively draws different forms of interface into alignment as a way of generating and reinforcing a fictional encounter. The fictional connection is the engine, and the commitment and attention of the interpreter may well be relatively indifferent to media boundaries.

Ownership, Mastery, and Control

One other issue arose in different forms across various media, and that was the question of ownership. It was Ben who first drew my attention to this issue. Ben was enrolled in a year-long computer course, so when we talked about the different advantages of having information in print and in online form, I carelessly assumed that he would favour the digital format. I was wrong. When asked whether he preferred a screen or a paper version of different texts, he often spoke of the portability of the book, pointing out that even a heavy book weighs less than a laptop. He was, however, enthusiastic about the electronic book and said if they made a lighter version he could see himself preferring such e-reading to dealing with print on paper. So it was not an aversion to screen reading that prompted his comments about a hypothetical *Spider-Man* encyclopaedia.

Ben was a big *Spider-Man* fan and had just finished telling me how he and his friends had finessed some free time at college to watch the newly issued DVD version. Later in the same session, we looked at a print encyclopaedia that billed itself as *The Interactive Book*. With icons in the margins to denote "links," this book attempts to combine the virtues of print with the value-added features of hypertext. Ben and I discussed the qualities of this book, and then I asked him whether he thought this book would provide a useful format for a *Spider-Man* encyclopaedia or whether a website would work better. Ben thought either format would work well, but said if he were obliged to choose between them he would pick the book—"just so I could have it." We talked about whether a CD-ROM or DVD text would work as well, and again he said he would take either in preference to a website. "Because it would be mine. I don't know, there—you can never go and say that you own a website or anything. That way it would be yours still. Something personal."

It is interesting but perhaps not surprising that in a society that conveys conflicting values about the priority of consuming and the virtues of the new and/or ephemeral, Ben came down on the side of owning what he especially valued in his constantly fleeting cultural world. Also not surprising, in light of this predilection, is the fact that Ben was one of the participants who spoke most frequently about the need to make money.

Our discussion about owning the *Spider-Man* book was one of those moments when actually talking to readers comes into its own. Asked about Ben, I would have been happy to assume that, as a net-savvy 21-year-old multiple-platform gamer, planning to earn his living by working with computers, he would be comfortable with a post-modern take on the cultural universe that surrounds him, happy to live with the short-term and the changeable. Instead, it would seem to be the consumer element of our culture that most clearly spoke to Ben, even on questions involving textual relationships. Ownership involved a different kind of connection for him, one in which permanence was an important feature.

Ben liked to "own" in other ways too. When the video of *Batman Forever* first appeared,

> I watched that *every* day for about two months. I could recite the entire movie. My friends would actually quiz me on this, they'd be like, okay, you know the scene where, yeah, okay, he says and I'll be like, yeah, and Batman says this and Two Face says this and Riddler says this, and they would just be in *awe*.

In fact, Ben gave priority to this form of mastery of the script over owning a print copy in a more conventional way. Asked whether he would buy a screenplay of the movie, he said, laughing, "Mmm, no, because I knew it already. I would be, like, heh no, these guys are wrong here, and that would be about it."

Ben's mastery of the entire script of *Batman Forever* corresponded with Drew's intense engagement with the soundtrack of *The Lord of the Rings* (and also with other soundtracks of favoured movies). I would be inclined also to make a comparison with Courtney's regular mounting of baby Joanna's pictures on the web; by publishing the record of the baby's life so assiduously, she "owned" it in a way that differs from the inevitably fleeting quality of daily experience with the child.

Isaac was another participant who, in many ways, shared Ben's take on the priority of ownership. As he looked at the *Sopranos* website, I asked Isaac whether he would prefer such information in book or online form. Isaac immediately questioned the terms of his commitment to the information: "To use or have?" he asked.

> If I was a big *Sopranos* fan and I wanted mmm . . . memorabilia, I would get the book even though I could print the exact same information off a website. If all I want to do is know the stuff then I would go with the website because I could just pick sections and just print that rather than having to print, you know, a hundred pages' worth. If all I wanted to do is find out some info, then I would just go to the website.

Isaac described himself as a "book hanger-onto." He was also a collector of CDs. Asked about downloading music, he sighed and said, "I'm a purchaser." Since he wanted to own every single recording ever made by a group he liked, this commitment to purchasing was a serious investment. Like Ben, Isaac said, "I would rather have it." He expanded this statement thus:

> I would rather have the whole album to get a better definition of the artist, um, because one song, especially if it is the one that the record company decides that it is going to be the single release to radio play doesn't necessarily define them and, ah, they could have some, the other nine songs could be more powerful or more appealing to me musically, but I'll never know because all you can get is best of, released twenty years later or something, or some of their newer stuff.

He cited the example of a group not available in North America any more. "They're apparently huge now in Japan, so all I can do is get them as a Japanese import for fifty, sixty bucks per CD. I'll pay that for them."

Isaac was without secure employment when I talked to him, and budget constraints caused him to watch movies on television, with the associated reduction in selectivity, rather than buying or renting them. But his passion for music extended to ownership. He was nervous about eBay because he could not be sure of the condition of his acquisitions and he liked them to be in mint condition. Just as Ben absorbed all the dialogue of his favourite movies, Isaac's ownership involved saturation; he played and replayed a new acquisition until he did not want to hear it any more. "But I won't part with any of them. . . . No, I won't part with it. I bought it. I could again one day want to listen to it."

At the time of our discussion, as we have seen, Isaac owned 2,200 CDs, all indexed on his computer. He also used the computer to research his bands, to track down every single recording they ever made. He judged the utility of a music website in part by the quality of its discography. His quest had musical, historical, and intellectual components, but the drive for complete ownership was clearly a major source of energy.

A Broader Picture

Vivian Howard and Shan Jin (2004), in a small-scale survey of Nova Scotia teenaged readers, discovered a similar preference for purchase. The young people who responded to their questionnaire expressed a particular preference for shopping in the big chain bookstores. Unlike Isaac, they did not do much online shopping, but this may be a factor of less disposable income or of less access to the Internet, particularly in rural areas, or simply as a result of not owning a credit card.

Broader statistics for Canadian borrowing and purchasing habits are suggestive. A 2005 survey of a random sample of nearly 2,000 Canadians found that 87% of them read and 54% read virtually every day (Createc+, 2005, 4): 40% of them reported borrowing a library book in the previous 12 months (Createc+, 2005, 14), but 81% said that they bought one or more books (new or used) during that time (Createc+, 2005, 15). Readers clearly have many sources of reading material, as "It is estimated that seven books out of ten that are read are not purchased" (Createc+, 2005, 15); on the other hand, more than one-third of the small fraction of Canadian non-readers actually also buy books (Createc+, 2005, 15). The report is extensive and raises very interesting questions about the appeal of ownership.

Once we get into the territory of owning your own reading material, we are in a complex and ill-understood space. Lynne McKechnie's (2004) fascinating account of the private book collections of 52 Canadian children aged from 4 to 12 is a reminder of how miscellaneous and serendipitous such ownership may be. Her list of sources is an engaging hotch-potch: children acquired books and non-book materials as gifts, from school and mail-order book clubs, from school book fairs, as new and used book purchases, as hand-me-downs, on loan from other readers, from school and public libraries, and as cereal box enclosures and prizes—and when these sources were not sufficient they sometimes made their own (McKechnie, 2004, 82). A list of the sources of an adult's private collection of reading materials would differ slightly (though it might well, of course, include some still cherished childhood relics from the very sources listed above), but it would undoubtedly bear some family resemblances in terms of variety and happenstance.

Why It Matters, and to Whom

Thick play, immersion and engagement, big worlds, reading outside the book, ownership, mastery, and control—what makes these ideas of more than local interest? I believe both librarians and teachers can find food for thought in this list. These themes arose from an exploration of text use with adults who are largely answerable only to themselves for their choices and behaviours. If such themes are important to them in this context, what are the implications for institutions of literacy? I will attempt some selective answers to this question.

In Libraries

For libraries, this list raises some significant issues. Libraries are good at offering access to materials, but if thick play is a component of learning how to make best use of materials, what can libraries do? Their record with reading is very good: libraries offer not only large quantities of material but also plenty of spaces for thick play, which in the case of reading involves access to quiet reading spaces. Libraries also lend DVDs but are less likely to provide access points for extended viewing. In many cases, they do not even lend games and it is a rare library indeed that provides extended access to playing space. If you do not have private access to a game-playing machine, your options for thick play are very poor.

Big worlds also posit some challenges for libraries. Here the record is patchy even with print. One common version of a big world story is a series of books. One common library practice is not to catalogue paperback books. If a paperback series (and many science fiction series in particular are never published in hardback) is distributed around the branches of a large library system, tracking all its titles can be surprisingly frustrating.

Libraries also have decisions to make about how many manifestations of a particular big world story they are prepared to buy and catalogue. What is repetition and what is an appealing reworking of a story? The financial implications are costly and the best decisions are based on thoughtful policy; there is much work to be done in this area.

Questions of ownership might seem to be irrelevant to libraries, but they are interested in attracting young users and it may well be that they should be marketing their potential as a sampling arena for the improvement of potential purchasing decisions. They need to address questions about what kinds of reading materials (inside and outside the book, so to speak) they want to make room for.

In Schools

For schools, the issues are slightly different. The idea of thick play is potent as a learning tool and teachers might consider whether their crowded schedules could be squeezed a bit harder to make room for one or two genuine sessions of thick play in a year.

The question of immersion is an important one for teachers of English in particular. By and large, immersed reading loses out in school. There is plenty of engaged reading, with much dipping in and out for exegesis and questioning, but too many classrooms make no room at all for the trance of immersed reading or confine it to limited instalments of a book read aloud by the teacher when all the other jobs are done. For those who experience this readerly commitment elsewhere, it may not matter very much—but there is an argument that the reading gains from thick play and immersion are too important to be overlooked by teachers. Children who read only in class settings may think that engaged reading is what it is all about and may miss entirely the other world of immersion.

Approaches to big worlds in the classroom could take many shapes. A single "big world" text and its satellites might make for interesting discussion or it may be more appealing to ask students to talk about their own favoured big world stories. Choosing a big world text for extended study may be productive of excellent work or it may close out students who dislike it for too long—the nature of the time commitment with a big world approach is something that calls for careful consideration.

The issue of reading outside the book is one with obvious educational significance. Teachers need to consider the implications of this idea for themselves, but it would also be useful to include students in a discussion of the priorities and significance of reading elsewhere than in a book.

Discussion

Obviously this overview is sketchy in the extreme, but it does perhaps point to the kinds of practical questions that may fruitfully be asked when we make use of a model of successful literate adults actually exploring and enjoying their interpretive options. Too often, the only adult models of literacy that professionals draw upon involve their own private behaviours, which are certainly illuminating but may also be limiting in their singularity. By investigating the behaviours of a number of adult readers, I hope to demonstrate ways of expanding on the private insular understanding of any one individual.

Change continues to happen very fast, and it seems reasonable to assume that these adults will continue to adapt most significantly in areas that are personally salient to them. To what degree change will be forced upon them by their own tastes and interests is a question worth pondering. To take a single example, let us return to Isaac and his preference for the complete works of a given group. What will Isaac do if he likes the Canadian group Barenaked Ladies? Here is a brief account of their approach to releasing a new "album" late in 2006:

> For the new album, *Barenaked Ladies Are Me* (read: army) McBride and BNL have reinvented the release campaign, starting with the music itself. The band wrote 29 new songs, which will be packaged and sold in a variety of formats, including a CD, four different digital versions, a 14-track collection for Starbucks in Canada, and a second full-length disc, *Barenaked Ladies are Men*, due early next year.
>
> And that's just the beginning. Between ringtones, acoustic versions, and concert recordings, those 29 songs have been multiplied into more than 200 "assets"—song versions—that can be used individually or in conjunction with others to create a product. "Because the copyrights are in one place [in BNL's hands], we can be really creative," McBride says. Hardcore fans can buy 45 of these assets on a USB drive; others can download the special *Sims* versions (recorded in Simlish, no less). (Howe, 2006, 180, 204)

Such a panoply of asset manipulation moves the goalposts in terms of Isaac's devotion to owning the complete repertoire; it also challenges the limits of a big world in shapeshifting ways. It is likely that all the terms I have collected in this section may undergo mutation over the course of the next 10 or 20 years, but I still find them a useful starting point for understanding the territory.

SECTION V
NEW MAPS

NEW MAPS: "DOING" MULTIMODALITY, EXPERIENCING SLIPPERY TEXTS

The participants in this study have spent a lifetime in meeting and exploring new forms of text. Their lifespan includes the advent of the Walkman, the video cassette recorder, the readily affordable and accessible home computer, the CD-ROM, the DVD, the Internet, the electronic reader and the electronic daytimer, the iPod, and the cell phone, to name only the most obvious. How have they *learned to learn* a new medium? Are there general strategies that we can observe in action or extrapolate from their comments?

We do have models for exploring how people learn new interpretive behaviours, and in my research I found insight in an unexpected quarter: a study of pre-readers imitating what they perceive as reading behaviours. Much of our understanding of how little children learn to read involves investigating their behaviours as they cooperate with helping adults. Marlene Barron was interested in looking at how children practised reading behaviours on their own. Her term for what she discovered in an ethnographic study of a Montessori classroom was that the children were "doing books" (2001, 42).

"Doing" Books

Barron's description of children's independent book-related activities makes a good starting point for drawing the threads of this study together, because in looking at adults on their own in a broad recreational culture, we are also investigating the self-directed behaviours of interpreters as they navigate territory that is sometimes familiar and sometimes new. In their recreational lives, these participants are not trying to "please teacher," nor is there any external arbiter of success or failure unless they invite one in.

So what can we learn from Barron's account of these pre-reading children? To begin with, she says that the children valued doing books very highly, and clearly considered books to be sources of power and authority. She describes an extended set of behaviours:

> Another shared characteristic was the variety of emergent reading strategies used, often recursively, by children. These ranged from those that focused on pictures to those that focused on print. Some children randomly flipped through pages, particularly in information books, stopping to look at a picture or two. Others looked systematically at each page. Many children carefully examined the pictures noting minute details. When two or more children were together, they sometimes talked about a page or two, other times they seemed to create a story from the pictures. With familiar books, some children retold the story either from memory or by using the pictures as cues to the text. A few times children compared versions of a story in different books. Some text readers ran their fingers under the lines, while others did not. (2001, 42)

These behaviours were informal and spontaneous, says Barron. Sometimes, they involved solitary immersion, "characterized by the deep involvement stances of the participants" (2001, 44). Sometimes it was a question of cooperation, "creating a social event with the book as the medium, . . . using the activity of doing a book as a way to foster their relationship with their partner" (2001, 44). Sometimes the behaviour involved performance to other children. The overall impression is of multifarious forms of moving in and out of connections with books.

"Doing" Multimodality

This project is not an ethnographic study and the evidence of participants' recreational media-related behaviours comes from two sources: self-reporting of home activities and observation of exercises set for them during the five sessions. It is important at the outset to assert a fundamental difference between Barron's busy classroom and the kinds of activities described by the nine subjects in my project: the small children she describes manifestly perceive themselves as apprentices. They are rehearsing behaviours with a view to mastering them. The adults in this study, while clearly open to the idea of learning more (a topic I will discuss shortly), do not appear to think of themselves overall as learners; in their accounts of their own preferences, they are describing behaviours that they perceive as already successful. In some of the exercises dealing with unfamiliar materials, however, we may see more tentative strategies at work, and it is possible to observe participants "doing" tactics that have worked elsewhere.

With such distinctions firmly in mind, it is interesting to look at the kind of activities described in this book that could be categorized as "doing multi-modality." In this context, two questions are inevitable: If an apprentice were to model external strategies on what could be perceived of the behaviours of these nine adults, what might that learner do? And what can we understand about invisible internal behaviours from what the subjects tell us?

Solitary immersion, cooperation, and performance all play a role in how these adults approach media, just as Barron discovered with her emergent readers.

To take just a few examples of *solitary commitment*, consider Jocelyn entranced by the unexpected in her ruthlessly selected books and movies, Seth absorbed in the unfamiliar territory of a book recommended by a colleague, Drew wrapped up in mastering the intricacies of the back story of *The Lord of the Rings*, Ben intent on his Goodkind novel, Damian engrossed in the flow of a game and playing for hours at a time, Isaac pursuing online information about musical groups. All appear to be caught up in the pleasures of being captivated.

Jeremy, of course, is overwhelmingly committed to the idea of *social cooperation* as part of his approach to just about any kind of text. But we also see Seth accepting any reading recommendation from his co-workers, Courtney looking for online help with mothering, Denise calling in her brother when technology defeats her.

There are also numerous examples of *performance*: Ben quoting long streams of dialogue from *Batman Returns*, Drew setting up his game scenario for his friends, Courtney posting her writing online, Jeremy creating his radio show.

This cursory comparison indicates, not surprisingly, that children who are exploring ways of using books manifest interpretive behaviours that can be seen again in the actions of these adult media users: physical manipulation of the text, meaning-making from whatever cues are available, reverting to a learner stance when new challenges appear, drawing on memory of successful exposure to previous texts. What other kinds of activities might a learner observe among these nine participants? To explore this question, I will return once again to insights offered by theoretical maps.

Unfinish

One striking element of the behaviours observed and described in this project is the repeated motif of what Peter Lunenfeld calls "an aesthetic of unfinish" (2000, 11). While the participants were vociferous in their rejection of the hypertext narrative of *Victory Garden*, they did take a context of "unfinish" for granted, in ways that Lunenfeld discusses when he speaks of

> situating open-ended hypernarratives in a broader context of unfinish. Just as the text has multiplied its own paths toward an internal form of unfinish, so the boundaries between the text and the context have begun to dissolve in the . . . universal solvent of the digital. Technology and popular culture propel us toward a state of unfinish in which the story is never over, and the limits of what constitutes the story proper are never to be as clear again. (2000, 14)

Lunenfeld talks about marketing arrangements within popular culture that result in "rigid demarcations between formerly discrete texts becom[ing] fluid, liminal zones and then simply markers within an ever-shifting nodal system of narrative information" (2000, 15). Stories are told and re-told, sold and re-sold. The adults in this project irritably resisted fluidity and uncertainty when they were manifested in a single hypertext story, but they displayed signs of ease, confidence, and considerable interest when stories they liked were multiplied across media boundaries. When they were given sufficient tools to feel some sense of control (such as in the very strict structure of *253*, a linked story arranged on far more tightly marshalled lines than *Victory Garden*), they were prepared to experiment even with hypertext.

At various points in this project, I pushed to see where participants would draw their personal limits with experimentation. To generalize broadly from diverse examples, they were open to and intrigued by new experiences if they felt comfortable with the level of scaffolding they perceived as available to them. For example, they all liked the film *Memento*, which is told backwards, considerably more than the film *Time Code*, which splits the screen into four quadrants telling related stories simultaneously. With *Memento*, they commented on a challenge to their wits that they had some chance of solving; *Time*

Code overwhelmed them. "Designing a Bird from Memory" intrigued them; *Victory Garden* annoyed them, almost universally.

An outside observer watching the kinds of behaviour described by these participants would soon notice that not every form of engagement with media was successful, even when (or perhaps especially when) that behaviour was highly time-consuming. Damian rejected his own history of hours of gaming. Jeremy gave up gaming altogether because it consumed so much of his life. Drew stopped reading fantasy because he found too much of it to be not worth his time. Isaac watched a movie a night on television over his long summer, but spoke in very deprecating terms about the negative impact of this activity on his life and well-being. The culture of unfinish, at least in terms of constant entertainment always on tap, can sometimes mutate into a culture of restless dissatisfaction. In these cases, it would seem to be not so much a case of stories where the yearning for an ending is frustrated as a case of too much and too many stories ("always more where that came from"), and the upshot appears to be discouragement and *ennui*—possibly a case of too little challenge.

More often, however, the participants described positive returns on their investment of time and attention. There were cases where, even if the original text was less than satisfactory (*The Lord of the Rings* in novel form for Drew, for example), the activity of constructing knowledge, even expertise, out of a collection of what might be called "outer texts" led to a different kind of satisfaction. In these cases, "unfinish" presented room for big world play and the potential to "thicken" the experience of the story in ways that were clearly satisfying to these adults.

Slippery Texts

If we are to understand the kinds of literacy demonstrated in this project, we need to find new ways of understanding the idea of *text*. These adult readers demonstrated an openness to unfamiliar forms at least to the extent of being willing to assess the kinds of demands new forms would make on them. Not every kind of new material passed the test of reasonable accessibility but the participants were willing to be attracted.

Kristie Fleckenstein offers a useful phrase based on her daughter's changing relationship with Pokémon: she talks about "slippery texts" and describes them, "loosely," as "artifacts that keep us positioned on the edges that blur, the edges where literacy evolves" (2003, 105). It is an amorphous concept, which, in conjunction with the baggy notion of "doing multimodality" may actually be fuzzy enough to help us pin down some of what is going on in the shapeshifting world of contemporary media technologies.

The idea of a slippery text fits well with the concepts I developed over the course of this project. A slippery text may often involve a big world; it very often entails reading outside the book and invites movement between immersion and engagement. Fleckenstein describes her daughter's Pokémon commitment in terms that could certainly be re-described as forms of thick play with mastery as part of the goal, and ownership an important component of the experience.

If you are dealing with a slippery text, with all its potential for mutation (aesthetically or commercially inspired) and you are content to start, at least, with some vague notion of "doing," you may actually develop a flexible skill-set that is open to adaptation as needed. At its best, this constitutes a mindset open to perceiving the challenges of multimodal aesthetics as offering the potential for flow.

Active Interpretation

P. David Marshall offers another useful lens when he talks about the ways in which new media blur old distinctions between reception/consumption and production.

> [N]ew media make us engage more directly with production even as we study consumption. From the internet to the ways that mobile phones are used, from games to chatrooms, new media implies a changed spectrum of what defines production and what defines consumption. . . . [N]ew media . . . are cultural forms that have expanded the capacity for the viewer/user to produce. (2004, 11)

Discussing the development of more active consumers, Marshall suggests,

> Thinking of the audience as active means that audience members "work" on media texts. Where we can see this activity most pervasively represented by audiences is in their "intertextual" work on media texts. Intertextuality acknowledges the presence in any media form of other texts. Those other texts help determine the interpretation and reading of the given text through comparisons of similarity and difference with other texts. Although these connections to other texts may be encoded by the producers of the text, they only become enacted through the audience's process of interpretation. The activity of the audience generally with traditional media is at the

point of consumption or reception even as the activity begins to change the meanings of these terms into something productive. (2004, 13)

I like this quote because of its sense of provisional transitions being, as it were, "felt through" by interpreters, either on their own or in interpretive communities. The nine people in this study were not necessarily at the front line of media change. They combined old and new media in ways that were useful and/or pleasing to themselves without necessarily feeling they had to try everything. I would describe much of their activity as having a conservative tinge to it; for the most part, I would not describe these individuals as dedicated early adopters—partly for financial reasons, partly because of their tastes and inclinations. Nevertheless, it is possible to see evidence of a significant attitude shift in their responses, just as Marshall describes it: their reception behaviours incorporated aspects of production, even if the main productive behaviour was often manifested as the active selection of intertextual references to support their interpretive actions. It seems to me that this shift is all the more powerful for being largely subliminal.

Tactics of "Doing"

What did the participants choose to "do" when offered an unfamiliar text? One example supplies a hint of how variegated their behaviour could be. Presented with the computer game *American McGee's Alice* (a violent re-working of *Alice's Adventures in Wonderland*), they manifested a broad range of actions (this game was acquired after Denise's pilot session so she is not represented here). Courtney's preference was to read the whole rulebook before starting. Jocelyn was keen to pick up expertise by following the embedded instructions in the game; Drew objected to such embedding and expressed a strong preference for explicit training. Isaac responded first to the cover art. Damian went straight to the technical settings to see what adjustments would make his play more comfortable before he even looked at the storyline. Jeremy began the game but soon paused it to finesse the settings. Seth paid close attention to the initial introductory scenes as the most likely source of useful information. And Ben decided to focus directly on the plot on the assumption that the behaviours necessary to make game play automatic would follow most readily if he paid attention to the story.

All of these are reasonable strategies but their variety is hard to encompass in a word less vague than "doing."

Experiencing

What ends do those "doers" have in mind as they bring their labile toolkit to bear on a slippery text? Here is Drew's answer to that question. During one session, I tried to prod Drew into expressing a preference among media activities. He dodged my artificial priorities in his reply and drew attention to a form of literacy practice that deserves further attention:

> Margaret : Let's take those four, reading, watching, listening, playing. Which means the most to you? If you could only have one of those, which do you keep? This is a totally artificial question.
>
> Drew   : I would pick the fifth one, which would be experiencing.

Experiencing as the main aim of fictional connection can subsume the media-neutral activities that I have described under the categories of thick play, big worlds, immersion and engagement, and reading outside the book. It suggests a frame of mind in which the channel of input is of less significance than the sense of being in or around the world of a particular fiction.

It is not really surprising that this very explicit statement should come from Drew. His notion of "experiencing" is extremely complex, sometimes almost baroque. He immerses himself very deeply in stories, but always with some of his mind held ready for switching into a more "engaged," un-immersed, multi-schematic relationship with his text. While he enjoys the story world very much, in all its absorbing detail, he is almost never oblivious to the craft that creates such a world. As a writer, as a game master, as a fiction creator himself, he is alert to the components that bind a world together. As an adult in his twenties who grew up with a plethora of narrative alternatives, he articulates the pleasures of "experiencing" as the driving force that relegates media specifics to second place in his mental hierarchy of interpretive processes. It is very tempting to postulate that Drew's enthusiasm for "experiencing" involves an inchoate notion of flow, a heightened form of orchestration that could be described as incorporating the pleasures of playing, conducting, and listening to the music all at once.

Experiencing Fiction Multimodally

Let us look more closely at some examples of Drew's preference for experiencing. For example, he creates his own personal soundtracks for his reading by selecting one CD to play over and over. He watches movies, then listens intensively to the soundtrack, and also reads the accompanying liner notes. He plays games that rely heavily on maps and rules and pays serious attention to their role in the game.

Drew is aware of narrative worlds as constructs, even as he becomes absorbed in exploring all their intricacies. He has thought about ways that an author may develop stories; for example, he compared being a virtual and an actual game master. As a virtual game master, he creates scenarios for an email game in ways that allow for subtler plotting and foreshadowing than are possible in the tabletop version. He described this form of email game and its virtues as follows:

> Well, a play-by-email game is simply, umh—. Well, *Dungeons and Dragons* in its most known form, you know, tabletop: four people get around, guy tells a story and the other three kind of react to it. Well, it's the same idea only it's done on email, but with email it's completely different because now you have—it becomes less action based, now you can start writing, you can start putting in a bunch of elements that you know, that might become relevant later. It becomes really a form for writing, which is a good thing and a bad thing, because games all of a sudden have a much different character.

Drew made numerous observations that indicate how alive he is to the physical affordances of the different media that he uses, commenting on the pleasures of the tactile qualities of paper, the importance of comfortable and intuitive game controls, the significance of certain kinds of musical instrument in establishing mood and cuing attention, the different styles of storymaking that are enabled by tabletop or email game structures. Nevertheless, it is clear that he has articulated an important priority for himself when he says that "experiencing" is his main objective. Even as he discriminates among media, establishing what is accomplished best by different formats, the aim of his encounters with media would seem to be something more holistic than the set of verbs I offered him: reading, watching, listening, playing. While not losing sight of the physicality of the vehicle, he also wants to move wholeheartedly into the narrative world. It is a delicate balancing act; he is aware of the different forms of set-up but he still wants to be swept away.

The experience Drew values is not an unauthored "given," a world existing "out there" that he wants to join thoughtlessly with no awareness of its *composed and created* nature. Perhaps because of his predilection for control, Drew certainly does not sacrifice the importance of the author as opposed to a generic creative force supplying the bubble of his preferred imaginary world. He is articulate, for example, about his dislike for collaborative game development:

> Some people, rather than have a game master who kind of sets the story and this is what's happening— umh, some games do it as a collaborative. So now it's four writers getting together and kind of building on each other's work on the same story as opposed to some guy directing the story. [But] I prefer the hierarchical system of somebody driving the story 'cause, I mean, it's really annoying if you have four writers, and you work hard to build up this one character of yours and all of a sudden, well, he does something out of character—that gets annoying and frustrating.

We can see clearly from Drew's comments that he is not indifferent to the material qualities and affordances of each different medium, nor does he devalue the role of the author in crafting the experience (a kind of ownership). Yet his attachment is to the overall commitment to the story rather than to particular modes of experiencing. He articulates and acknowledges these issues but still puts them in second place to finding ways of enriching his committed experience of a story.

If we take the idea of readers, viewers, and players finding different ways of doing slippery texts with a focus on achieving something that can be called experience, are we making useful progress or are we stuck in a fog of utter vagueness? One problem is that even the process of creating this kind of description actually privileges words and makes it more difficult to move beyond what words make possible. Are there any ways we can get around this bias?

Narrative Across Media

What theoretical maps offer any guidance to an attitude towards story that privileges the final experience over the specific components that create it and the words that describe it? I believe it is possible to recognize Drew's "experiencing" in Marie-Laure Ryan's analysis of the relationship between narrative and words. In her 2004 exploration of narrative across media, she looks at the role of language in narrative and finds it significant but not all-encompassing; she suggests forms of "experience" that cannot be conveyed simply by words.

> Yes, language is the privileged medium of summaries because it can articulate the logical structure of a story; yes, language all by itself can support a wider variety of narratives than any other single-track medium, not just because of its logical superiority but also because only words can represent language and thought. But this does not

mean that media based on sensory channels [other than print] cannot make unique contributions to the formation of narrative meaning. There are, quite simply, meanings that are better expressed visually or musically than verbally, and these meanings should not be declared a priori irrelevant to the narrative experience. (2004, 12)

Drew, like the other participants in this study, spoke mainly of texts from popular culture, and a particular high-budget example of that culture offers a fine example of Ryan's kinds of meaning. Speaking about the Peter Jackson films of *The Lord of the Rings*, Mark Sinker discusses the differences between media versions in illuminating ways:

One of the differences between a film and a book is that a good book requires good making of words, different registers of words, you have poems, you have songs, you have conversations, but films don't really deal with words. They deal with images, music, the binding together of stories told by other means than verbal story telling. (2005, 47)

Sinker goes on to explore elements of story telling without words, focusing on visual components of the films and how they replace Tolkien's vast verbal accounts of cultural nuances in his created world:

Peter Jackson and his vast team of back-up artisans . . . poured tremendous resources into sub-creating the immediate believability of this secondary world, the world that we're in when we're watching. . . . Every object on the screen, large or small, carries this sense of a physical, cultural past, of rival worlds of culture. . . . The film project employed several artists, crafts people, technicians and designers, object-makers like potters, people making cups and bowls for the Rohirrim, cups and bowls for the dwarves, cups and bowls for elves. (2005, 47)

This element of visual craft operates literally on the basis of "show not tell" and supports the narrative of different cultures coming together to fight a great menace.

Ryan's observations about non-verbal narrative meanings apply to classical culture as well, and include components other than the visual. For many years I thought the words "God said, Let there be light and there was light" were as sublime a piece of storytelling as it was possible to put together. But then I listened to Haydn's *Creation*. In this oratorio, the musical majesty of the moment when the light emerges from the darkness conveys sublimity at least equal to that expressed in the verbal version, but in a different register and with a more primal call to the emotions to register the extraordinary, spine-chilling nature of that change. The chord that calls light into being is untranslatable into words, but it is unquestionably a narrative moment of overwhelming power. It is a form of experiencing that goes beyond the information supplied by the words of the story, though it indubitably acts in concert with those words.

Other Multimodal Experiences

The participants in this study, as I have been at pains to emphasize, were all quite different one from another. However, I think that in many significant ways, Drew spoke for many of them in this vote for experiencing as more important than the discrete categories I offered him. It is possible to discern a multimodal approach to texts in many of the tastes and habits they described. Jeremy, playing his game of *Half-Life* and spending much of his time online chatting with other players, is experiencing his fiction through playing, and through very interactive forms of reading and writing. Seth, enjoying *The Sopranos* and going online to read the HBO website with its *faux* FBI files, email correspondences, and so forth, is extending his grasp of a fictional world through both viewing and reading. Ben, systematically working his way through the extra materials on the deluxe DVD version of *Spider-Man* is enhancing his understanding and enjoyment of the fiction through careful perusal of background material about the craft of the making. Isaac, interested in listening to his contemporary Christian music, also reads as much as he can find on the Internet to make sure his collection is exhaustive and to learn about the history and development of his favourite groups. Comfort with slipperiness is apparent in all these examples, as is active choice of intertexts.

Not everybody approaches a particular fiction in this multimodal way; Jocelyn, as so often, speaks for the opposing point of view when she says she is not remotely interested in any kind of background material. She immerses herself in her fictional world, whether book, film, or game, and then she steps right out of the fiction zone, often without much of a backward glance. But even Jocelyn is not completely immune to the charm of different interpretations; when she likes a song, she will often watch the music video version (once only, she stressed) to gain some insight into a take on the song that is different from her own.

Jocelyn serves as a helpful reminder that not everybody goes in for the multiple-version form of commitment to a text (and raises an interesting question about gender that cannot be answered on the basis of the data collected here). But for many of these participants, a fictional commitment overrides media boundaries. It is not that they are unmindful of the possibilities and constraints of different media, or that they do not have preferences, but it would appear to be that the commitment to the experience is often the primary engine that drives the connection. And that commitment often runs to engagement as well as immersion. These "experiencers" want to know how their story was put together—as long as such knowledge does not fracture the connection (as Drew found to be a problem when he learned how the makers of *The Lord of the Rings* reduced the size of the hobbits and then could not get that background information out of his mind when he next watched the film). They want to *think about* their story as well as understand it directly (again, except for Jocelyn, who values that direct and visceral connection very highly, and does not really want to probe what makes it tick, and Jeremy who is more interested in his social world than the background material). Such *thinking about* is part of the overall experience to them, and it is quite clear that most of these interpreters enjoy and value what might be described as the metatextual component of their encounters with stories.

Critical Resistance and Creative Production

Drew went to some lengths to create conditions for experiencing his narratives in multiple media. Such efforts aligned him smoothly with the impact of contemporary synergistic marketing of narratives. As Henry Jenkins points out,

> For this synergy-based strategy to be successful, media audiences must not simply buy an isolated product of experience, but rather, must buy into a prolonged relationship with a particular narrative universe, which is rich enough and complex enough to sustain their interest over time and thus motivate a succession of consumer choices. (2004/2003, 284)

Drew clearly "bought into" to some of these rich and multimodal narrative worlds, although he was selective in his choices. As Pierre Bourdieu points out, "The experience of a world that is 'taken for granted' presupposes agreement between the dispositions of the agents and the expectations or demands immanent in the world into which they are inserted" (1997, 147). Drew's predilection for multimodal forms of experience over single-medium activities and his passion for big worlds that cross media boundaries were readily catered to in a world of convergent marketing. What he took for granted was part of his interpretive toolkit.

This project focused on issues of reception and found the participants interested in developing expertise in favoured texts. Resistance generally took the form of rejection rather than any kind of critical or analytical engagement. What about questions of production? It was not a significant component of the study, but participants volunteered a few examples of using the raw materials of language and other communicative tools to express their own imaginative priorities. Courtney exploring different sites for her online writing, Jocelyn building websites to back her interest in preventing cruelty to animals, Jeremy using downloaded music to create the text of an online radio program, and Drew composing his fantasy games in a variety of media are all examples of creative engagement and production. Circumstances impeded certain endeavours: Seth more than once lamented what he perceived as an absence of talent that prevented him from achieving a cherished ambition to draw caricatures. Drew outlined the frustrations of not having extended time and solitude to devote to writing. Ben described the deep satisfaction he gained from high school acting and suggested that he might one day return to the pleasures of amateur drama but indicated that a lack of time and secure income made it impossible for the present.

In a commercial culture that places a major priority on the consumption of texts, it is encouraging to catch glimpses of these productive energies. But it is important not to exaggerate or over-romanticize the creative actions of these participants. Jocelyn stopped having fun with her websites and ceased production. Ben looked back with fondness on his school acting career but currently was taking no steps to continue with dramatic work. Jeremy's radio station broadcast only intermittently. With the exception of Courtney and Drew, I think it is fair to say that reception mattered much more to this group of adults than did production.

Nevertheless, it is hardly fair to label even their receptive behaviours as passive. The complex acts of selecting and responding, while not necessarily overtly critical, do contribute to the shaping of each individual. And the plural nature of contemporary representations introduces rather more in the way of critical consumption than readily meets the eye. Once a text becomes plural or slippery, it becomes easier to question it, or to resist certain implications of a particular version. The assumptions and affordances of our multimodal world invite forms of comparing and contrasting even if they are not always articulated in critical terms.

Navigating Texts and Experiences with New Guides

My aim in this book has been to collect a portfolio of guides to the landscape of contemporary media use: theoretical maps of the conceptual markers, snapshots of individual trips across the terrain, notes of particular landmarks. At one level, as is often the case with work that has ethnographic tendencies, much of this collection is of merely local interest. These are the activities of nine particular human beings as observed by a tenth, in a particular time, in a particular place. I hope the descriptions convey some of the vividness of the engagements with media stories and songs that these nine people enjoy. But how are these accounts of any import on a scale larger than the local? How may we take the literacy events described in this book and use them to improve our understanding of the broader nature of new literacy practices?

Pierre Bourdieu (Wacquant, 1989, 50) talks about using theories as "thinking tools." The materials accumulated in this book may offer guides into new ways of thinking about the role of media fictions in our culture. When we look at the kinds of activities described under the headings of thick play, big worlds, ownership, reading outside the book, how can we best consider their contribution to changing fields of literacy?

The Development of New Literate Behaviours: The Big Map

The participants in this study have grown up in a world of varied and ubiquitous media. At school they learned to read and write, and perhaps to develop some basic competence with computers, but, clearly, along the way they also picked up many other ways to interpret and respond to media texts. The ease with which they handled any text I gave them testified to a comfort developed out of many forms of practice in encountering multimodal materials and a willingness to experiment with "doing."

What can we learn from such ease developed outside of school? It is not simply that reading is harder and exclusively requires actual teaching or that other media are simplistically geared to be interpretable by intuition alone. Other media also throw up interpretive barriers to the amateur. We know that small children need to learn *how* to make sense out of television (Robinson & Mackey, 2003), and that adults over 40 often balk at the complexities of the digital game screen. Clearly more than simple exposure is required to master different media. We need an account of multimodal literacies that will make sense of the gradual and comfortable accrual of expertise, in domestic surroundings as well as in school.

To begin with, let us look for a large-scale map. One account of exactly this process of the gradual accrual of expertise comes from Pierre Bourdieu in his summation of the roles of agency and practice. Bourdieu says we are never truly passive, that "all knowledge, and in particular all knowledge of the social world, is an act of construction implementing schemes of thought and expression." He highlights "the structuring activity of the agents" who create an understanding of the world not from

> a system of universal forms and categories but a system of internalized, embodied schemes which, having been constituted in the course of collective history, are acquired in the course of individual history and function in their *practical* state, *for practice* (and not for the sake of pure knowledge). (1984/1979, 467, emphasis in original)

Bourdieu's vocabulary offers us a very precise way to describe the enticements of thick play, the enjoyment and expansion of big worlds, the enablement (and restriction) of ownership, the use of reading in various forms and format, the cognitive and affective charge of alternating between immersion and engagement. To understand the participants in this study in Bourdieu's terms is to see them as both shaped and shaping.

Bourdieu's complex term of *habitus* describes some of the ways in which people are shaped. Habitus

> is sometimes described as a "feel for the game," a "practical sense" (*sens pratique*) that inclines agents to act and react in specific situations in a manner that is not always calculated and that is not simply a question of conscious obedience to rules. Rather, it is a set of dispositions which generates practices and perceptions. The habitus is the result of a long process of inculcation, beginning in early childhood, which becomes a "second sense" or a second nature (Johnson, 1993, 5).

Thus, in Johnson's gloss on Bourdieu's terms, we may see the participants in this study as accreting a "feel" for the orchestration of complex media, as developing dispositions to particular forms of behaviour, often in service to the interpretation of a particular story or as routes to the accumulation of Drew's kind of "experience."

Bourdieu is illuminating in describing the physical nature of the attributes of habitus. His observations on the role of the body as "memory-jogger" are especially helpful:

> There is no better image of the logic of socialization, which treats the body as a "memory-jogger," than those complexes of gestures, postures and words—simple interjections of favourite clichés—which only have to be slipped into, like a theatrical costume, to awaken, by the evocative power of bodily mimesis, a universe of ready-made feelings and experiences. (1984/1979, 474)

This project presented explicit moments of just such a slipping on of bodily posture. One occurred when Isaac, who claimed he had little experience of computer games, took hold of the mouse in the first game I showed him. His demeanour shifted, perceptibly and immediately. From his very first movement of that mouse, he was purposeful and experimental. It turned out that he had spent his high school years playing arcade games. As a result, although he did not feel any explicit familiarity with "computer games" per se, he had a repertoire of both bodily and cognitive responses to the larger category of interactive digital gaming, on which he instantly and visibly began to draw. A similar change in physical attitude and confidence happened when Denise picked up the GameBoy. All her previous encounters with digital games on the computer and on the PlayStation had been marked by great tentativeness. Suddenly her whole body knew what it was doing. She described long journeys across the prairies with a GameBoy in the back seat, and the sudden disappearance of all diffidence was a testimony to her jogged memory.

German has a word for the knowledge of the hands: *Fingerspitzengefühl*. The word is not really translatable into English; dictionaries provide alternatives, such as "flair" or "sure instinct," that do not make any reference to the hands' role in our knowledge of the world. But Isaac's hands, very surely, took over the mouse, Denise's fingers raced over the GameBoy, and the skill of those hands manifestly affected their owner's posture (and possibly vice versa).

Here we see two small, explicit examples of Bourdieu's "memory-jogging" bodies in action. The comfort of sliding into familiar bodily knowledge and psychological perspective can often provide an important element of enjoyment. Bourdieu himself uses the helpful phrase, "reading routines" (1996/1992, 327) to describe some of the implicit "certainties" of body and mind that we often apply without much attention.

Routines are developed, not innate, and they occur in the process of reading as well. The brain activity associated with reading actually changes as readers develop competence. When word recognition calls for "effortful atten-tion," beginning readers use different parts of their brain from those used in the automatic routines of experienced readers. Brain activity actually changes as readers become fluent (McCandliss & Posner, 2003).

Clearly, competence, routine, and their associated forms of automaticity contribute to the ease of understanding that fosters connection and enjoy-ment. For the most part, the adults in this study had already put in the efforts necessary to automatize their gestures and responses, but there were moments, especially in the playing of *Black & White* and in their baffled reaction to the hypertext novel, when the effortfulness of the performance was apparent. But their varying approaches to *American McGee's Alice* show them making strong efforts to slide into the game and not to be distracted into effortfulness, either by diving head-first into the plot or by getting some of the technical questions out of the way first so as to reduce the chance of later interrup-tion. We can see them using a variety of scaffolds to enable this imaginative transfer to begin.

Bourdieu describes habitus as bodily; but the more we learn about the mind the more we realize that its physical aspects and habits are also crucial, and that the slipping on of familiar stances is a mental as well as a corporeal issue. The mental equivalent of the body knowing what to do may perhaps be well represented by the time-honoured test for a competent and committed reader of sitting in front of a cereal box on the breakfast table and *not* reading its print contents. The brain knows how to behave in front of the stimulus of print and it charges into action through sheer force of familiarity, paying little heed to the conscious intentions of the breakfast-eater.

Multimodal readers develop other dispositions and skills in mind and hand and body, often as a by-product of thick play. They absorb attitudes (social and physical) through contact with their multimodal friends and siblings. The big theoretical map and the jottings from the individual tours across the land-scape both show a gradual assumption of routines, of embodied knowledge, of *Fingerspitzengefühl* and of flow.

Thus a map of multimodal learning that includes ideas about the exten-sive and intensive qualities of thick play, about the capacity to slide between immersion and engagement, about the priorities of big worlds, about the way that reading moves inside and outside the book covers, and about the signifi-cance of ownership and access can provide new ways of observing the creation of a habitus. Explicit cognitive theories about teaching and learning, while also essential, may overlook the invisible and implicit accretion of social and physical understandings. The nine participants in this study demonstrated the significance of implicit as well as explicit learning in many different ways.

But at the heart of it all remains an impenetrable mystery. Just as the complex process of decoding print is still incomprehensible to the pre-readers "doing" their books, so the alchemy by which any text user creates live working mental images out of the stimuli on offer remains ultimately opaque to us. It was clear that every participant in this study was familiar with this mystery and they articulated what they could of the processes that bring words, sounds, images, and represented movement to vivid life in their minds. Their hands and minds worked together in a variety of ways and the end result was a form of experience that could be shared only partially.

The nine participants reported on rich and satisfying textual lives, though sources of satisfaction were individual and idiosyncratic. All of them were interested in exploring something new, and readily drew on a tacit toolkit for dealing with the unfamiliar. In no case, did this predilection for idiosyncrasy and novelty preclude a deep understanding of the pleasures of reading. These nine adults overthrew many stereotypes, and they offer models for developing text users that are full of interest and promise.

APPENDIX: THE SESSIONS

What follows is the list of texts on offer to participants by the end of the sessions. Denise and Damian, as pilot participants, worked with a slightly variant set of titles. Even with the seven main participants, there was some slight variation in texts on offer, usually in the form of an addition acquired as it became available (particularly in the sets of graphic novels and the games for the PlayStation and the GameBoy). It was important to me that each participant should look at current materials. In a project extended over 18 months and dealing with popular culture, this called for updates. It is noteworthy that in areas where I did not add any new materials, most notably the set of computer game openings in the second session, the participants were most likely to comment on the datedness of the options.

The sessions, by the end of the project, included the following texts:

Session 1: Books and Movies

Books

Cat's Eye by Margaret Atwood
Middlemarch by George Eliot
Sophie's World by Jostein Gaarder

The Constant Gardener by John LeCarre
Atonement by Ian McEwan
Monster by Walter Dean Myers
The Light Fantastic by Terry Pratchett

Movies

Galaxy Quest
The Matrix
Memento
Moulin Rouge
The Purple Rose of Cairo
Time Code

Books about Movies

Moulin Rouge (a book containing many photographs and some background
   commentary)
The Matrix: The Shooting Script by Larry & Andy Wachowski (the movie script,
   no photos)
The Matrix and Philosophy, ed. William Irwin
The Making of Memento by James Mottram (analysis, background story of the
   filming, black-and-white photos)

DVD about Movie

The Matrix Revisited (behind-the-scenes, interviews, etc.)

Session 2: Computer Games, Television and the Internet

Computer Games

Oni

> "action thriller . . . anime style characters and storyline. . . . revolutionary gameplay
> blend of hand to hand and weapons combat" (back of box). Rated T (Teen)/animated
> violence.

The Sims

"create dozens of original Sims. . . . design your Sims' homes. . . . watch your Sims. . . . or take direct control" (back of box). Rated T (Teen)/comic mischief, mature sexual themes, mild animated violence.

Shadoan

"mysterious and intricate J.R.R. Tolkien-typeworld. . . . gather five lost pieces of ancient amulet. . . . attempt to destroy evil wizard" (back of box). No rating.

Sophie's World

"challenging adventure through 3,000 years of philosophical thought" (front of box). "learn about the meaning of life and participate in a mystery about the secrets of human existence—all will be revealed as you progress through the adventure" (back of box). No rating.

American McGee's Alice

"Wonderland, once merely odd, evilly altered by anger and dread. . . . stunning third-person, 3D action based on enhanced *Quake* ® III Technology" (back of box). M (Mature)/animated violence, animated blood and gore.

Television

Scene from *The Sopranos*, season 1, episode 3, "Denial, Anger, Acceptance."

Books about Television

The Sopranos: A Family History by Allen Rucker.
The New York Times on the Sopranos, introduction by Stephen Holden.

Magazines about Televison

"The Complete *Sopranos* Viewer's Guide," *Entertainment Weekly*, September 6, 2002.
"All theUnderworld's a Stage Department: A *MAD* Peek behind the Scenes on the Set of *The Sopranos*," *MAD Magazine*, October 2002.

Internet Sites about Television

Sites concerning *The Sopranos* selected by the participant using google.ca

Internet Sites Generally

Display of personal preferences by the participant using google.ca

Session 3: Picture Book, Graphic Novels, Playstation 2, and Gameboy Advance Games

Picture Book

The Three Pigs by David Wiesner

Graphic Novels

Ethel & Ernest: A True Story by Raymond Briggs
The A-Z of Judge Dredd: The Complete Encyclopedia from Aaron Aardvark to Zachary Zziiz by Mike Butcher
David Boring by Daniel Clowes
Watchmen by Alan Moore, Dave Gibbons & John Higgins
Fax from Sarajevo: A Story of Survival by Joe Kubert
Mort: A Discworld Big Comic by Terry Pratchett, illus. Graham Higgins
Persepolis: The Story of a Childhood by Marjane Satrapi
Gemma Bovary by Posy Simmonds
Maus: A Survivor's Tale (2 vols.) by Art Spiegelman
The Tale of One Bad Rat by Bryan Talbot
Judge Dredd, featuing Judge Death by John Wagner & Brian Bolland
Jimmy Corrigan, or, The Smartest Kid on Earth by Chris Ware

CD-ROM

The Complete Maus by Art Spiegelman

PlayStation 2 games

NHL 2K3 (Sega Sports). Rated E (Everyone)
NHL 2001 (EA Sports). Rated E (Everyone)

NASCAR 2001 (EA Sports). Rated E (Everyone)

Baldur's Gate: Dark Alliance (Interplay). Rated T (Teen)/Blood, Violence, Use of Alcohol.

EverGrace (agetec). Rated T (Teen)/Animated Violence.

Batman Vengeance (Ubi Soft). Rated T (Teen)/Violence.

Men in Black II: Alien Escape (Infogrames). Rated T (Teen)/Blood, Comic Mischief, Violence.

The Lord of the Rings: The Two Towers (EA Games/New Lane Cinema). Rated T (Teen)/Blood, Violence.

GameBoy Advance games

Super Mario Advance (Nintendo). Rated E (Everyone).

Spider-Man: Mysterio's Menace (ActiVision/Marvel). Rated E (Everyone).

Harry Potter and the Philosopher's Stone (EA Games/Warner Bros.) Rated E (Everyone)

The Lord of the Rings: The Fellowship of the Ring (Black Label Games/Vivendi Universal). Rated E (Everyone).

Computer games

Harry Potter and the Philosopher's Stone (EA Games/Warner Bros.) Rated E(Everyone).

Lego Creator Harry Potter (Lego Software). Rated E(Everyone).

Session 4: Print and Electronic Reading

Short Stories on Paper

"Defenseman" by Russell Banks, from *The Angel on the Roof*

"Lies" by Ethan Canin from *Emperor of the Air*

"The Red Queen" by Katherine Govier from *The Immmaculate Conception Photography Gallery*

Electronic Text

Victory Garden by Stuart Moulthrop (a hypertext fiction on disk)

253 by Geoff Ryman (a hypertext fiction online)

Designing a Bird from Memory in Jack's Skin Kitchen by Eliot Khalil Wilson (an online poem with images, music and soundtrack)

Hypertext-related Print on Paper

253: The Print Remix by Geoff Ryman (the book version of the online fiction, identical in wording with a single page for each link in the hypertext)
The Interactive Book by Celia Pearce (a book with pseudo-hyperlinks in the margin connecting different sections)

Print on Paper with CD

We Now Know Who: McSweeney's Six (hardback literary magazine with CD "soundtrack" for different entries)

Electronic Book

Rocket E-Book loaded with

The Secret Garden by Frances Hodgson Burnett
Alice's Adventures in Wonderland by Lewis Carroll
Unleashing the Killer App by Larry Downes and Chunka Mui
The Age of Innocence by Edith Wharton

PDA (personal data assistant)

Sony Clié with MobyPocket loaded with

The Secret Garden by Frances Hodgson Burnett
Alice's Adventures in Wonderland by Lewis Carroll
Kubla Khan by Samuel Taylor Coleridge
Frankenstein by Mary Shelley
The Time Machine by H.G. Wells

Session 5: Computer game, Live Performances/CD-Rom

Computer game

Black & White (EA Games).

Cover opens two ways. One side reads, "Raise a kind and gentle giant to do your bidding. Perform benevolent Miracles and bring peace to the land. Preside over 5 different lands from high atop your Citadel. Seek sanctuary in a home fit for a god." (cover). The other side reads, "Raise an enormous creature of mass-destruction. Perform malevolent Miracles to wreak havoc upon the land. Terrorize 8 different tribes from high atop your Citadel. Battle up to 8 other deities online in the ultimate test of your divine powers." (cover) Rated T(Teen)/Comic Mischief, Violence.

CD-ROM

The Geek Disc by Three Dead Trolls in a Baggie.

BIBLIOGRAPHY

Adams, Douglas. (1998) *Starship Titanic*. CD-ROM computer game. New York: Simon & Schuster Interactive/The Digital Village.

Alphonso, Caroline. (2003, October 14) "Students See Grim Job Market." Toronto: *Globe & Mail*, A8.

Arizpe, Evelyn & Morag Styles. (2003) *Children Reading Pictures: Interpreting Visual Texts*. With contributions from Helen Bromley, Kathy Coulthard & Kate Rabey. London: RoutledgeFalmer.

Atkins, Barry. (2006, April) "What Are We Really Looking At? The Future-Orientation of Video Game Play." *Games and Culture* 1(2), 127–140.

Babiak, Todd. (2004, May 13) "Art, Youth Appeal Aren't Always Mutually Exclusive." *The Edmonton Journal*, C1, C3.

Baldick, Chris. (1990) *The Concise Oxford Dictionary of Literary Terms*. Oxford: Oxford University Press.

Barron, Marlene. (2001, Fall) "Doing Books: Children 'Reading' Without Teachers." *Montessori Life* 13(4), 42–47.

Barthes, Roland. (1974/1970) *S/Z: An Essay*. Trans. Richard Miller. New York: Hill and Wang/Noonday Press.

Bartle, Richard. (1996) "Hearts, Clubs, Diamonds, Spades: Players Who Suit MUDs." http://www.mud.co.uk/richard/hcds.htm, accessed January 26, 2004.

Barton, David & Mary Hamilton. (1998) *Local Literacies: Reading and Writing in One Community*. London: Routledge.

Bourdieu, Pierre. (1997) *Pascalian Meditations*. Trans. R. Nice. Stanford, CA: Stanford University Press.

Bourdieu, Pierre. (1996/1992) *The Rules of Art: Genesis and Structure of the Literary Field*. Trans. Susan Emanuel. Stanford, CA: Stanford University Press.

Bourdieu, Pierre. (1984/1979) *Distinction: A Social Critique of the Judgement of Taste.* Trans. Richard Nice. Cambridge, MA: Harvard University Press.

Broucek, Paul. (2002) Liner notes for*The Lord of the Rings: The Two Towers*. Original motion picture soundtrack. Music composed, orchestrated, and conducted by Howard Shore. Reprise Records, Warner Music Group.

Bruner, Jerome. (1986)*Actual Minds, Possible Worlds.* Cambridge, MA: Harvard University Press.

Calvino, Italo. (1981) *If on a Winter's Night a Traveler.* Trans. William Weaver. New York: Harcourt Brace Jovanovich.

Carrier, David. (2000) *The Aesthetic of Comics.* University Park, PA: Pennsylvania State University Press.

Cleary, Beverly. (1984) *Ramona Forever.* New York: William Morrow.

Cox, Roger. (1996) "Audiotaped Versions of Children's Stories." *Children's Literature in Education* 27(1), 23–33.

Crago, Hugh. (1982, September) "The Readers in the Reader: An Experiment in Personal Response and Literary Criticism." *Signal* 39, 172–182.

Createc+ (2005) *Reading and Buying Books for Pleasure: 2005 National Survey, Final Report.* Ottawa: Department of Canadian Heritage.

Csikszentmihalyi, Mihaly. (1997) *Finding Flow: The Psychology of Engagement with Everyday Life.* New York: Basic Books.

Damasio, Antonio. (1999) *The Feeling of What Happens: Body and Emotion in the Making of Consciousness.* New York: Harcourt Brace.

DeNora, Tia. (2000) *Music in Everyday Life.* Cambridge: Cambridge University Press.

DiPardo, Anne & Pat Schnack. (2004, January/February/March). "Expanding the Web of Meaning: Thought and Emotion in an Intergenerational Reading and Writing Program." *Reading Research Quarterly* 39(1), 14–37.

Douglas, Susan J. (1999) *Listening In: Radio and the American Imagination.* New York: Random House Times Books.

Douglas, J. Yellowlees & Andrew Hargadon. (2001) "The Pleasures of Immersion and Engagement: Schemas, Scripts, and the Fifth Business." *Digital Creativity* 12(3), 153–166.

Ellis, Sue, Lynda Graham, & Guy Merchant. (2004) "Children and Their Multimodal Texts at Home and School." Presentation at the United Kingdom Literacy Association, Manchester, England.

Elsaesser, Thomas. (1998) "Digital Cinema: Delivery, Event, Time." In Thomas Elsaesser & Kay Hoffman (Eds.), *Cinema Futures: Cain, Abel or Cable? The Screen Arts in the Digital Age.* Film Culture in Transition. Amsterdam: Amsterdam University Press, 201–222.

Eskelinen, Markku & Ragnhild Tronstad. (2003) "Video Games and Configurative Performances." In Mark J.P. Wolf, & Bernard Perron (Eds.),*The Video Game Theory Reader.* New York: Routledge, 195–220.

Evans, Dean. (2001)*Black & White: Prima's Official Strategy Guide.* Roseville, CA: Prima Games.

Fischer, Steven Roger. (2003)*A History of Reading.* Globalities. London: Reaktion Books.

Fleckenstein, Kristie S. (2003)*Embodied Literacies: Imageword and a Poetics of Teaching.* Carbondale: Southern Illinois University Press.

Frasca, Gonzalo. (2003) "Simulation versus Narrative: Introduction to Ludology." In Wolf, Mark J.P. & Bernard Perron (Eds.), *The Video Game Theory Reader.* New York: Routledge, 221–235.

Frasca, Gonzalo (2001) *Videogames of the Oppressed: Videogames as a Means for Critical Thinking and Debate*. Masters thesis (Georgia Institute of Technology), available at http://www.jacaranda.org/frasca/thesis/ (pdf version), accessed April 21, 2004.

Gee, James Paul. (2003) *What Video Games Have to Teach Us about Learning and Literacy*. New York: Palgrave Macmillan.

Geertz, Clifford. (1975) *The Interpretation of Cultures: Selected Essays*. New York: Basic Books.

Gitlin, Todd. (2001) *Media Unlimited: How the Torrent of Images and Sounds Overwhelms Our Lives*. New York: Metropolitan Books/Henry Holt.

Goffman, Erving. (1959) *The Presentation of Self in Everyday Life*. New York: Doubleday.

Grodal, Torben. (2003) "Stories for Eye, Ear, and Muscles: Video Games, Media, and Embodied Experiences." In Wolf, Mark J.P. & Bernard Perron (Eds.),*The Video Game Theory Reader*. New York: Routledge, 129–155.

Hagood, Margaret C., Kevin M. Leander, Carmen Luke, Margaret Mackey, & Helen Nixon. (2003, July/August/September) "New Directions in Research: Media and Online Literacy Studies." *Reading Research Quarterly* 38(3), 386–413.

Hatt, Frank. (1976) *The Reading Process: A Framework for Analysis and Description*. London: Clive Bingley.

Heppell, Stephen. (1993, June 18) "Hog in the Limelight." *The Times Educational Supplement*, Computer Updates Section, 3–4.

Holland, Norman N. (1975) *5 Readers Reading*. New Haven: Yale University Press.

Holland, Walter, Henry Jenkins, & Kurt Squire. (2003) "Theory by Design." In Wolf, Mark J.P. & Bernard Perron (Eds.),*The Video Game Theory Reader*. New York: Routledge, 25–46.

Howard, Vivian and Shan Jin. (2004) "What Are They Reading? A Survey of the Reading Habits and Library Usage Patterns of Teens in Nova Scotia." *Canadian Journal of Information and Library Science* 28(4), 25–44.

Howe, Jeff. (2006, September) "No Suit Required." *Wired*14.09, 176–180, 204.

Jacobson, M.J. & R.J. Spiro. (1995) "Hypertext Learning Environments, Cognitive Flexibility, and the Transfer of Complex Knowledge: An Empirical Investigation." *Educational Computing Research 12*, 301–333.

Jae Soo Liu. (2003) *Yellow Umbrella*. Dong-Il Sheen, composer. New York: Kane/Miller.

Jenkins, Henry. (2004/2003) "Quentin Tarantino's Star Wars? Digital Cinema, Media Convergence, and Participatory Culture." In David Thorburn & Henry Jenkins (Eds.), *Rethinking Media Change: The Aesthetics of Transition*. Cambridge, MA: MIT Press, 281–312.

Johnson, Randal. (1993) "Editor's Introduction: Pierre Bourdieu on Art, Literature and Culture." In Pierre Bourdieu, *The Field of Cultural Production: Essays on Art and Literature*. Cambridge: Polity Press, 1–25.

Juul, Jesper. (2001, July) "Games Telling Stories?-A Brief Note on Games and Narratives." *Game Studies 1*(1), n.p. http://www.gamestudies.org/0101/juul-gts/, accessed February 3, 2004.

King, Brad & John Borland. (2003) *Dungeons and Dreamers: The Rise of Computer Game Culture from Geek to Chic*. New York: McGraw-Hill Osborne Media.

Knobel, Michele & Colin Lankshear. (2005) " 'New' Literacies: Research and Social Practice." In Beth Maloch, James V. Hoffman, Diane L. Schallert, Colleen M. Fairbanks, & Jo Worthy (Eds.), *54th Yearbook of the National Reading Conference*. Oak Creek, WI: National Reading Conference, 22–50.

Koontz, Dean. (2002/2001) *One Door Away from Heaven*. New York: Bantam Books.

Krashen, Stephen. (2005/1993) *The Power of Reading: Insights from the Research*. Englewood, CO: Libraries Unlimited.

Kress, Gunther. (2003) *Literacy in the New Media Age*. London: Routledge.

Laurel, Brenda. (1993/1991) *Computers as Theatre*. Boston: Addison-Wesley.

Lewis, David. (2001) *Reading Contemporary Picturebooks: Picturing Text*. London: RoutledgeFalmer.

The Lord of the Rings. (1978) Dir. Ralph Bakshi. United Artists.

The Lord of the Rings. (2001) *The Fellowship of the Ring*. Dir. Peter Jackson. New Line Cinema.

The Lord of the Rings. (2003) *The Return of the King*. Dir. Peter Jackson. New Line Cinema.

The Lord of the Rings. (2002) *The Two Towers*. Dir. Peter Jackson. New Line Cinema.

Lunenfeld, Peter. (2000) "Unfinished Business." In Peter Lunenfeld (Ed.), *The Digital Dialectic: New Essays on New Media*. Cambridge, MA: MIT Press, 7–22.

Macaulay, David. (1998)*The Way Things Work 2.0*. CD-ROM. London: Dorling Kindersley Multimedia.

Mackey, Margaret. (2003) "At Play on the Borders of the Diegetic: Story Boundaries and Narrative Interpretation." *Journal of Literacy Research* 35(1), 591–632.

Mackey, Margaret. (2002) *Literacies across Media: Playing the Text*. London: RoutledgeFalmer.

Mackey, Margaret. (2001, February) "Literacy in the Zone of Corporate Development: The Cultural and Commercial World of *Men in Black*." *SIMILE: Studies in Media & Information Literacy Education* 1(1), http://www.utpjournals.com/simile/issue1/Mackey1.html, accessed April 3, 2007.

Mackey, Margaret. (1999, January) "Playing in the Phase Space: Contemporary Forms of Fictional Pleasure." *Signal: Approaches to Children's Books* 88, 16–33.

Mackey, Margaret. (1995) *Imagining with Words: The Temporal Processes of Reading Complex Fiction*. Unpublished dissertation. Edmonton, Alberta: University of Alberta.

Mann, Charles C. (2006, September) "Spam Blogs = Trouble."*Wired*14.09, 104–116.

Manovich, Lev. (2002/2001) *The Language of New Media*. Cambridge, MA: MIT Press.

Marshall, P. David. (2004) *New Media Cultures*. London: Arnold.

McCandliss, Bruce D & Michael I. Posner. (2003, Spring) "Fostering Literacy through Understanding Brain Mechanisms." *Education Canada* 43(2), http://proquest.umi.com/pqdweb?ind ex=42&did=000000545452441&SrchMode=1&sid=6&Fmt=3&VInst=PROD&VType =PQD&RQT=309&VName=PQD&TS=1097616296&clientId=12301#fulltext, accessed October 12, 2004.

McCloud, Scott. (1993) *Understanding Comics: The Invisible Art*. Northampton, MA: Kitchen Sink Press.

McKechnie, Lynne E.F. (2004) " 'I'll Keep Them for My Children' (Kevin, Nine Years): Children's Personal Collections of Books and Other Media." *The Canadian Journal of Information and Library Science* 28(4), December, 73–88.

McMahan, Alison. (2003) "Immersion, Engagement, and Presence: A Method for Analyzing 3-D Video Games." In Wolf, Mark J.P. & Bernard Perron (Eds.),*The Video Game Theory Reader*. New York: Routledge, 67–86.

McNeely, Joel. (1996) *Star Wars: Shadows of the Empire*. CD. Studio City, CA: Varese Sarabande Records.

Meek, Margaret. (1988) *How Texts Teach What Readers Learn*. Stroud, GL: Thimble Press.

Morgan, David. (2000) *Knowing the Score: Film Composers Talk about the Art, Craft, Blood, Sweat, and Tears of Writing for Cinema*. New York: HarperEntertainment.

Murray, Janet H. (2004) "From Game-Story to Cyberdrama." In Noah Wardrip-Fruin & Pat Harrigan (Eds.), *First Person: New Media as Story, Performance, and Game*. Cambridge, MA: MIT Press, 2–11.

National Endowment for the Arts. (2004, June) *Reading at Risk: A Study of Literary Reading in America*. Research Division Report #46. Washington: National Endowment for the Arts.

Nevins, Jess. (n.d.) "On Crossovers." http://ratmmjess.tripod.com/crossovers.html, accessed November 17, 2003.

Newkirk, Thomas. (1997) *The Performance of Self in Student Writing*. Portsmouth, NH: Boynton/Cook: Heinemann.

Newman, James. (2004) *Videogames*. London: Routledge.

Nielsen, Jakob. (2006, November 20) "Digital Divide: The Three Stages." Jakob Nielsen's Alertbox, http://www.useit.com/alertbox/digital-divide.html, accessed December 8, 2006.

Nussbaum, Emily. (2004, January 11) "My So-Called Blog." *The New York Times*, http://www.nytimes.com/2004/01/11/magazine/11BLOG.html?ex=1074840110&ei=1&en=36132f769 3f2b8d9, accessed January 11, 2004.

Pavel, Thomas G. (1986) *Fictional Worlds*. Cambridge, MA: Harvard University Press.

Pullman, Philip. (1989, September) "Invisible Pictures." *Signal: Approaches to Children's Books* 60, 160–186.

Purves, Alan. (1998) "Flies in the Web of Hypertext." In David Reinking, Michael C. McKenna, Linda D. Labbo, & Ronald D. Kieffer (Eds.), *Handbook of Literacy and Technology: Transformations in a Post-Typographic World*. Mahwah, NJ: Lawrence Erlbaum Associates, 235–251.

Rabinowitz, Peter J. (1987) *Before Reading: Narrative Conventions and the Politics of Interpretation*. Ithaca: Cornell University Press.

Robinson, Muriel & Margaret Mackey. (2003) "Film and Television." In Nigel Hall, Joanne Larson, & Jackie Marsh (Eds.), *Handbook of Early Childhood Literacy*. London: Sage, 126–141.

Ronen, Ruth. (1994) *Possible Worlds in Literary Theory*. Literature, Culture, Theory 7. Cambridge: Cambridge University Press.

Rosen, Charles. (2001) "On Playing the Piano." In Robert B. Silver, (Ed.), *Doing It: Five Performing Arts*. New York: New York Review of Books, 15–44.

Ross, Catherine Sheldrick. (2001) "Making Choices: What Readers Say about Choosing Books to Read for Pleasure." In Bill Katz, (Ed.), *Readers, Reading and Librarians*. New York: Haworth Information Press, 5–21.

Rucker, Allen. (2003) *The Sopranos: A Family History*. Updated for the 4th Season. Series created by David Chase. New York: New American Library.

Ryan, Marie-Laure. (2004) "Introduction." In Marie-Laure Ryan (Ed.) *Narrative across Media: The Languages of Storytelling*. Lincoln: University of Nebraska Press, 1–40.

Ryan, Marie-Laure. (2001) *Narrative as Virtual Reality: Immersion and Interactivity in Literature and Electronic Media*. Baltimore: Johns Hopkins University Press.

Saenger, Paul. (1997) *Space between Words: The Origins of Silent Reading*. Stanford, CA: Stanford University Press.

Salvatore, R.A. (2000/1998) *The Dark Elf Trilogy*. Collector's Edition. Renton, WA: Wizards of the Coast.

Sinker, Mark. (2005, March) "Talking Tolkien: The Elvish Craft of CGI." *Children's Literature in Education* 36(1), 41–54.

Sipe, Lawrence R. (1998a) "Individual Literary Response Styles of First and Second Graders." *National Reading Conference Yearbook* 47, 76–89.

Sipe, Lawrence R. (1998b) "How Picture Books Work: A Semiotically Framed Theory of Text-Picture Relationships." *Children's Literature in Education* 29(2), 97–108.

Smith, Frank. (1998) *The Book of Learning and Forgetting*. New York: Teachers College Press.

Smith, Greg M. (2003) *Film Structure and the Emotion System*. Cambridge: Cambridge University Press.

Smith, Michael W. & Jeffrey D. Wilhelm. (2002)*"Reading Don't Fix No Chevys": Literacy in the Lives of Young Men*. Portsmouth, NH: Heinemann.

Strate, Lance. (2002) "No(rth Jersey) Sense of Place: The Cultural Geography (and Media Ecology) of *The Sopranos*." In David Lavery (Ed.), *This Thing of Ours: Investigating The Sopranos*. New York: Columbia University Press. London: Wallflower Press, 178–194.

Strawson, Galen. (2004, October 15) "A Fallacy of Our Age." *Times Literary Supplement*, 13–15.

Sundén, Jenny. (2003) *Material Virtualities: Approaching Online Textual Embodiment*. New York: Peter Lang.

Thompson, Kristin. (2003) *Storytelling in Film and Television*. Cambridge, MA: Harvard University Press.

Varley, Pamela. (2002) "As Good as Reading? Kids and the Audiobook Revolution." *Horn Book Magazine* 78(3), 251–262.

Vygotsky, L.S. (1978) *Mind in Society: The Development of Higher Psychological Processes*. (Ed.) Michael Cole, Vera John-Steiner, Sylvia Scribner, & Ellen Souberman Cambridge, MA: Harvard University Press.

Wacquant, Loic J. D. (1989, Spring) "Towards a Reflexive Sociology: A Workshop with Pierre Bourdieu." *Sociological Theory* 7(1), 26–63.

Walton, Kendall L. (1990) *Mimesis as Make-Believe: On the Foundations of the Representational Arts*. Cambridge, MA: Harvard University Press.

Wiesner, David. (2001) *The Three Pigs*. New York: Clarion Books.

Wright, Robert. (2001) *Hip and Trivial: Youth Culture, Book Publishing, and the Greying of Canadian Nationalism*. Toronto: Canadian Scholars' Press.

INDEX

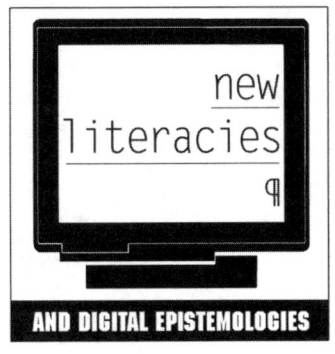

Colin Lankshear, Michele Knobel,
Chris Bigum, & Michael Peters
General Editors

New literacies and new knowledges are being invented "in
the streets" as people from all walks of life wrestle with
new technologies, shifting values, changing institutions,
and new structures of personality and temperament emerging
in a global informational age. These new literacies and
ways of knowing remain absent from classrooms. Many education administrators, teachers, teacher educators, and aca-
demics seem largely unaware of them. Others actively
oppose them. Yet, they increasingly shape the engagements
and worlds of young people in societies like our own. The
New Literacies and Digital Epistemologies series will explore this terrain with a view to informing educational
theory and practice in constructively critical ways.

For further information about the series and submitting
manuscripts, please contact:

Michele Knobel & Colin Lankshear
Montclair State University
Dept. of Education and Human Services
3173 University Hall
Montclair, NJ 07043
michele@coatepec.net

To order other books in this series, please contact our
Customer Service Department at:

(800) 770-LANG (within the U.S.)
(212) 647-7706 (outside the U.S.)
(212) 647-7707 FAX

Or browse online by series at:

www.peterlang.com